GMAT®
Verbal
Workbook

Ninth Edition

Lead Editor

Craig Harman

Contributing Editor

Paula L. Fleming, MA, MBA

Special thanks to

Kim Bowers, Harry Broome, Chris Cosci, Robin Garmise, Rita Garthaffner, Joanna Graham, Laurel Haines, Mandy Luk, Jennifer Moore, Camellia Mukherjee, Monica Ostolaza, Carly Schnur, Gordon Spector, Jay Thomas, Oscar Velazquez, Ethan Weber, Michael Wolff, Amy Zarkos, and the many others who made this book possible.

GMAT® is a registered trademark of the Graduate Management Admission Council™. Kaplan materials do not contain actual GMAT items and are neither endorsed by nor affiliated in any way with GMAC.

This publication is designed to provide accurate information in regard to the subject matter covered as of its publication date, with the understanding that knowledge and best practice constantly evolve. The publisher is not engaged in rendering medical, legal, accounting, or other professional service. If medical or legal advice or other expert assistance is required, the services of a competent professional should be sought. This publication is not intended for use in clinical practice or the delivery of medical care. To the fullest extent of the law, neither the Publisher nor the Editors assume any liability for any injury and/or damage to persons or property arising out of or related to any use of the material contained in this book.

Kaplan Publishing print books are available at special quantity discounts to use for sales promotions, employee premiums, or educational purposes. For more information or to purchase books, please call the Simon & Schuster special sales department at 866-506-1949.

TABLE OF CONTENTS

How to Use This Book vii

PART ONE: **GETTING STARTED**

Chapter 1: **Introduction to GMAT Verbal** 3

How Verbal Is Scored on the GMAT 4

Test Overview 4

Computer Adaptive Testing 6

PART TWO: **VERBAL STRATEGIES**

Chapter 2: **GMAT Sentence Correction** 11

The Fundamental Rules of GMAT English 12

The Kaplan Method for Sentence Correction 16

The Question and Answer Choices 17

Practice Questions 20

Answers and Explanations 24

Chapter 3: **GMAT Reading Comprehension** 27

The Basic Principles of GMAT Reading 28

Get the Gist of Each Paragraph 29

Exercises: Getting the Gist 31

Reading Comprehension Question Types 34

The Kaplan Method for Reading Comprehension 37

Practice Questions 39

Answers and Explanations 44

Chapter 4: **GMAT Critical Reasoning** 47

Breaking Down an Argument 48

Critical Reasoning Question Types 51

The Kaplan Method for Critical Reasoning 56

Practice Questions 59

Answers and Explanations 64

PART THREE: **PRACTICE SETS**

    Chapter 5: **Sentence Correction Practice** 71

        Sentence Correction Practice Set One 71

        Answers and Explanations 76

        Sentence Correction Practice Set Two 78

        Answers and Explanations 84

        Sentence Correction Practice Set Three 87

        Answers and Explanations 92

        Sentence Correction Practice Set Four 94

        Answers and Explanations 98

    Chapter 6: **Reading Comprehension Practice** 101

        Reading Comprehension Practice Set One 101

        Answers and Explanations 106

        Reading Comprehension Practice Set Two 109

        Answers and Explanations 114

        Reading Comprehension Practice Set Three 118

        Answers and Explanations 122

        Reading Comprehension Practice Set Four 125

        Answers and Explanations 130

    Chapter 7: **Critical Reasoning Practice** 133

        Critical Reasoning Practice Set One 133

        Answers and Explanations 138

        Critical Reasoning Practice Set Two 142

        Answers and Explanations 148

        Critical Reasoning Practice Set Three 151

        Answers and Explanations 156

        Critical Reasoning Practice Set Four 160

        Answers and Explanations 166

    Chapter 8: **GMAT Verbal Practice** 171

        Practice GMAT Verbal Section 171

        Answers and Explanations 188

PART FOUR: **ANALYTICAL WRITING ASSESSMENT**

    Chapter 9: **Analytical Writing Assessment** 199

        Essay Format and Structure 200

        The Basic Principles of Analytical Writing 200

How the AWA Is Scored 202

The Kaplan Method for Analytical Writing. 205

Breakdown: Analysis of an Argument 207

GMAT Style Checklist 212

Practice Essays 214

Chapter 10: **Analytical Writing Assessment Practice Set** 223

Practice Essay Prompts 224

Sample Essays and Analyses. 228

PART FIVE: **APPENDIXES**

Appendix 1: **Grammar Reference Guide** 251

Sentence Structure. 251

Subject-Verb Agreement 252

Modification 254

Pronouns 256

Verbs. 259

Parallelism 263

Comparisons 265

Ellipsis. 267

Appendix 2: **Guide to Usage and Style** 269

Be Concise 270

Be Forceful 274

Be Correct 279

Appendix 3: **Common GMAT Idioms** 291

GMAT Strategy Sheet. 299

How to Use This Book

WELCOME TO KAPLAN'S *GMAT VERBAL WORKBOOK*

Congratulations on your decision to pursue an MBA or other graduate management degree and thank you for choosing Kaplan for your GMAT preparation. You've made the right decision in acquiring this book—Kaplan has prepared students to take standardized tests for over 80 years, and our researchers and editors know more about preparing for the GMAT than anyone else.

This book is designed to benefit anyone who is looking to score higher on the GMAT. Within these pages, you'll see concrete advice to help you drive your Verbal Section score higher and improve the way you construct and write your Analytical Writing Assessment (AWA). And, because this is a Workbook, you'll be presented with practice questions—lots and lots of practice questions.

If you are looking for a book that provides even more extensive advice and covers the entire GMAT (including the Quantitative section), we recommend purchasing our comprehensive compendium of GMAT test knowledge, Kaplan's *GMAT Prep Plus*. If, on the other hand, you are looking for a book that provides GMAT math strategies and lots of math practice, pick up a copy of Kaplan's *GMAT Math Workbook*.

YOUR BOOK AND YOUR ONLINE RESOURCES

There are two components of your *GMAT Verbal Workbook* study package: your book, which includes instruction and practice, and your online resources, which include more practice sets and a free practice test. We here at Kaplan strongly encourage you to utilize these resources. Since the GMAT is taken on a computer, getting comfortable tackling questions in that format is a valuable way to prepare you for what you will encounter on Test Day. To register your online resources, follow these simple steps:

GO ONLINE

kaptest.com/login

1. Go to **kaptest.com/moreonline**.
2. Follow the onscreen instructions.

Each part of your *GMAT Verbal Workbook* serves a purpose in helping you improve your performance. Following are brief descriptions of the different sections of this book.

Part One: Getting Started

The first step to a higher score is to know exactly what you can expect to find on the GMAT Verbal and AWA Sections. In the *Introduction to GMAT Verbal* section of this book, we'll provide you with background information on these sections, what skills they measure, and how they're organized. We'll also explain how the Computer Adaptive Test (CAT) format differs from traditional paper-and-pencil tests in the way it determines your score, and we'll tell you how you can use this system to your advantage.

Part Two: Verbal Strategies

Once you understand how the GMAT is structured and scored, it's time to focus on the specific type of questions you will see in the Verbal section of the GMAT: Sentence Correction, Reading Comprehension, and Critical Reasoning. For each of these different question types, we devote a chapter that details the skills and methods needed to tackle each question type effectively and efficiently. Finally, to allow you to put into practice the new insights and skills you've learned, each of these chapters ends with a short practice set of questions.

Part Three: Practice Sets

Once you've learned Kaplan methods and strategies for handling each of the different question types, it's time to put your knowledge into practice. Indeed, this is why you purchased a workbook: to get in some work.

The practice sets contained in part three contain hundreds of Sentence Correction, Critical Reasoning, and Reading Comprehension questions complete with detailed explanations. Let's start with a description of how *not* to tackle this section of the book: doing all of the Practice Sets at once and *then* looking through the explanations. If you were to do this, then how would you know if you were approaching questions incorrectly? How would you be able to learn from your mistakes and adjust your thinking? Instead, take one Practice Set at a time, letting the explanations act as further instruction.

A strategic way to approach a Practice Set would be like this: first, work through the set of questions contained in a practice set. When you are finished, review your results and read through the explanations of *every* question in the set. Many students only ever review questions they answered incorrectly, but by doing so they miss out on the guidance and insights that can be found in reviewing questions that were answered correctly. Here's why: in your review, you should be looking for patterns in the questions that you tend to get wrong *and* in those you tend to get right. Pattern recognition will help you get more questions correct and get them correct more quickly. As you continue to practice, take note of your areas of strength, and areas of weakness. Knowing your strenghts will help you be a more strategic test-taker, and knowing your weakness will help you target what to continue studying.

Part Four: Analytical Writing Assessment

Part four focuses on the essay portion of the GMAT, known as the Analytical Writing Assessment (AWA). It contains descriptions and examples of Argument essay prompts, along with an explanation of how the essay is graded and strategies for writing a successful essay. You'll then have a chance to practice writing some essays of your own and compare them to high-scoring sample essays to gauge your progress.

Part Five: Appendixes

At the end of your *GMAT Verbal Workbook* you will find three appendixes that contain additional instruction to help you fine-tune your skills and address any verbal weak spots. We especially recommend that all readers take a look at the list of common GMAT idioms in Appendix 3. There is also an extensive grammar reference guide, as well as a guide to usage and style that presents the principles of good writing and exercises to help you sharpen your writing skills. Spending time with these guides will help you develop skills that will serve you long after you've taken the GMAT.

If, at the end of working through this book, you would like to explore more Kaplan practice resources, you can look into the variety of course options available at **kaptest.com/gmat**.

Thanks for choosing Kaplan. We wish you the best of luck on your journey to business school.

PART ONE

Getting Started

CHAPTER 1

Introduction to GMAT Verbal

If you have ever taken any kind of standardized admissions test, it's highly likely you encountered some form of a verbal section, and the GMAT is no different. On this test, you will tackle questions that test your ability to read and understand written passages, evaluate arguments, and make corrections to poorly written or structured sentences. In addition, the GMAT includes an Analytical Writing Assessment that allows you to demonstrate your ability to write effectively and to demonstrate logical reasoning. The purpose of the Verbal section of the GMAT is to test skills that are necessary for an aspiring business school student. But what if it's been a while since you've had an English class? What if you barely remember what grammar is, much less its intricacies in the English language? What if reasoning of *any* kind scares you, especially the *critical* kind?

Don't worry. As a standardized test, one of the great things about the GMAT is that it's required to test the same limited number of core verbal concepts over and over in predictable ways. That means no matter when you take the GMAT, you will be tested on your ability to apply the same rules of grammar, analyze the same types of passages, engage in the same kinds of reasoning, and write the same type of essay. Even the way questions are phrased will often be the same. Such predictability allows us to teach you, for example, only the rules of grammar that will be tested rather than every obscure rule of grammar in existence. This book combines instruction with practice on test-like questions so you will be ready for the real thing before you know it.

In the box below, we have provided a checklist of the core verbal concepts you'll need to know. These concepts are vital, not only because they are tested directly on every GMAT administration, but also because knowing how to perform these simpler tasks provides the foundation for tackling more complicated ones. For instance, you won't be able to figure out an argument's unstated assumption if you can't correctly identify the conclusion and evidence that are presented. Over the next few chapters, we will help you build your understanding of these vital GMAT concepts.

GMAT VERBAL BASICS

- Use correct subject-verb agreement. (Chapter 2)
- Distinguish between independent clauses and sentence fragments. (Chapter 2)
- Get the gist of a reading passage. (Chapter 3)
- Identify key words that reveal the author's purpose. (Chapter 3)
- Read an argument for its conclusion and evidence. (Chapter 5)
- Combine statements to determine what must, can, or cannot be true. (Chapter 5)
- Dissect an argument for its flaws and weaknesses. (Chapter 6)
- Propose ways to strengthen a weak argument. (Chapter 6)

How Verbal Is Scored on the GMAT

The GMAT provides a scaled Verbal score from 0 to 60 and an Analytical Writing Assessment (AWA) score from 0 to 6. These scores and their accompanying percentile values reflect your performance on the verbal and AWA portions of the test compared to all other GMAT test takers.

You will also receive an overall score that reflects your performance on both the Quantitative and the Verbal portions of the test. This is a scaled score from 200 to 800. Note that the AWA score is not factored into this scaled score.

Test Overview

The GMAT is a Computer Adaptive Test, or CAT. You take this test on a computer at special testing centers. Here's a quick overview of the AWA and Verbal Sections.

The AWA is 30 minutes long with one essay question: the Analysis of an Argument.

The Verbal Section contains 36 multiple-choice questions to be answered in 65 minutes. Roughly one-third of the questions will be Sentence Correction, a third will be Reading Comprehension, and a third will be Critical Reasoning.

So-called "experimental" questions will be scattered throughout. These are questions that are being tested for use in future tests and are not scored. However, there is no way of telling the experimental questions from the scored questions, so you should treat all questions as if they are scored.

Analytical Writing Assessment: Argument Essay

Analysis of an Argument essay prompts ask you to critique a given argument. Here's a sample Argument essay prompt.

Example:
The following appeared in a memo from the CEO of Hula Burger, a chain of hamburger restaurants:

"Officials in the video games industry report that over 60 percent of the video games released last year targeted an age 7–13 audience. Moreover, sales data indicate that, nationally, hamburgers are the favorite food among this age group. Since a branch store of Ultimate Video Games opened in town last year, hamburger sales at our restaurant next door have been higher than at any other restaurant in our chain. Because the sale and rental of video games seem to stimulate hamburger sales, the best way to increase our profits is to open new Hula Burger restaurants as near to other Ultimate Video Games stores as possible."

Consider how logical you find this argument. In your essay, be sure to discuss the line of reasoning and the use of evidence in the argument. For example, you may need to consider what questionable assumptions underlie the thinking and what alternative explanations or counterpoints might weaken the conclusion. You may also discuss what types of evidence would strengthen or refute the argument, what changes in the argument would make it more logically sound, and what, if anything, would help you better evaluate its conclusion.

Sentence Correction Questions

Sentence Correction questions feature a statement that is partially or completely underlined. You are asked to choose the answer choice that is the most grammatically and stylistically correct replacement for the underlined portion. Here's a sample Sentence Correction question.

Example: The box of plastic bottles, which the inspector will find on the bottom shelf, <u>seem to have taken on</u> damage during transit.

- O   seem to have taken on
- O   seem to have been taking
- O   seemingly took after
- O   seems to have taken
- O   seems to be taking

Answer: The underlined portion is referring to the singular *box* and not the plural *bottles*, so use the singular *seems*. Additionally, the correct idiom is *to take damage*, not *to take on damage*. Only (D) and (E) fix both these issues. (E) makes it sound as though the damage is occurring right now, so (**D**) is correct.

Reading Comprehension Questions

Reading Comprehension questions can ask a limited variety of things about an accompanying passage, including: main point, purpose, details, and inferences. Passages are usually three to four paragraphs long and cover topics such as the sciences, humanities, and business. Here's a sample Reading Comprehension question.

Example: With which of the following would the author most likely agree?

- O   Supermarkets generally lose money on tomato sales.
- O   Most people could improve their health by consuming more tomatoes.
- O   Stocking tomatoes will always result in more sales for vegetables such as carrots.
- O   Supermarkets should never stock tomatoes.
- O   Rotten tomatoes should not be sold.

Answer: While you cannot be sure of a correct answer without referring to the accompanying passage, wrong answers often use extreme language to push an idea beyond that which is discussed in the passage. Words like *always* and *never* make choices (C) and (D) difficult to select.

Critical Reasoning Questions

Critical Reasoning questions test your ability to dissect the logic that underlies an argument. Here is a sample Critical Reasoning question.

Example: Consumer electronics manufactured and sold by Rappel Inc. seldom cater to the masses. This decision has by and large been a conscious one due to the difference in profit margins Rappel can command in its chosen niche relative to the mainstream market. Because Rappel's business model is focused on gaining the largest possible share of the young professional market, they sell only what would appeal to these individuals. Consequently, all of Rappel Inc.'s products tend to be minimalistic in design.

The author assumes that

○ Rappel executives prefer more flamboyant designs

○ college students are more likely to purchase electronics with flashier designs

○ Rappel's project managers enjoy designing products with minimalistic designs

○ young professionals generally find a minimalistic design to be appealing

○ many consumers who cannot afford Rappel's products often express utter disdain toward the brand

Answer: The author assumes that there is a link between a minimalistic design and that which appeals to young professionals. The only choice that connects these two ideas is (D).

Computer Adaptive Testing

The GMAT is a computer-based test known as a computer adaptive test. In this kind of test, your performance on one question affects the question you will see next. In other words, the test adapts to your ability level. This means that as you answer more questions correctly, you will see more difficult questions. On the other hand, if you answer a series of questions incorrectly, you will begin to see questions that are less difficult.

How a CAT Finds Your Score

Because of the adaptive nature of the test, your score is not calculated by the raw number of questions you answer correctly. Instead, your score is determined by the difficulty level of the questions you are answering at the end of the section. Here's how it works.

When you start a section, the computer:

- Assumes you have an average score.
- Gives you a medium-difficulty question.

If you answer a question correctly:

- Your score goes up.
- You are given a harder question.

If you answer a question incorrectly:

- Your score goes down.
- You are given an easier question.

After a while you will reach a level where most of the questions will seem difficult to you. At this point you will get roughly as many questions right as you get wrong. This is your scoring level. The computer uses your scoring level in calculating your scaled score.

Another consequence of the test's adaptive nature is that for the bulk of the test you will be getting questions at the limit of your ability. While every question is equally important to your final score, harder questions generate higher scores and easier questions generate lower scores. You want to answer as many hard questions as possible. This is a reason to concentrate your energies on the early questions. Get these right and you are into the harder questions, where the points are. The sooner you start to see harder questions, the higher your final score is likely to be.

There are a few other consequences of the adaptive nature of the test that you should consider.

- There is no preset order of difficulty; the difficulty level of the questions you're getting is dependent on how well you have done on the preceding questions. The harder the questions are, the better you are doing. So, if you seem to be getting only hard questions, don't panic: it's a good sign!

- Once you leave a question, you cannot return to it. That's it. Kiss it good-bye. This is why you should never rush on the CAT. Make sure that you have indicated the right answer before you confirm it and move on. The CAT rewards meticulous test takers.

- In a CAT, you must answer a question to move on to the next one. There's no skipping around. If you can't get an answer, you will have to guess in order to move on. Consequently, intelligent guessing can make the difference between a mediocre and a great score. Guess intelligently and strategically—eliminate any answer choices that you determine are wrong and guess among those remaining. The explanations to the questions in this book will demonstrate techniques for eliminating answer choices strategically.

- One final, important point. There is a penalty for unanswered questions on the CAT. Every question you leave unanswered will decrease your score by a greater amount than a question that you answered incorrectly! This means that you should answer all the questions on the test, even if you have to guess randomly to finish a section.

Verbal Strategies

CHAPTER 2

GMAT Sentence Correction

LEARNING OBJECTIVES

After studying this chapter, you will be able to:

- Recognize Sentence Correction questions by their format
- List the six fundamental areas of grammar tested on the GMAT
- State the steps of the Kaplan Method for Sentence Correction
- Apply the Kaplan Method for Sentence Correction to a set of practice questions

---

You'll probably see about 12 or 13 Sentence Correction questions among the 36 questions on the Verbal section of your GMAT, so this question type accounts for about a third of your Verbal score.

Why is grammar such a big deal on the GMAT? Because business schools believe that the best managers are those who can communicate effectively, and knowing the rules of standard written English is part of being an effective communicator. Beyond that, the GMAT is evaluating your ability to apply general rules to particular cases: Can you identify and apply the relevant big-picture principle without overlooking any details? You'll need to do this frequently in your business career—apply principles of good management, regulatory guidance, or organizational policies to a particular situation with a unique twist.

Sentence Correction on the GMAT covers a range of grammar and style errors, some of which are so obscure that even some good writers commit them. But here's the good news: you don't need to be a grammar maven to become proficient on these types of questions. While there are many rules of standard written English, the GMAT concentrates on the following six types of errors:

- Verbs—proper agreement and correct tense
- Pronouns—correct relationship to a noun
- Modifiers—correct form and placement
- Parallel structure and comparisons—consistency among items in a list or comparison
- Idioms and style—conventional, clear, and concise usage of words and phrases
- Connectors—logical relationships between ideas

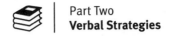

The Fundamental Rules of GMAT English

Since the GMAT tends to test your understanding of these six kinds of errors over and over, learning these fundamental rules will let you do well on Sentence Correction.

Verbs

While the concept of subject-verb agreement isn't a difficult one, the GMAT will often turn it into a challenge, either by separating the verb from the subject or by putting the verb before the subject. Additionally, the verb tense must agree with the sequence of events in the sentence. Depending on the sentence, the appropriate verb tense may be past, present, future, or something a bit more complicated.

Have a look at the following sentences and choose the correct verb in each:

1. Each of the entertainers involved in the festivities (was, were) paid in advance.
2. Neither the prosecutor's eloquent closing argument nor the mountains of incriminating evidence (was, were) able to convince the jury to find the defendant guilty.
3. I (did not see, had not seen, have not seen) him since last Saturday.
4. She already (closed, has closed, had closed) the door behind her when she realized that she (was not, will not be, would not be) able to get back in later.

Answers and Explanations

1. *Each . . . was* paid in advance.

    Each is always singular. While the prepositional phrase "of the entertainers" does contain a plural noun, it is only there to describe the singular subject *each*.

2. Neither the prosecutor's eloquent closing argument nor the *mountains* of incriminating evidence *were* able to convince the jury to find the defendant guilty.

    In *neither . . . nor* constructions, the verb has to agree with the subject following *nor*—in this case *mountains*, which is plural. By the way, the same rule applies in *either . . . or* sentences: the verb must agree with the subject following *or*.

3. I *have not seen* him since last Saturday.

    The "since last Saturday" in the sentence tells you that the (non)activity under discussion began in the past and continues into the present; thus, you should use the present perfect tense *have not seen*.

4. She already *had closed* the door behind her when she realized that she *would not be* able to get back in later.

    When the rest of the sentence is in the past tense (as in "she realized") and the verb in question refers to an action that occurred *before* that, use the past perfect tense (here, it's *had closed*). And when the verb in question refers to the future as contemplated in the past (a future that is still speculative in the time frame of the sentence), use the subjunctive mood, as in *would not be*.

Pronouns

When you see a pronoun underlined (especially *it, its, they, them, their, that, those,* and *which*), look for two things. First, does the pronoun agree with the noun it is replacing (singular for singular or plural for plural)? Second, is it absolutely clear what noun the pronoun is replacing? If there's any doubt or ambiguity, the pronoun use is wrong. Modifying phrases must also clearly and correctly refer to what they modify, which means they should be placed as close as possible to what they modify. On the GMAT, these phrases most often begin the sentence and are followed by a comma; what follows the comma should be the subject of the phrase.

See if you can complete each of the following sentences correctly:

1. Although the company had promised to maintain operational factories within the city limits, (it, they) later reneged on the agreement.

2. After Orson Welles created an unflattering portrait of newspaper mogul William Randolph Hearst in the movie *Citizen Kane*, (he, Hearst) set about to destroy (his, Welles's) career and reputation.

Answers and Explanations

1. Although the *company* had promised . . . , *it* later reneged on the agreement.

    Watch out for collective nouns like *company, committee, group, gang*, etc., which require singular pronouns.

2. After Orson Welles created an unflattering portrait of newspaper mogul William Randolph Hearst in the movie *Citizen Kane, Hearst* set about to destroy *Welles's* career and reputation.

    Using pronouns would have led to ambiguity in this sentence as either man could have set out to destroy the other's reputation.

Modifiers

Misplaced modifiers can occur anywhere in a sentence, so the best rule once again is to avoid any possibility of ambiguity. As you scan the answer choices, if a word or phrase moves from one part of the sentence to another, ask: What does that word or phrase modify? What word or idea should it be next to?

In addition, you may have to choose between an adverb (which usually ends in –*ly*) and an adjective. If so, ask whether the word modifies a noun (in which case it must be an adjective) or a verb, an adverb, or another adjective (in which case it must be an adverb).

Complete each of the following sentences:

1. While eating spaghetti, (a meatball rolled, I let a meatball roll) off my plate.

2. He hung the damp laundry (careful, carefully) over the balcony rail.

Answers and Explanations

1. While eating spaghetti, *I let a meatball roll* off my plate.

    If the meatball were eating spaghetti as it rolled off the plate, that would be a very talented meatball! You can infer that the subject of the modifying phrase "While eating spaghetti" is "I."

2. He hung the damp laundry *carefully* over the balcony rail.

    The modifier refers to how he *hung* the laundry out to dry (the laundry itself is not careful), so the adverb *carefully* is correct.

Parallel Structure and Comparisons

Ideas with the same importance and function in a sentence should be expressed in the same grammatical form. Any time you see items arranged in a list, be on the lookout for parallel structure. Also, constructions such as *between one thing and another, either do this or do that, not only this but also that*, and the like require parallel structure.

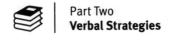
Likewise, comparisons must exhibit parallel structure—and more than that. Most faulty comparisons on the GMAT relate to the notion that you can't compare apples and oranges. Thus, comparisons must be not only grammatically similar but also logically similar. You have to compare one individual to another, one quality to another, one action to another, and so on.

Try giving these sentences parallel, logical structure:

1. The city's decay stems from governmental mismanagement, increasing unemployment, and (down-town businesses are relocating, the relocation of downtown businesses) outside the city.

2. To visualize success is not the same as (to achieve, achieving) it.

3. Even though the franchises stood side by side, one had greater sales volume than (did the other, the other).

4. The article compared the popularity of jazz to (classical music, that of classical music).

Answers and Explanations

1. The city's decay stems from governmental *mismanagement*, increasing *unemployment*, and *the relocation of downtown businesses* outside the city.

    The list here is of nouns: mismanagement . . . unemployment . . . relocation.

2. *To visualize* success is not the same as *to achieve* it.

    "To visualize" is the phrase that begins the sentence, and the appropriate, parallel match among the choices is "to achieve."

3. Even though the franchises stood side by side, *one* had greater sales volume than *did the other*.

    When comparing actions (how much sales volume *one had* to how much *the other had*), you need to include that second verb "did" to make the comparison clear. Otherwise, the sentence technically compares one store's sales volume to the other store.

4. The article compared *the popularity of jazz* to *that of classical music*.

    Without the pronoun "that," the author would be saying that the article compared popularity to music.

Idioms and Style

As anyone who's ever studied a foreign language can attest, learning proper idioms can be extremely frustrating. That's because, when it comes to idioms, there is no general rule—only lists to memorize. The main way to get questions right that deal with idioms is to be alert for them; in particular, pay attention to which prepositions are used with verbs. Also, take the time to learn the idioms that tend to show up frequently on the GMAT.

Try the following:

1. Matthew Brady is regarded (as, to be) one of the greatest 19th-century American photographers.

2. The destruction of the tropical rain forest is generally (considered, considered as, considered to be) a major threat to the environment.

3. It took me four times as long to write the report collaboratively (as, than) I would have taken working by myself.

4. I (either must read, must either read, must read either) the newspaper or listen to the radio before I go to work.

Answers and Explanations

1. Matthew Brady is regarded *as* one of the greatest 19th-century American photographers.

    The correct idiom is *regarded as.*

2. The destruction of the tropical rain forest is generally *considered* a major threat to the environment.

    It is not idiomatically correct to include "to be" after *considered*.

3. It took me four times *as long* to write the report collaboratively *as* I would have taken working by myself.

    When comparing the lengths of two different events, the correct idiom usage is *as long . . . as.*

4. I *must either read* the newspaper or *listen* to the radio before I go to work.

    Because "listen" comes right after "or," the verb "read" must come right after "either."

For a more exhaustive list of idioms that commonly appear on the GMAT, check out the list of common GMAT idioms in the appendixes of this book.

Other errors involving the author's choice of words are best classified as problems of style—that is, as problems of ineffective expression. The most common of these on the GMAT is using too many words to get an idea across. Sometimes the problem is outright redundancy, but more often the wording is just needlessly verbose. Another common style error is using a passive verb when the sentence could easily be written using an active verb.

Try rewriting the following sentences to correct for errors of style. Then compare your final versions to ours.

1. There are many children who believe in Santa Claus, but there are few adults who do.

    _____

2. The country's procedures for the processing of visas are extremely inefficient.

    _____

3. The shrine is at least 2,000 years old or older.

    _____

4. *A Confederacy of Dunces* has been bought and enjoyed by millions of readers since it was first published in 1974.

    _____

Answers and Explanations

1. Many children believe in Santa Claus, but few adults do.

    "There is/are" sentences are often needlessly wordy.

2. The country's procedures for processing visas are extremely inefficient.

    Removing *the* and *of* does not alter the meaning of the sentence, and a more concise sentence is preferable to a more verbose sentence.

3. The shrine is at least 2,000 years old.

    The redundant phrase *or older* is already implied by *at least*.

4. Millions of readers have bought and enjoyed *A Confederacy of Dunces* since it was first published in 1974.

    Active voice is preferable to passive voice.

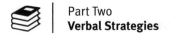

Connectors

The GMAT test makers will also test you on your ability to pay attention to small details, such as the connector words that often get overlooked because they don't seem to carry as much meaning as the nouns and verbs.

As noted in the discussion of redundancy in the previous section, correct choices on the GMAT will use just one connector, not two, to join ideas. A sentence need not say that one thing happened *and also* another thing happened. Just *and* does the job.

Moreover, the connecting word needs to make sense given the context. For example, if the author is saying that one thing caused another, a connector such as *because* or *since* would properly communicate that idea. However, if the author is contrasting ideas, *despite* or *even though* might work. Pay particular attention to the very short connector words, such as *and*, *but*, *so*, *for*, and *yet*, when they are underlined, as these are easily overlooked.

In the following sentences, select the best connecting word or phrase.

1. Although the bridge was overused, (but it, it, and it) did not show signs of wear and tear.
2. (Because, Although) the new medication uses a rare ingredient, it is expensive.
3. The marathon is grueling, (for, so) runners must train diligently for it.
4. The dire environmental consequences of plastics (and, yet) how to curtail their use are the topics of the conference.

Answers and Explanations

1. Although the bridge was overused, *it* did not show signs of wear and tear.

   "Although" establishes the relationship between clauses, so no connector word is needed after the comma.

2. *Because* the new medication uses a rare ingredient, it is expensive.

   It follows that the medication is expensive if it uses a rare ingredient, so use a connector that establishes the correct logical relationship between clauses.

3. The marathon is grueling, *so* runners must train diligently for it.

   A runner must train hard *because* the marathon is a tough race, not the other way around.

4. The dire environmental consequences of plastics *and* how to curtail their use are the topics of the conference.

   The two ideas are simply the topics of the conferences, so use a connector that describes that relationship.

As you work through the Sentence Correction practice questions in this book, be on the lookout for sentences that commit these six fundamental errors. Always consult the explanations after you tackle a set of questions to build your knowledge of common patterns in these types of questions.

The Kaplan Method for Sentence Correction

In a moment, we'll discuss a step-by-step approach to tackle these questions, but first, let's take a quick look at the various parts of a Sentence Correction question.

The Directions

The directions for Sentence Correction questions look something like this:

> **Directions:** Each Sentence Correction question presents a sentence, part or all of which is underlined. Below each sentence, you will find five ways to phrase the underlined portion. The first answer choice repeats the original version, while the other four choices are different. If the original seems best, choose the first answer choice. If not, choose one of the revisions.
>
> In choosing an answer, follow the norms of standard written English: grammar, word choice, and sentence construction. Choose the answer that produces the most effective sentence, aiming to eliminate awkwardness, ambiguity, redundancy, and grammatical error.

First, note that the first answer choice repeats what's underlined in the original sentence. Since the first thing you should do on a Sentence Correction question is to read the entire original sentence, this means you should *never bother reading the first answer choice.*

Second, always remember that you are looking for the answer that is correct, not necessarily the one that sounds the best. GMAT test makers are skilled at making sentences that obey the rules of standard written English without sounding particularly appealing. If a choice doesn't make a sentence sound great, but you can't find anything specifically wrong with it and the other choices are stylistically no better, stick with that choice.

Finally, note the wording the test makers use to distinguish what makes one answer correct. It should be a choice that "[aims] to eliminate awkwardness, ambiguity, redundancy, and grammatical error." Basically, this boils down to following the basic rules of GMAT grammar, but if you're still left with more than one answer choice, go for the shortest answer that doesn't sound awkward and doesn't leave the author's meaning in doubt.

The Question and Answer Choices

Here's an example of a Sentence Correction question:

> A recent spate of news reports questioning the long-term health benefits of high-fat diets <u>have done little to convince its practitioners that they should</u> follow more traditional weight-loss plans.

> The first thing you should do is to *read the sentence in its entirety and try to spot an error*. If you spot an error, eliminate choice (A). Can you spot any errors in this sentence? If you can't, there's another way to get to the correct answer . . .

- O   have done little to convince its practitioners that they should
- O   have done little to convince their practitioners to
- O   has done little to convince its practitioners to
- O   has done little to convince practitioners of these diets to
- O   has done little to convince practitioners of these diets they should

Go to the answer choices! Here's where you can isolate any error being tested, even if you couldn't spot it in the original sentence. The key is to scan the answer choices vertically, looking for differences. What's the first difference you spot? You may have noticed the split between *have* and *has*. Figure out which verb is correct and eliminate choices with the wrong verb. Here, the verb must agree with "*a spate* of news reports," so *has* is correct. Eliminate (A) and (B).

Time to read vertically again and spot differences among the remaining choices. Eliminate choices as soon as you find a mistake. When only one choice remains, read it back into the sentence to confirm that it makes sense. Here, (C) uses the singular pronoun "its" to stand for "high-fat diets," and (E) uses the wordy and redundant "convince practitioners . . . they should." The correct choice is **(D)**. Read it back into the sentence to confirm you didn't miss anything:

> A recent spate of news reports questioning the long-term health benefits of high-fat diets *has done little to convince practitioners of these diets to* follow more traditional weight-loss plans.

This is the gist of the Kaplan Method for Sentence Correction.

THE KAPLAN METHOD FOR SENTENCE CORRECTION

1. Read the original sentence carefully, looking for errors.
2. Scan and group the answer choices.
3. Eliminate choices until only one remains.

STEP 1: READ THE ORIGINAL SENTENCE CAREFULLY, LOOKING FOR ERRORS

As you read the sentence, keep your eyes peeled for signs of the classic errors that the GMAT loves to test. If you spot an error, eliminate (A) immediately. If you don't spot an error the first time through, don't bother rereading. You're no more likely to spot a problem the second time around—especially because there may not be an error at all! Instead, move straight to Step 2.

STEP 2: SCAN AND GROUP THE ANSWER CHOICES

Instead of wasting time reading each choice individually, quickly scan and compare the answers with one another. If you spotted an error in Step 1, sort the choices into two groups: those that do not correct the error (which you can eliminate) and those that do correct it.

If you *didn't* spot an error, try to zero in on a grammatical or stylistic difference that splits the answer choices into distinct groups. This will let you identify one of the issues that the question is testing. Once you know what is being tested, you can apply your knowledge of grammar and usage to determine which group is correct, potentially eliminating multiple choices at once.

STEP 3: ELIMINATE CHOICES UNTIL ONLY ONE REMAINS

If more than one choice remains, go back to Step 2 and scan again to find another difference, then eliminate accordingly. Repeat this process until only one choice remains.

Important Pacing Tip: If more than one choice remains after you have eliminated all of the answer choices you know to be wrong, just go with your best guess. If you don't know the rule by Test Day, you probably won't successfully teach it to yourself while taking the exam. You'll get a much higher score by investing that time in other questions.

Apply the Kaplan Method to this question:

Several consumer protection agencies have filed suit, seeking to bar distributors from advertising treatments for baldness <u>that brings no discernible improvement and may even result in potential harm</u>.

- ○ that brings no discernible improvement and may even result in potential harm
- ○ that bring no discernible improvement and may even prove harmful
- ○ bringing no discernible improvement and even being harmful
- ○ that brings no discernible improvement and may even potentially result in harm being done
- ○ that bring no discernible improvement, maybe even resulting in harm

STEP 1: READ THE ORIGINAL SENTENCE CAREFULLY, LOOKING FOR ERRORS

The underlined text is a clause that describes something in the first part of the sentence. (The use of the pronoun *that* is a good clue.) What in the first part of the sentence "brings no discernible improvement" and may cause harm? *Treatments.* But it's not proper grammar to say *treatments brings*.

You've found a problem with this sentence (subject-verb agreement), so (A) can't be correct.

STEP 2: SCAN AND GROUP THE ANSWER CHOICES

Quickly scan the choices, looking for any that repeat the error. Since (D) also uses *brings*, eliminate it.

If you didn't spot the error, you'd now say to yourself, "Hmm . . . two answer choices say *brings*, two say *bring*—one is plural, the other singular. This is very likely about subject-verb agreement. So, what *brings* no improvement? Is it *baldness*? There's an *of* before *baldness*, so *baldness* can't be the subject. Plus "baldness brings no discernible improvement" just doesn't make sense. It has to be *treatments*. Now that makes sense! Sneaky, GMAT, but I figured it out! Now you'd eliminate (A) and (D) and turn your attention to *bring/bringing*.

STEP 3: ELIMINATE CHOICES UNTIL ONLY ONE REMAINS

Now eliminate *bringing*, either because you recognize that the continuous tense is awkward and unnecessary here or because you know that on the GMAT, *–ing* forms are almost always wrong in verb questions.

Finally, comparing (B) and (E), you spot a difference at the end: *and may even prove harmful* versus *maybe even resulting in harm. Prove* is parallel with *bring*, while *resulting* is not. Eliminate (E). That leaves only **(B)**. Read it back into the sentence to confirm:

Several consumer protection agencies have filed suit, seeking to bar distributors from advertising treatments for baldness *that bring no discernible improvement and may even prove harmful.*

That contains no errors. Select (B) and move to the next question.

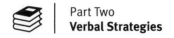

Practice Questions

Now that you know the six types of grammar errors that the GMAT loves to test, it's time to test your knowledge on some Sentence Correction practice questions. Although the six common types of errors explain the great majority of Sentence Correction questions, the Grammar Reference Guide in Appendix 1 of this book offers a more thorough treatment of the possible grammatical rules and errors that could appear in these questions. Make sure to apply the Kaplan Method as you answer the following questions. Answers and explanations follow.

1. Nineteenth-century authors often included encyclopedic information in their novels; Melville's famous chapter on the physiology of whales, <u>contained as it is in</u> his masterwork *Moby-Dick*, serves as a perfect example of this phenomenon.

   O contained as it is in

   O contained as it is within

   O contained in

   O found contained in

   O being found contained in

2. Due to the limitations imposed on scientists' observations by the speed of light, the visible universe <u>is estimated as</u> a mere fraction of the total universe.

   O is estimated as

   O is estimated to be

   O is estimated at

   O estimated to be

   O estimated at

3. For over forty years, Dr. Jane Goodall has conducted field studies of large primate species and <u>shares her findings with the general public in an effort</u> to promote conservation of these species and their habitats.

   O shares her findings with the general public in an effort

   O sharing her findings with the general public so as

   O shared her findings with the general public in an effort

   O will share her findings with the general public so as

   O would share her findings with the general public in an effort

4. Cattle were domesticated both for the uses made of the animal—food and leather—<u>but also for</u> the labor the animal could provide.

   O but also for

   O and for

   O or for

   O but also

   O and also

5. Just as studying Latin helps students with English vocabulary—many English prefixes, suffixes, and roots are derived from Latin words—<u>so basic math skills are useful to those interested in taking classes</u> in science or economics.

   O so basic math skills are useful to those interested in taking classes

   O so learning basic math skills is useful to those interested in taking classes

   O so the basic skills of math are useful to those interested in taking classes

   O learning basic math skills is useful to those interested in taking classes

   O basic math skills are useful to those interested in taking classes

6. During World War II, "code talkers" were Native American soldiers <u>that were specifically recruited to develop codes based in the Navajo language;</u> these codes made any intercepted communications virtually indecipherable.

   O that were specifically recruited to develop codes based in the Navajo language

   O who were specifically recruited to develop codes based in the Navajo language

   O that used the Navajo language to develop the codes they were specifically recruited for

   O that, when specifically recruited, developed codes based on the Navajo language

   O who were specifically recruited to develop codes based on the Navajo language

7. Increasingly, standardized tests include logic puzzles to test students' problem-solving skills; while these puzzles can be difficult, they can be solved <u>where students are able to visualize abstract concepts, quick to note relationships between disparate ideas, and are</u> willing to take the time to learn a few basic rules.

   O where students are able to visualize abstract concepts, quick to note relationships between disparate ideas, and are

   O where a student is able to visualize abstract concepts, quick to note relationships between disparate ideas, and is

   O if students are able to visualize abstract concepts, quick to note relationships between disparate ideas, and

   O where students being able to visualize abstract concepts and quick to note relationships between disparate ideas, along with being

   O if students are being able to visualize abstract concepts, quick to note relationships between disparate ideas, besides being

8. In many coastal New England towns, <u>the fisherman still operates as they have</u> for generations, displaying and selling their catch dockside at the end of each day.

   O the fisherman still operates as they have

   O the fisherman still operates as was done

   O fishermen still operate as they have

   O the fisherman still operates as he has

   O fishermen still operate as they had

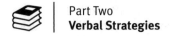
9. The average salary for new jobs <u>is expected to rise in the future as jobs become available in high-paying industries</u>.

   ○ is expected to rise in the future as jobs become available in high-paying industries

   ○ are expected to rise in the future as jobs become available in high-paying industries

   ○ are expected to rise in the future through jobs becoming available in high-paying industries

   ○ would be expected to rise in the future through jobs becoming available in high-paying industries

   ○ will rise in the future because jobs in high-paying industries are expecting to become available

10. In addition to being more expensive than manual research, <u>the compounds identified by machine-based research are often of lower quality than those identified by</u> manual research.

    ○ the compounds identified by machine-based research are often of lower quality than those identified by

    ○ machine-based research often identifies compounds that are of lower quality than those identified by

    ○ machine-based research is lower in quality than those compounds identified by

    ○ the compounds identified by machine-based research are often lower in quality than

    ○ compounds identified by machine-based research often had lower quality than those identified by

11. Many climatologists now suspect that the effects of global warming will include unusual temperature fluctuations throughout the Northern and Southern Hemispheres that <u>far exceeds what scientists were predicting only a few years ago</u>.

    ○ far exceeds what scientists were predicting only a few years ago

    ○ far exceeds those predicted by scientists only a few years ago

    ○ exceeds by far that which scientists had predicted only a few years ago

    ○ exceed by far those that scientists had predicted only a few years ago

    ○ far exceed what scientists were predicting only a few years ago

12. The ancient Sumerians are credited <u>as having created</u> the first phonetic writing system as long ago as 3100 B.C.

    ○ as having created

    ○ to have created

    ○ for creating

    ○ with creating

    ○ as being the ones who created

13. A stock market analyst now reports that the plummeting <u>values of many stocks have fallen so as to make</u> these stocks once again attractive to investors.

    ○ values of many stocks have fallen so as to make

    ○ stock values have fallen, making

    ○ descent of many stock values have made

    ○ values of many stocks are making

    ○ values of many stocks have fallen, which has made

14. Compared to the 1930s, when each animation cel had to be separately hand drawn, today's computerized process is much more time- and cost-effective.

   O   Compared to the 1930s, when each animation cel had to be separately hand drawn

   O   When comparing it to each cel, which was separately hand drawn in the 1930s

   O   Compared to animation in the 1930s, when each cel had to be separately hand drawn

   O   In comparison to the 1930s, with each animation cel having to be separately hand drawn

   O   In comparison to the separately hand-drawn animation cels of the 1930s

15. By the number of carbons in the compound's longest chain, a hydrocarbon's standard name is partly determined.

   O   By the number of carbons in the compound's longest chain, a hydrocarbon's standard name is partly determined.

   O   The number of carbons in the compound's longest chain enables partial determination of the standard name of a hydrocarbon.

   O   The standard name of a hydrocarbon is partly determined by the number of carbons in the compound's longest chain.

   O   Counting the number of carbons in the compound's longest chain enables partially determining a hydrocarbon's standard name.

   O   As the carbons on a hydrocarbon's longest chain are counted, so that partially determines the compound's standard name.

Answers and Explanations

1.	C	5.	B	9.	A	13.	D
2.	B	6.	E	10.	B	14.	C
3.	C	7.	C	11.	E	15.	C
4.	B	8.	C	12.	D		

1. C

When you suspect that excess verbiage may be at issue, check to see whether the shortest choice makes sense. In this case, it does.

2. B

The correct idiom is "estimate(d) to be," eliminating (A), (C), and (E). Choice (D) is incorrect because without the word "is," it sounds like the universe is doing the estimating.

3. C

Sometimes determining the proper verb tense is simply a matter of maintaining the same tense as the other verbs in the sentence, as in "Dr. Jane Goodall has *conducted* . . . and *shared* . . . ." Note that the auxiliary verb "has" applies to both verbs in the parallel structure.

4. B

The key here is to recognize that the "both" in the sentence sets up the parallel-structure idiom "both *A* and *B*," so anticipate the correct answer here to be "*both* for the uses . . . *and* for the labor," which is exactly what (B) says. By the way, "and also" is considered redundant on the GMAT. Moreover, phrases between dashes, as in "—food and leather—" here, are usually thrown into Sentence Correction sentences just to confuse the issue. They should always be ignored on your first reading of the sentence.

5. B

The sentence begins with the first part of a two-part construction—"just as . . . so." (D) and (E) drop the needed "so" and can therefore be eliminated. "Just as . . . so" signals a comparison, so check the items being compared. The first, "studying Latin," is not in the underlined portion, so the second item must be in parallel form. Note the verb "studying" along with the subject "Latin." Only (B)'s "learning basic math skills" is parallel. Both (A)'s "basic math skills" and (C)'s "the basic skills of math" omit a verb and are therefore not parallel.

"Just as . . . so" signals a comparison, so check to see what's being compared. Here, it's "studying Latin" and "basic math skills," which is not a logical comparison, so eliminate (A). Eliminate (C) because it illogically compares "studying Latin" and "the basic skills of math." Adding "learning" (and changing the verb from "are" to "is" to agree with its new singular subject), as (B) does, makes the comparison both logical and parallel.

6. E

The underlined portion in this sentence begins with the pronoun "that," so you should make sure it's being used correctly. Even if this had not occurred to you as a potential error, the 3–2 split in the choices between "that" and "who" should make you think about which pronoun is appropriate here. The original sentence uses the pronoun "that" to refer to "Native American soldiers"; however, "who" is correct when referring to people. Therefore, eliminate (A), (C), and (D).

In the remaining two choices, the only difference is idiomatic: (B) has "codes based in the Navajo language," and (E) has "codes based on the Navajo language." The idiom "based in" is generally used to refer to a location (Kaplan Test Prep is *based in* New York); "based on" is the appropriate idiom in this context.

7. C

The underlined portion contains a list of skills that help students solve logic puzzles. That list must be in parallel form for the sentence to be correct. Also, the underlined portion begins with "where," which on the GMAT can only refer to a specific location. Since this sentence does not reference a physical location, the use of "where" is incorrect. (A), (B), and (D) begin with "where," so eliminate these choices. (C) and (E) begin with "if."

The three requirements to solve logic puzzles are to be (1) *able to visualize*, (2) *quick to note*, and (3) *willing to take the time*. Only (C) lists these elements correctly. In addition to leaving the items in the list unparallel ("besides being"), (E) contains "students are being able," which is not grammatically correct usage.

8. C

You have to read the entire sentence to know whether to go singular or plural here. Because the sentence refers to "their catch," you need plural "fishermen" and plural "they." That eliminates everything but (C) and (E). And (E) is out because under discussion is a practice that has continued from the past into the present, so the proper verb tense is present perfect, as in "fishermen still operate as they *have* . . ."

9. A

The subject is "salary," so the verb should be singular, which eliminates (B) and (C). As written, "is expected to rise in the future" makes good sense; there's no need to complicate the verb tense, as (D) does. (E) changes "expected" to "expecting," illogically suggesting that the jobs are expecting themselves to become available.

10. B

If you noticed the comparison error as you read, that's great. Otherwise, seeing the 3-2 split between "[the] compounds" and "machine-based research" would have led you to test the agreement with the preceding modifying phrase, which makes a comparison with "manual research." Compounds can't logically be compared to research, so eliminate all choices except (B) and (C).

(C) changes the meaning of the sentence, incorrectly making machine-based research of lower quality; it is the *compounds* identified by manual research that are of lower quality. (B) is correct.

11. E

A vertical scan reveals a choice between *exceeds* and *exceed*, so ask yourself, what is the subject of the verb? The answer is *fluctuations*, which is plural, so the proper verb form is *exceed*—(A), (B), and (C) are out. And (D) is not only wordier than (E), but it also makes inappropriate use of the past perfect verb tense *had predicted* (which should be used only when discussing two past events, one of which happened before the other, and referring to the earlier event).

12. D

The proper idiom here is "credit(ed) with."

13. D

In this sentence, there's an out-and-out redundancy; "plummeting" means falling, so get rid of any answer choices that discuss falling, including (A), (B), and (E). Choice (C) is also a bit off, with its "plummeting descent." Choice (D) is the only choice that avoids redundancy and makes sense.

14. C

As soon as you read "compared to," you know that this sentence is offering a comparison. On the GMAT, items compared must be in parallel form and logically comparable. This sentence illogically compares "the 1930s" to "today's computerized process." Since "today's computerized process" isn't underlined, you need to find something about the 1930s to which it can logically be compared. Each answer choice retains the comparison, so examine each choice quickly to see if the comparison is logical.

(A) is incorrect because the 1930s cannot be compared to a process. (D) also compares the 1930s to today's computerized process. (B) and (E) compare the cels drawn in the 1930s to the animation process today, another illogical comparison. Only choice (C) makes a logical comparison between "animation in the 1930s" and "today's computerized process."

15. C

When the entire sentence is underlined, style problems are often found in many of the answer choices, so read and eliminate aggressively. Here, choice (A) needlessly complicates the sentence by sticking the long and confusing prepositional phrase "By the number . . ." at the beginning of the sentence (it's also a misplaced modifier, as the phrase should be next to "determined"). In choice (B), does the wording "enables partial determination of the standard name" strike you as a bit awkward? Surely there must be a better way of phrasing this sentence. Choice (C) is the first version that makes sense. Choice (D) is awkward, as well: "Counting . . . enables . . . partially determining . . . ." And (E) not only mangles the sense of the sentence but is not even a complete sentence. Moral of the story: you don't have to know what stylistic error a sentence is committing, so long as your ear can distinguish effective expression from ineffective expression. (Also, note that the passive voice is not *always* wrong. In this case, the clearest way to express the idea was to use the passive "*is . . . determined.*")

CHAPTER 3
GMAT Reading Comprehension

LEARNING OBJECTIVES

After studying this chapter, you will be able to:

- Read GMAT Reading Comprehension passages strategically
- Recognize different question types associated with Reading Comprehension passages
- State the steps of the Kaplan Method for Reading Comprehension
- Apply the Kaplan Method for Reading Comprehension to a set of practice questions

Reading Comprehension passages and questions on the GMAT will test your critical reading and thinking skills. Among other things, these types of questions assess whether you can do the following:

- Summarize the main idea of a passage
- Understand logical relationships between facts and concepts
- Make inferences based on information in a text
- Analyze the logical structure of a passage
- Deduce the author's tone and attitude about a topic from the text

Therefore, you can improve your performance on these questions by doing two things: strategically reading GMAT passages and strategically answering the associated questions. If that advice sounds simple, that's because it is. But working to improve those two skills can be hard, and many students who prepare for the GMAT choose not to address them in their practice. Don't let that be you. If you work to improve the way you read GMAT passages and the way you tackle questions on those passages, you will see your performance in this section improve. In this chapter, you will learn both skills. First, though, a few facts about Reading Comprehension on the GMAT.

In the 36-question GMAT Verbal section, you'll probably see four Reading Comp passages, and each will likely have three or four questions associated with it. Passages on the GMAT address a topic in the areas of business, the social sciences and humanities, and the biological and physical sciences. The passages have the tone and content that one might expect from a scholarly journal or serious journalism. All the information you need to answer the questions correctly is contained in the text in front of you, so you don't need any knowledge of the topics beforehand.

After you read the passage, you will usually be asked three or four questions about it. The passage will be visible on one side of the screen and the questions on the other. You will see only one question at a time, and you will have to answer each question before you can see the next question. If the text is longer than the available space, you'll be given a scroll bar to move through it.

Before each passage, you will see directions similar to these:

> **Directions:** The questions in this group are based on the content of a passage. After reading the passage, choose the best answer to each question. Answer all questions following the passage on the basis of what is stated or implied in the passage.

Notice two important things here. First, even when directions speak to a "best" answer, remember that there is one and only one correct answer to each question. Each of the four wrong choices contains something that makes it objectively wrong. While you might read through the correct answer without immediately thinking, "Aha! That's right!" you can always eliminate choices that are definitely *not* correct. Once you've eliminated four choices, the one remaining must be the right one.

The other thing to notice here is the instruction to answer each question based solely on what is stated or implied in the passage. Applying outside knowledge of the topic can get you into trouble, leading you to choices that aren't supported by the passage. In GMAT Reading Comp questions, it is vital to refrain from making unwarranted inferences and assumptions.

The Basic Principles of GMAT Reading

In everyday life, you likely read for a number of different reasons. Maybe you're looking to learn something new, or you're passing the time, or you're following the instructions that tell you how to assemble the new gadget you just purchased. On the GMAT, however, you read for only one goal: to answer as many questions correctly as you can. That requires a different approach in the way that you read and digest information. While you absolutely need to read GMAT passages with intensity and focus, the goal is not to read for details. After all, since the passage remains on the screen even while you're answering questions, trying to memorize facts, dates, and names is a waste of time. Instead, focus on the big picture of the passage—the overall gist. Try to understand the author's purpose in writing the passage and the structure of the passage.

To read more strategically, there are a number of skills you can work to improve as you prepare for the GMAT. First, when you read, try to determine the overall big picture of the passage. What's the author's broad topic? And what about that topic is the author interested in? Additionally, summarize the passage as you read and determine the gist of each paragraph. Finally, look out for opinions, theories, and points of view and keep track of whether they are the author's or someone else's.

Identify Topic and Scope

As you read, stay engaged by asking yourself questions about the passage. One of the first questions to ask is: What is the main thing that the author wants to discuss in this passage? That is the passage's topic, and it almost always shows up in the first couple of sentences. It will be something broad, far too big to discuss in the 350 words or so of most GMAT passages. Here's an example of how a passage might begin:

> The great migration of European intellectuals to the United States in the second quarter of the 20th century prompted a transmutation in the character of Western social thought.

After just one sentence, the author's topic seems clear: the migration of European intellectuals to the United States during a certain time period. Specifically, the author cares about the effect of this migration on Western social thought—that's an important clue to the scope.

As you read, you'll refine your understanding of the passage's scope. It could be "several of the effects of a migration on Western social thought." More likely it will be more specific: "one aspect of Western social thought affected by the migration." But maybe the passage will compare two different migrations, or contrast two different effects. Think critically about what's coming and look for clues in the text that tell you what direction the author is taking with the topic.

Get the Gist of Each Paragraph

The paragraph is the main structural unit of any passage. At first, you won't know the passage's topic or scope, so you will be reading that first paragraph closely. But once you get a sense of the direction the passage is headed, all you need to do is understand the role of each new paragraph. As you read, continue asking yourself questions. For each paragraph, ask:

- Why did the author include this paragraph?
- What's discussed here that's different from the content of the paragraph before?
- What bearing does this paragraph have on the author's main idea?
- What role do the details play?

Notice that last question isn't about the details themselves but how they function. Instead of asking, "What does this mean?" (or, even less usefully, trying to learn the details), ask, "Why did the author include this?" Many GMAT passages try to swamp you with boring, dense, and sometimes confusing details. But if you stay focused on understanding the overall purpose of each paragraph, you'll be able to see the author's larger intent. As an example, consider this paragraph, which might show up in a difficult science-based passage:

> The Burgess Shale yielded a surprisingly varied array of fossils. Early chordates were very rare, but there were prodigious numbers of complex forms not seen since. *Hallucigenia*, so named for a structure so bizarre that scientists did not know which was the dorsal and which the ventral side, had fourteen legs. *Opabinia* had five eyes and a long proboscis. This amazing diversity led Gould to believe that it was highly unlikely that the eventual success of chordates was a predictable outcome.

Pretty dense stuff. But don't worry about understanding all of the science jargon; instead, focus on the gist of the paragraph and *why* the details are there. When you do that, things get easier. The first sentence isn't that bad:

> The Burgess Shale yielded a surprisingly varied array of fossils.

Okay, the "Burgess Shale," whatever that is, had a lot of different kinds of fossils.

> Early chordates were very rare, but there were prodigious numbers of complex forms not seen since. *Hallucigenia*, so named for a structure so bizarre that scientists did not know which was the dorsal and which the ventral side, had fourteen legs. *Opabinia* had five eyes and a long proboscis.

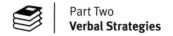

Part Two
Verbal Strategies

Oh, this is just a list of different kinds of fossils and some facts about them—not a lot of "chordates," whatever they are, but lots of other stuff.

> This amazing diversity led Gould to believe that it was highly unlikely that the eventual success of chordates was a predictable outcome.

Notice the emphasis key words in this sentence: "amazing" and "highly." These let you know to pay close attention, because the author is probably expressing an important idea—one that you'll likely see a question about. Indeed, this sentence tells you *why* those annoyingly dense details are there. They are the facts that led Gould to a belief—namely that the rise of "chordates" couldn't have been predicted. So, on your noteboard, you'll jot down something like this:

> Evidence for Gould's belief—chordate success not predictable.

Doing this for every paragraph allows you to create a map of the passage's overall structure. This passage map will help you keep a clear understanding of the big picture. And making it will give you a sense of mastery over the passage, even when it deals with a subject you don't know much about.

Look for Opinions, Theories, and Points of View

An important part of critical reading is distinguishing between factual assertions and opinions or interpretations. Reading Comprehension passages are organized around an author's opinions and interpretations, and you should pay the most attention to them.

Consider how the critical reader would react to this:

> Abraham Lincoln is traditionally viewed as an advocate of freedom because he issued the Emancipation Proclamation and championed the Thirteenth Amendment, which ended legal slavery in the United States. While these achievements cannot be denied, Lincoln also set uncomfortable precedents for the curtailment of civil liberties.

"Ah," the GMAT expert says, "that phrase *traditionally viewed* lets me know how other people typically think about Lincoln. But the author probably doesn't completely agree. Sure enough, I see that she brings up the fact that he restricted civil liberties. And the word *uncomfortable* is a big clue that the author is not pleased with Lincoln. I note, though, that the phrase *this achievement cannot be denied* means she won't go so far as to say that Lincoln was an enemy of freedom."

"In fact," the critical reader continues, "I bet I know what the author is going to do structurally. She'll use at least one paragraph to describe these *precedents* and how they restricted civil liberties. It might even be possible, since she uses the word *precedents*, that she goes on to describe how later presidents used Lincoln's actions as justification for their own restrictions. Wow! Three sentences in, and I bet I've got the passage already!"

Put together, the passage's structure and its opinions and theories (especially the author's) will lead you to understand the author's primary purpose in writing the passage. This is critical, as most GMAT passages have a question that directly asks for that purpose, and many questions are most effectively answered by viewing the passage through the lens of the author's purpose.

Exercises: Getting the Gist

Now it's time for you to try to "get the gist" of a GMAT passage. Keeping in mind topic, scope, and purpose, sum up the gist of this paragraph in one sentence, using your own words as much as possible.

> The "robber baron" industrialists of the late 19th and early 20th centuries are often portrayed as having had no interest in the well-being of society as a whole in their ruthless pursuit of power and personal fortunes. Quite apart from the incidental benefits they provided to society through industrial development, this view ignores the philanthropic endeavors with which most of the robber barons were associated. Admittedly, a good deal of their philanthropy took the form of bequests; still, these industrialists are responsible for many of our best museums and symphony halls, and the foundations they established continue to rank among the most important sources of charity to this day.

What this author is basically saying is:

_____

_____

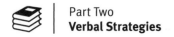

How did that go? Were you able to take that dense paragraph and "get the gist" in just one sentence or so? Here is one way to sum up that paragraph:

> Contrary to popular belief, turn-of-the-century robber barons did a lot of things (like donating money) to make society better.

This version has hit on the right topic (robber baron industrialists) and scope (their concern, or lack of it, for society during the late 19th and early 20th centuries). Just as importantly, it's got the author's purpose right. It would be a distortion, for instance, to say that this author is out to whitewash the robber barons, to argue that they were totally selfless. There's no attempt here to deny that these guys were out to make money for themselves. What the author wants to do is acknowledge that they also score some points on the "Helping Society" side of the ledger, in contrast to the prevailing view. "They weren't all bad" is the bottom line.

What's important to note is that this paragraph, like so many other GMAT passages (in both Reading Comprehension and Critical Reasoning), is contrasting a commonly held view with the author's own view. As long as you get the gist of each of those viewpoints, you'll be okay. You don't have to underline or memorize all the details—all the specific ways the robber barons demonstrated their philanthropy, for example—unless and until questions demand it. As long as you've gotten the gist of the text, you're armed well enough to move on.

When it becomes second nature to you to tackle GMAT prose in this way, your timing improves—you get through the passages much faster—and your ability to answer questions improves as well, because getting the gist is all about interpreting and digesting difficult prose until you "get it."

Try the same process with the following paragraphs, reading and distilling them one at a time. Remember:

- Look for the topic and scope of the passage.
- Get the gist of each paragraph and its structural role in the passage.
- Look for opinions, theories, and points of view—especially the author's.
- Don't obsess over details.

1. It is a commonplace observation that people have become much more sophisticated about evaluating media-delivered messages than used to be the case. But take a closer look. Media celebrities still act as spokespeople to persuade the public to buy every kind of product from automotive parts to cell phones. Political campaigns are waged entirely on the basis of social media memes. People can be stirred to favor foreign intervention in response to television images. How sophisticated is that?

What this author is basically saying is:

_____

_____

_____

2. Observers moved by the plight of a country in the throes of famine will sometimes call for the international community to act. Unfortunately, the solution is often more complicated than it first appears; if it weren't, the country would be able to solve the problem itself. Famines are usually caused by civil strife. In order to alleviate the famine, the international community must send a "peacekeeping force" to resolve the dispute. That means the mediators must either come down in favor of one side, often without understanding the issues at stake, or try to keep either side from winning and, as a result, artificially prolong the war.

What this author is basically saying is:

_____

_____

_____

3. When people get older, their memories of "the good old days" are not always accurate. They may remember that a movie cost a quarter and a trolley ride cost a nickel, but they forget that those amounts represented an appreciable part of the average person's hourly wage. They remember living in close-knit communities, but they forget the depressions and wars that sometimes struck those communities.

What this author is basically saying is:

_____

_____

_____

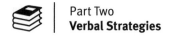
Answers and Explanations

Below, you'll see some sentences that sum up the gist of each of the previous paragraphs. Compare your work to these examples. Note that it's possible, even likely, for you to have picked up correctly on the same key ideas but to have worded your answer differently from what you see here.

1. People probably are no better at resisting sales pitches than they used to be.

Once again, the "commonplace" view is contrasted with the author's view. She uses several examples of how the media sells us products or ideas in quick, unsophisticated snippets and ends with a rhetorical question "How sophisticated is that?" to evoke the response: not very. It's easy to overlook the implied comparison in the first sentence ("much more sophisticated . . . *than used to be the case*"), but that comparison is important to the scope.

2. Would-be international rescuers of countries suffering from famine often do more harm than good.

The author's point is conveyed by the painful choice offered in the last sentence: the international community must send in peacekeepers and either ill-advisedly favor one side or prolong the war by remaining neutral. Other issues raised in the paragraph—the motives for international relief efforts, the deceptive complexity of the situations, the causes of famine—are secondary to, or supportive of, the key point made.

3. Older people sometimes remember only the "good parts" of their youth.

The gist of this paragraph is a paraphrase of the first sentence; the second and third sentences act as evidence for the opening assertion.

Reading Comprehension Question Types

After reading a GMAT passage, you should have a solid understanding of the author's purpose, the passage's main idea, and the way in which the passage is organized. If so, excellent work! Now you're ready to answer the questions associated with that passage.

But what is the most effective way to answer these questions? How can you find the correct answer quickly and confidently, and why do so many wrong answers tempt even the strongest test takers? The key point to remember when tackling these questions can be traced back to the specific directions you'll see before each passage, similar to these:

> **Directions:** The questions in this group are based on the content of a passage. After reading the passage, choose the best answer to each question. Answer all questions following the passage on the basis of what is stated or implied in the passage.

Even though the directions refer to a "best answer," remember that every question comes with four answer choices that are definitively *incorrect*. There is only one *correct* choice. This will be the only choice that answers the question asked and is supported *on the basis of what is stated or implied in the passage*. The four incorrect choices will contain ideas the author doesn't address, present ideas the author does discuss but distort them in some way, or accurately restate part of the passage but not a part that answers the particular question.

In addition to understanding how to read passages strategically, it's invaluable to know the different types of questions that will be asked and how to strategically tackle each of them. There are four main categories of Reading Comprehension questions: Global, Detail, Inference, and Logic. Occasionally, Critical Reasoning-style questions, such as questions that ask for an assumption the author makes or for evidence to strengthen or weaken the author's argument, appear with Reading Comp passages as well. Review the chapter on Critical Reasoning to better understand these question types.

Global Questions

Any question that asks you to consider the passage as a whole is a Global question. Here are some examples:

- Which one of the following best expresses the main idea of the passage?
- The author's primary purpose is to . . .
- Which of the following best describes the organization of the passage?
- Which of the following would be an appropriate title for this passage?

The correct answer will be consistent with the passage's topic, scope, purpose, and structure. If you identified those as you read the passage, then you'll need only a few seconds to select the right answer. Most wrong answers will either get the scope wrong (either too narrow or too broad) or misrepresent the author's point of view.

Detail Questions

Detail questions ask you to identify something the passage explicitly says. Here are some sample Detail question stems:

- According to the passage, which of the following is true of X?
- The author states that . . .
- The author mentions which of the following in support of X?

Detail questions ask you to use your research skills. Because you didn't read for details in your first pass through the passage, you likely haven't memorized exactly what the author stated about a specific thing. That's good! The passage is still right there, on your screen, ready for you to find the correct answer.

Use your understanding of the structure of the passage to help you narrow your search. Then read for context to determine the best response to the specific question.

Consider this question:

> According to the passage, which of the following is true of the guinea pigs discussed in line 17?

Here, your initial research step is easy: go to line 17 and find the reference to guinea pigs.

> . . . a greater percentage of the guinea pigs that lived in the crowded indoor heated area survived than of the guinea pigs in the outdoor cages.

Be careful, though. It's not enough to find the phrase "guinea pigs" in the passage and focus on the first thing you see. You have to answer the specific question asked. If you don't read for context, you might think that the right answer was this:

> Guinea pigs survive better indoors.

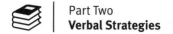
But look at the full context, starting one sentence before:

> Until recently, scientists had no evidence to support the hypothesis that low temperature alone, and not other factors such as people crowding indoors, is responsible for the greater incidence and severity of influenza in the late fall and early winter. Last year, however, researchers uncovered a journal from a Yellowstone Park camp that suffered an influenza outbreak in October of 1945; this journal documented that a greater percentage of the guinea pigs that lived in the crowded indoor heated area survived than of the guinea pigs in the outdoor cages.

So, the right answer will look something like this:

> Researchers discovered that some guinea pigs survived better indoors than outdoors during a flu outbreak.

By reading not just line 17 but the information that came before it, you realize that not all guinea pigs survived better outdoors; only a specific subset did. An answer that matched your first prediction would have been distorting the facts; to get the question correct, you need to understand the information in context.

Inference Questions

Reading Comprehension Inference questions ask you to find something that must be true based on the passage but is not mentioned explicitly in the passage. To tackle these questions, keep in mind that the right answer is not just something that *might be true* according to the passage—it will be something that is demonstrably correct *on the basis of what is stated or implied by the passage.* Stick to that rule: eliminate all but the one choice that must be true based on information in the passage.

Inference questions on the GMAT almost always ask about a specific idea in the passage. Like Detail questions, these prompts will use key phrases and even highlighted text to guide you to a part of the passage. Like Detail questions, they are best answered by reviewing the context of that detail and then predicting the answer.

Here are some sample Inference question stems:

- It can be inferred from the passage that which of the following is true about cardiac tissue?
- The author would most likely recommend that scientists undertake which of the following experiments?
- The passage suggests that which of the following is a valid comparison of literature from different eras?

Logic Questions

Logic questions ask *why* the author does something—why she cites a source, why she includes a certain detail, why she puts one paragraph before another, and so forth. Another way of thinking of this is that a Logic question asks not for *what* a part of the passage says but *why* the author included it. As a result, any choice that focuses on the content of the text will be incorrect.

Here are some sample Logic question stems:

- The author mentions "the psychosocial complexity of elephant behavior" most probably in order to . . . ?
- Which of the following best describes the relationship of the second paragraph to the rest of the passage?
- What is the primary purpose of the third paragraph?

Most Logic questions can be answered right from your passage map—the brief written summary of each paragraph—as informed by the passage's overall topic, scope, and purpose. If the question references a detail, as does the first sample question stem above, then you should also read the context of that detail—just as you should for any Detail or Inference question that references a specific detail.

The Kaplan Method for Reading Comprehension

Now that you understand how to read GMAT passages and how to answer the questions based on those passages, it's time to learn a methodical, step-by-step approach that will allow you to tackle every passage in a systematic way. Following this method will take the guesswork out of your performance in Reading Comprehension, allowing you tackle each passage confidently and with purpose.

> **THE KAPLAN METHOD FOR READING COMPREHENSION**
>
> 1. Read the passage strategically.
> 2. Analyze the question stem.
> 3. Research the relevant text.
> 4. Make a prediction.
> 5. Evaluate the answer choices.

STEP 1: READ THE PASSAGE STRATEGICALLY

To read strategically, read for the overall gist of the passage. In particular, be on the lookout for structural key words and phrases. These signposts will help you distinguish opinions from details and help you understand the author's purpose and point of view.

As you read, jot down a passage map—a brief summary of each paragraph and its function in the passage's structure. Then identify the passage's overall topic, scope, and purpose. To prepare for the questions the test will ask you, ask yourself the following questions while you read:

- Why did the author include this paragraph?
- Why did the author include these details?
- Is the author continuing the discussion along the same lines, or has the author introduced a different idea?
- Is this a fact or an opinion? If it's an opinion, is it the author's or someone else's?

Like most sophisticated writing, the prose you will see on the GMAT often takes twists and turns in its path through the topic. Remember: if ideas were laid out in a clear, easy-to-follow way, the test makers couldn't ask challenging questions about them. So, to set up the questions—to test how you think about what you read—the GMAT uses passages in which authors hide or disguise their statement of purpose and challenge you to extract it. That's why it's so important to stay curious and to ask probing questions as you read.

Some students are concerned that this approach will take too much time. But in fact, asking questions and considering the author's purpose and intent is a way for you to read more quickly, not more slowly. It's a way to skim the details and get through the passage to leave time to answer the questions. Digesting the passage by interrogating it, mentally paraphrasing, and jotting down some notes should take roughly 3 to 4 minutes. This will leave ample time for the questions, especially since you'll be so well prepared to answer the questions.

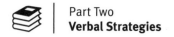

STEP 2: ANALYZE THE QUESTION STEM

After you've read the passage, it's time to attack the questions. For each question, your first goal is to identify the type: Global, Detail, Inference, Logic, or Critical Reasoning. Ask yourself, "What should I do on this question? What is being asked?" Here are some guidelines:

If you see "purpose of the passage" or "main idea" = Global question.

If you see direct language like "according to" or "states" = Detail question.

If you see indirect language like "agree" or "suggest" = Inference question.

If you are asked for the purpose of a detail or paragraph = Logic question.

Be sure to focus on exactly what the question is asking about. Let's say you see this question:

The passage states which of the following about the uses of fixed nitrogen?

It's not enough to just look for what the passage says about "nitrogen" in general. The whole passage might be about nitrogen. In fact, it's not enough to look for "fixed nitrogen." Be precise. The question asks about the *uses* of fixed nitrogen, so that's what you need to find.

STEP 3: RESEARCH THE RELEVANT TEXT IN THE PASSAGE

Here's the great news about Reading Comprehension passages: they don't disappear after you read them. Answering Reading Comprehension questions on the GMAT is like taking an open-book test. Many students rely on their memory of the passage to answer questions, but since incorrect choices often contain very subtle distortions of information in the passage, memory can be a poor guide. Instead, use your understanding of the passage's structure to find direct support for any answer that you select.

STEP 4: MAKE A PREDICTION

Don't make the mistake of reading the answer choices immediately after reading the question stem. Since your task is to find the correct answer, your brain will attempt to justify each choice as being correct. Doing this without a prediction can lead to confusion, as your mind works to mount arguments for why multiple choices could be correct. Instead, flip it around. Read the question stem, research the passage, and then make a quality prediction of what the answer choice should say. Once you've done that, *then* you're ready to jump into the answer choices. After all, it's much easier to find what you're looking for if you have an idea what that thing is.

STEP 5: EVALUATE THE ANSWER CHOICES

Once you've researched the passage and made a prediction, it's time to find a match in the answer choices. If you can't find a match for your prediction, if more than one seems to fit your prediction, or if you weren't able to form a prediction at all (it happens!), then you'll need to work by elimination. Fortunately, eliminating four wrong choices is the same as finding the one right answer!

Practice Questions

Apply the Kaplan Method for Reading Comprehension to the following passages and questions. Focus on the big picture as you read each passage and try to determine its topic, scope, and purpose. Then work through each question systematically by first identifying the question's type. Don't be in a rush to evaluate the answer choices; research the passage and phrase a prediction first, then try to find a match. After you finish, check the answers and explanations that follow.

Questions 1–3 refer to the following passage.

The search for an explanation of the historically weak status of U.S. third-party movements is illuminated by examining the conditions that have favored the growth of a strong two-party
5 system. Different interests and voting blocs predominate in different regions, creating a geographically fragmented electorate. This heterogeneity is complemented by a federal political structure that forces the major parties
10 to find voter support at state and local levels in separate regions. For example, the Democratic Party long sought and drew support simultaneously from northern black urban voters and from segregationists. Such pressures
15 encourage the major parties to avoid political programs that are too narrowly or sharply defined. The nondoctrinal character of U.S. politics means that important new issues and voting blocs tend to be initially ignored by the
20 major parties. Such issues—opposition to immigration and the abolition of slavery are two historic examples—tend to gain political prominence through third parties.

Ironically, the same factors that lead to the
25 emergence of third parties contribute to the explanation of their failure to gain national political power. Parties based on narrow or ephemeral issues remain isolated or fade rapidly. At the same time, those that raise increasingly
30 urgent social issues also face inherent limits to growth. Long before a third party can begin to broaden substantially its base of voter support, the major parties are able to move to attract the minority of voters that it represents. The
35 Democratic Party, for instance, appropriated the agrarian platform of the Populist Party in 1896, and enacted Socialist welfare proposals in the

1930s, in both cases winning much of the popular bases of these parties. Except for the
40 Republican Party, which gained national prominence as the Whigs were declining in the 1850s, no third party has ever achieved national major-party status. Only at state and local levels have a handful of third parties been sustained
45 by a stable voting bloc that remains unrepresented by a major party.

1. The primary purpose of this passage is to

    O   examine the appeal of U.S. national third parties to the electorate at state and local levels

    O   trace the historical rise and decline of third-party movements in the United States

    O   explain why most U.S. third-party movements have failed to gain major-party status

    O   demonstrate that U.S. politics has traditionally been non-ideological in character

    O   suggest a model to explain why certain U.S. third-party movements have succeeded while others have failed

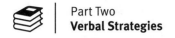

2. Which of the following does the author suggest was an important factor in the establishment of the Republican Party as a major national party?

○ the polarization of national opinion at the time of a major social crisis

○ the unique appeal of its program to significant sectional interests

○ the acceptance of its program by a large bloc of voters unrepresented by a major party

○ the simultaneous decline of an established major party

○ the inability of the major parties of the era to appeal to all sectional interests

3. According to the author, the major factor responsible for the rise of third parties in the United States has been the

○ domination of major parties by powerful economic interests

○ inability of major parties to bring about broad consensus among a variety of voters and interest groups

○ slow response of major parties to new issues and voting groups

○ exclusion of immigrants and minorities from the mainstream of U.S. politics

○ variety of motivations held by voting blocs in different regions

Questions 4–7 refer to the following passage.

Despite increasing enrollments of women in medical schools, feelings of isolation among women medical students persist. Women students still have to contend with the social
5 stereotype of a male doctor. In addition, institutions themselves may unintentionally foster feelings of separateness. Comparatively few women are hired for faculty positions, thus offering women students few role models. The
10 pervasive sexual humor of male doctors and students further intensifies the women students' alienation. Alienation, in turn, negatively affects individual self-perception.

As women enter medical study in increasing
15 numbers, they may feel less at odds with their peers and the teaching establishment. Institutional bias will, no doubt, also change in response to changing societal values. However, we should not wait passively for gradual social
20 processes to bring changes; schools must provide current students with support services designed to meet women's needs. In a recent study, 48 percent of the women questioned rated a student support group as the most
25 important support service a school can provide.

4. The passage cites all of the following as causing psychological problems for women medical students EXCEPT

○ feelings of alienation from teachers and fellow students

○ prevailing societal conceptions about doctors

○ declining enrollments of women to medical schools

○ expressions of sexism by peers and superiors

○ absence of positive female models for women students

5. The author of the passage would be most likely to agree with which of the following?

   O Medical schools practice widespread discrimination on the basis of sex.

   O Gender-based stereotyping encourages feelings of isolation among women medical students.

   O Some medical school policies are deliberately designed to make women students feel isolated.

   O Social norms must change before institutional bias can decline.

   O The majority of women medical students have a negative self-image.

6. The passage suggests that which of the following would likely reduce the isolation felt by women medical students?

   O requiring men doctors and students to participate in sexual harassment awareness training

   O adopting a unisex medical school dress code in order to minimize the appearance of sterotypical male doctors

   O greater support services designed to meet men's needs so that women students don't feel they are the only ones receiving support services

   O a change in medical school hiring practices that results in an equal percentage of women and men hired as professors

   O more studies on what types of support services women medical students feel they need

7. In terms of its tone and content, the passage is most appropriately described as

   O an impassioned polemic

   O an indignant protest

   O a reasoned appeal

   O a detached summary

   O a biased speculation

Questions 8–12 refer to the following editorial published in an academic journal relating to modern economics.

There is an intriguing note to the current call upon civil rights law to help remedy the undervaluation of women's work. Until fairly recently, government was not expected to solve
5 workers' economic grievances, however valid they might be. Many assumed that the responsibility lay with workers themselves. Collective bargaining was the preferred instrument for pursuing pay equity for women.
10 Rather than call upon the law to regulate the market from the outside, one could try to reshape or otherwise influence the market so that women themselves would be better able to address the problem. This could be done by
15 raising absolute wage levels in low-paying, predominantly female industries (such as retail clothing) or by changing the pay relationship between largely female and largely male occupations within a single industry, such as
20 auto manufacturing. Through union representation, employees in traditionally female jobs in an industry could identify the actual degree of underpayment of their work and then, as a group, pressure their employer to remedy
25 it. In addition, this process would encourage those affected—men and women alike—to be sensitive to the limits of available resources, to be pragmatic about the pace at which the wage structure could be revised.

30 This is not meant to suggest that collective
bargaining is a foolproof means for closing the
gender gap in wages. To the extent that the
problem involves the undervaluation of
nonunion female occupations in an otherwise
35 unionized industry, political hurdles will
discourage unionized employees from
supporting revisions in the wage structure. And
to the extent that the problem is the
concentration of women in low-paying
40 industries—textiles, for example—the product
market imposes serious economic constraints on
a substantial closing of the wage gap.

Despite the imperfections of tools like collective
bargaining for redressing wage disparities
45 between men and women, a reliance on law or
government is favorable for neither individual
firms nor the economy as a whole. Nonetheless,
although opponents of mandatory public
remedies may correctly fear those remedies as
50 being a cure worse than the disease, they are
wrong when they imply that the current system
of wage determination by business management
is perfectly healthy.

8. In line 14, "This" most likely refers to

O increasing the wages of women and
men in a single industry

O bringing about changes in market
conditions

O changing the dynamic of collective
bargaining

O relying on civil rights law to remedy
economic grievances

O applying group pressure on an
employer

9. According to the author, the process of
unionization and collective bargaining could do
all of the following EXCEPT

O overcome market pressures that keep
wages in some industries lower than in
others

O encourage worker flexibility in
adjusting a new pay scale to economic
conditions

O help workers to apply group pressure
on employers

O aid in determining the degree to which
women are being underpaid

O sensitize workers to the limits of their
industry's ability to institute change

10. Which of the following best summarizes the
author's main point?

O Pay inequity for women exists because
of the lack of unionization in
traditionally female occupations.

O Government regulation of industry to
achieve pay equity for women is
unnecessary because management has
the power to effectively determine
wages.

O Unionization would solve all industry
problems relating to the valuation of
women's work.

O Government regulation of women's
wages is necessary only in those
industries where collective bargaining
is ineffective.

O Collective bargaining is preferable to
government actions in redressing the
undervaluation of women's work.

11. The author mentions textiles (line 40) in order to

- O demonstrate the potential harm of government regulation of industry
- O outline a strategy for achieving pay equity for women
- O indicate how quickly employees can reasonably expect to achieve pay equity
- O give an example of a situation in which collective bargaining may be ineffective
- O show why civil rights laws are the most important tool for increasing women's wages

12. In the final paragraph, the author addresses "opponents of mandatory public remedies" (lines 48–49) by

- O arguing that those remedies would benefit the economy
- O implying that alternative methods of correcting wage disparities would be worse
- O asserting that the present approach to setting wages is flawed
- O defending civil rights legislation as a solution to social problems
- O insisting that those remedies are a viable means of correcting wage disparities

Answers and Explanations

1. C	4. C	7. C	10. E
2. D	5. B	8. B	11. D
3. C	6. D	9. A	12. C

1. C

Here, the "primary purpose" is fairly clearly articulated in the very first sentence of the passage. "The search for an explanation of the historically weak status of U.S. third-party movements is illuminated by examining the conditions that have favored the growth of a strong two-party system." In other words, the purpose of the passage is to explain why most U.S. third-party movements have failed to gain major party status (C).

A quick vertical scan of the verbs knocks out a few answer choices. GMAT passages are never comprehensive enough to "trace the historical rise and decline" (B) or "demonstrate" (D) anything exhaustively—(D) is also out because it doesn't mention third-party movements, clearly the topic of this passage. (A) is out because the passage is primarily concerned with the failure of third parties to rise above the state and local levels, not their success there. Finally, (E) is out because no "model" is given to explain the success of some third-party movements; again, the passage is about the general failure of third-party movements nationally.

2. D

This is an Inference question, so you just have to scan the passage to find where the Republican Party is mentioned: near the end of the passage. The exact line states: "Except for the Republican Party, which gained national prominence as the Whigs were declining in the 1850s, no third party has ever achieved national major-party status." Clearly, it doesn't take much to infer that the party's establishment was facilitated by the "simultaneous decline of an established major party."

Because this is an Inference question, answers from the wrong part of the passage can be counted out, including (C), an irrelevant detail from the second paragraph. (A) is nowhere mentioned, nor is (B) or (E). *Note*: Just because the question uses the word *suggest*, don't overthink it; just locate the information in the passage—the correct answer will still very often be almost a paraphrase of what you locate.

3. C

You're looking for factors to explain the rise of third parties, not their ultimate failure, so you want to research the first paragraph. There it states: "important new issues and voting blocs tend to be initially ignored by the major parties. Such issues . . . tend to gain political prominence through third parties." (C) represents a close paraphrase of this thought.

(A) is out; "powerful economic interests" are not mentioned. (B) is off base; in fact, one of the primary reasons third parties never get off the ground is that major parties swoop in to steal their voter support (lines 31–34). And (D) is out; if minorities were excluded from the mainstream of U.S. politics, black urban voters would not have been a significant voting bloc of the Democratic Party. Finally, (E) is out; major parties generally deal successfully with the variety of motivations held by voting blocs in different regions by avoiding narrowly defined political programs.

4. C

You're looking for the one answer choice not cited by the passage. According to line 1, enrollments of women in medical schools are increasing, not declining. Choice (C) is correct.

Choice (A) is the major problem mentioned in the passage, described variously as feelings of "isolation," "separateness," and "alienation" (lines 2, 7, and 12) from "peers and the teaching establishment" (paragraph 2). Choices (B), (D), and (E) all contribute to this major problem.

5. B

This is one form of Inference question, but on the GMAT, you aren't expected to infer too much. Lines 4–5 mention "the social stereotype of a male doctor." Since this comes right after the reference to "feelings of isolation" in line 2, you can infer that the author thinks gender-based stereotypes are one cause of such feelings (B).

Of the wrong choices, (A) is not supported; enrollments of women are increasing, though there are still few women faculty members—at worst there's a mixed picture, and nothing in the passage supports the idea of "widespread discrimination." (C) contradicts lines 6–7, which say institutional policies may "unintentionally" foster feelings of separateness. (D) distorts lines 17–18 in the second paragraph; to say changing values will cause institutional bias to decline is not to say that social norms *must* change before bias will decline. (E) exaggerates the last sentence in paragraph 1; you can infer that some women medical students have a negative self-perception, but not that they are the majority.

6. D

This is an Inference question, so find the choice that, while not directly stated in the passage, is supported by the passage. Paragraph 1 says that one reason for women's isolation is that they don't have many role models, since "comparatively few women are hired for faculty positions." In other words, the schools hire more men than women. Changing the hiring practices as described in correct choice (D) would result in as many women being hired as men, and this would provide more women role models. (A) and (E) sound reasonable, but there is simply no support for them in the passage. Don't pick a choice to an Inference question unless you can point to support in the passage itself. (B) distorts paragraph 1's reference to the *social* stereotype of a male doctor. The passage only refers to support services for women, so (C) is incorrect.

7. C

The question asks about both tone and content. The *tone* of the passage is quiet; the author summarizes facts, cites a statistic, and does not yell or scream. The *content*, however, is not disinterested; the author definitely advocates changes—medical schools should not "wait passively" for society to change but should do more to address the problems of "current students." (C) is the choice that best fits this combination of a quiet, persuasive tone and clear-cut advocacy. "Impassioned" and "indignant" in (A) and (B) are both too shrill, and the passage is not really a "polemic" (a sharply phrased argument directed against some person or position) or a "protest" (the author is *for* certain changes, but that's not the same thing). "Detached" (D) misses the author's involvement in the subject—this author *cares*—and "summary" misses her advocacy. In (E), although some persons might feel the author is "biased," the passage is not primarily a "speculation," but a plea for changes, or an "appeal," as in correct choice (C).

8. B

Since "This" is the first word in the sentence, you have to check the previous sentence to determine its meaning. The previous sentence says that instead of invoking civil rights law, one could try to influence the market so that women could address their own problems. The correct answer will paraphrase "influence the market," (B).

(A) and (E) appear after "This," and thus cannot be what the pronoun refers to. (C) mentions collective bargaining, but "changing its dynamic" is never discussed. (D) goes against the main idea, by favoring use of civil rights law over collective bargaining.

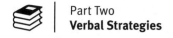

9. A

Figuring out where in the passage to look for an answer is vital! For something that collective bargaining *can't* do, you look at paragraph 2, which lists the shortcomings. There the author states that "the product market imposes serious economic constraints on a substantial closing of the wage gap," which makes (A) correct. Choices (B), (C), (D), and (E) are identified in paragraph 1 as things that collective bargaining *can* accomplish.

10. E

The main idea in the initial analysis of the passage is that collective bargaining isn't perfect, but it's preferable to civil rights law for addressing women's labor issues. (E) is a close paraphrase of this idea and is correct.

As for the wrong answers, (A) offers a detail. (B) distorts the passage—the author believes that government regulation is bad, but not that management should have unlimited power to set wages. (C) is a sweeping generalization—a negative sign in itself. Correct choices seldom use absolute words such as "all," "never," "always," and "every." And the passage explicitly states that unionization doesn't solve all problems. (D) runs counter to the author's attitude: the author never endorses any type of government remedy.

11. D

The textile industry is mentioned in the course of the author's admission that collective bargaining is not "foolproof." The passage says that "the concentration of women in low-paying industries" raises problems that are not easily resolved by collective bargaining. Thus, (D) is the correct answer.

Choice (A) is wrong because the second paragraph is not where the author makes a case against government regulation. Choices (B) and (C) refer to matters discussed earlier in the passage. (E) contradicts the author's argument.

12. C

In researching the previous question, you may remember examining the last paragraph to find that the author agrees that public remedies are potentially harmful but sharply questions the opponents' assumption that the present system is adequate. (C) restates this latter point. The four wrong choices run counter to the author's argument—at no point does the author endorse any form of government regulation or civil rights law.

GMAT Critical Reasoning

In Critical Reasoning questions, you'll be tasked with analyzing short arguments or proposals. Specific directions may ask you to strengthen or weaken an argument or to identify an appropriate inference that can be drawn from a set of facts.

In business, managers need to evaluate arguments and proposals with a critical eye. The ability to argue persuasively—to understand the logic of an argument, evaluate its merits, and be able to respond to its strengths and weaknesses—requires critical thinking skills that any business manager should have. That's precisely why these skills are tested on the GMAT!

The 36-question Verbal section contains about 10 Critical Reasoning questions. Critical Reasoning tests reasoning skills involved in making arguments, evaluating arguments, and formulating or evaluating a plan of action.

Specifically, you are measured on your ability to reason in the following areas:

- **Argument construction:** Recognizing the basic structure of an argument, properly drawn conclusions, underlying assumptions, or explanatory hypotheses
- **Argument evaluation:** Analyzing an argument, recognizing elements that would strengthen or weaken it, identifying reasoning errors committed in the argument or aspects of the argument's development
- **Formulating and evaluating a plan of action:** Recognizing the relative appropriateness, effectiveness, and efficiency of different plans of action as well as factors that would strengthen or weaken a proposed plan of action

To succeed in these question types, you must improve your ability to deconstruct arguments into evidence and conclusion, as well as to determine the assumptions that connect those two pieces together.

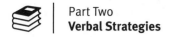

Breaking Down an Argument

A typical GMAT Critical Reasoning question stem is presented as a paragraph-length argument. But just what do we mean by "argument" on the GMAT? We mean an attempt at a reasoned appeal—a piece of text in which an author puts forth a claim and tries to support it. Thus, every GMAT argument contains the following parts:

- The conclusion is the author's claim, or the point the author is trying to make. The conclusion is always an opinion.

- The evidence is the support the author offers for the conclusion. Evidence may be fact or opinion.

Identifying the Conclusion and Evidence

To find an argument's conclusion, it's important not to make the mistake of thinking that the *conclusion* must come at the *end* of the stimulus. In fact, an author's conclusion can show up anywhere in an argument—it could be the first sentence, followed by the evidence; it could be the last sentence, with evidence preceding it; or it could be in the middle, sandwiched between two pieces of evidence. Since you can't use location to find conclusion, you'll have to use something else.

The easiest way to find the conclusion in an argument is to look for conclusion key words. These include *therefore, thus, as a result, hence, clearly, so,* and *consequently.* Whatever comes after those key words is the author's conclusion.

However, the author may not use a conclusion key word to signal their point. Fortunately, another way to find the conclusion is to look for evidence key words. The author uses these to clearly indicate the reasoning or support for a conclusion. Once you know where the evidence is, you can more easily locate the author's conclusion. Common evidence key words include *because, since,* and *for.*

But what if there are no explicit key word signals in the argument? Fortunately, there are other ways to determine the structure of the argument.

The One-Sentence Test

To give the stimulus the one-sentence test, ask yourself what the author would say if limited to a single sentence. The statement you come up with (which may be a recommendation or prediction) should be the conclusion.

The "What" Versus "Why" Test

Another technique that can help you to distinguish between evidence and conclusion is based on the fact that the evidence and the conclusion answer different questions, as you can see:

This part:	Answers the question:
Conclusion	What does the author believe?
Evidence	Why does the author believe this?

So, if you're unsure whether a particular statement is evidence or a conclusion, ask yourself: Does this sentence express *what* the author believes? Or does it explain *why* the author believes it? Once you locate the conclusion, the rest of the stimulus is either background information that provides contextual information, or evidence that supports the conclusion.

Now it's time for some practice. In the following arguments, identify the author's conclusion and the evidence used in support of the conclusion:

1. *Get Going* magazine surveyed its readers and found that three out of every four people who want to visit the Andaman Islands wish to do so on a package tour provided by a tour operator. Since tour operators currently in business can provide tours for only 60 percent of those who wish to visit the Andaman Islands, setting up a travel company that offers tours to the Andaman Islands is a relatively risk-free way to make money.

   Conclusion: _____

   Evidence: _____

2. In a recently published study, researchers asserted that steady chromium intake, even in small doses, can significantly lower the life expectancy of some primates. In the study, 250 chimpanzees were reared in a laboratory and given small, but constant, doses of chromium. Within 17 years, all of the chimps had died. Moreover, their average life span was just over 11 years, whereas the average life span for untreated chimps in the wild is approximately 40 years.

   Conclusion: _____

   Evidence: _____

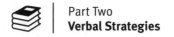
Compare your analysis of the two arguments to ours:

1. **Andaman Islands Argument**

    The conclusion is the last half of the last sentence: "[S]etting up a travel company that offers tours to the Andaman Islands is a relatively risk-free way to make money." This conclusion is based on a survey, which found that 75 percent of potential visitors would like to do so on a package tour, whereas package tour providers can accommodate only 60 percent of the demand.

2. **Chromium Chimps Argument**

    Here, the conclusion is in the first sentence: "[S]teady chromium intake, even in small doses, can significantly lower the life expectancy of some primates." This conclusion is based on a study in which chimps given small, but constant, doses of chromium in a lab had lower average life spans than did chimps in the wild.

Finding evidence and conclusion in an argument is a key skill for success in Critical Reasoning questions. But there's a third crucial component to these arguments. Because the evidence in these arguments is never strong enough to fully support the conclusion, you will need to consider additional evidence or reasoning that would be necessary for the argument to be convincing. These unspoken pieces of evidence and logic are the argument's assumptions.

Assumptions

Assumptions act as additional, unstated evidence. They are statements that must be true for the argument to be valid.

To find assumptions, compare the terms in the conclusion with the terms in the evidence. Then ask yourself: What's missing? Every GMAT argument contains a logical gap between the evidence and the conclusion, even if it's a small one. The author's assumptions fill that gap. With practice, the author's assumptions should start to jump right out at you. This is because the same types of assumptions appear over and over again in GMAT arguments.

Take another look at the two arguments you just analyzed. Weigh the conclusions you identified against the evidence and ask yourself what's missing. Is the author overlooking anything? Is he taking anything for granted? Remember to read critically. See if you can put the author's assumptions in your own words and then see whether you identified the same assumptions that we did.

1. In the Andaman Islands Argument, the author assumes that:

    _____

    _____

    _____

2. In the Chromium Chimps Argument, the author assumes that:

    _____

    _____

    _____

Here are some assumptions we found:

1. **Andaman Islands Argument**

   This author assumes that everyone who *wishes* to visit the Andaman Islands will in fact *do* so. If some of the people who would like to visit the islands won't actually do so, then the present tour providers may be more than sufficient to handle the people who actually purchase package tours.

   The author also assumes that the survey is not biased. What if *Get Going* magazine specializes in reviewing package tours and its readership is much more likely to prefer package tours than the average tourist? If the survey is not representative, the conclusion is not valid.

2. **Chromium Chimps Argument**

   This argument follows a common pattern that we call a *causal argument*: in general, these arguments assume that because two things are related, one must have caused the other. Here, the author assumes that chimps raised in a lab and chimps in the wild would normally have similar life expectancies and, even more important, the author assumes that there wasn't something else that caused the chimps in the study to die prematurely. Maybe most of the chimps succumbed to a virus that spread rapidly in crowded laboratory conditions, or maybe something else happened. The point is that in a causal argument, the author always assumes that there's not another plausible explanation for what happened.

When you break down an argument on the GMAT, begin by identifying the author's conclusion (what the author wants you to believe) and evidence (why the author thinks you should accept the conclusion). From there, seek to identify the missing steps or gaps between the evidence and the conclusion. These are the author's assumptions, and uncovering them is the key to confidently tackling most Critical Reasoning questions.

Critical Reasoning Question Types

GMAT Critical Reasoning questions come in a variety of types; knowing what makes each unique will help you phrase predictions and more easily find the correct answers.

Assumption Questions

As previously discussed, an assumption is a piece of support that isn't explicitly stated but is necessary for the argument to remain valid. When a question asks for what's missing from the argument or what the argument depends on, then it's asking you to find the assumption.

Here are some Assumption question stems:

- Which one of the following is assumed by the author?
- Upon which one of the following assumptions does the author rely?
- The argument depends on the assumption that . . .
- Which one of the following, if added to the passage, would make the conclusion logical?
- The validity of the argument depends on which one of the following?
- The argument presupposes which one of the following?

In these types of questions, your task is to find the answer choice that contains an assumption in the argument. Consider this brief stimulus:

> Allyson plays volleyball for Central High School. Therefore, Allyson must be over 6 feet tall.

The conclusion is the second sentence, and the evidence is the first. But what is the disconnect? Well, who's to say that all high school volleyball players have to be over 6 feet tall? You can confidently predict that an answer would say something like this:

> All volleyball players at Central High School are over 6 feet tall.

But what if an assumption doesn't just jump out at you? Can you track it down? Of course you can! One of the most common ways the GMAT uses assumptions is to cover over a scope shift in the argument. Notice that the argument discusses playing volleyball in the evidence, then jumps to a claim about being over 6 feet tall. The only way the argument makes sense is for these two ideas to be connected.

Therefore, when tackling Assumption questions on the GMAT, be sure to look closely at the terms in each part of the argument. Is there a shift in scope from the evidence to the conclusion?

Consider this seemingly solid argument:

> Candidate A won the presidential election, carrying 40 out of 50 states. Clearly, Candidate A has a strong mandate to push for her legislative agenda.

On the surface, it sounds pretty good. But take a closer look at the terms of the argument. The evidence is a win representing a sizeable majority of states. The conclusion is about a strong mandate for an agenda. Even if you don't immediately see why those two things don't have to be the same, you could still make a prediction like this: "Candidate A's **big victory** means she has a **mandate** for her agenda." You'd be much more likely to recognize the right answer between these two possibilities:

1. No other candidate in the last 24 years has won as many states as did Candidate A.
2. Most of the people who voted for Candidate A support her legislative agenda.

The first answer choice doesn't deal with Candidate A's agenda at all. But the second one shows a connection between her victory and her agenda, so it must be the right answer.

Strengthen and Weaken Questions

The ability to find an argument's assumption can you help you answer another common type of GMAT Critical Reasoning question: Strengthen or Weaken.

You can recognize these types of questions because the question stem will ask you to find a choice that strengthens or supports the argument (Strengthen question), or weakens or damages the argument (Weaken question). Here are some examples:

Weaken

- Which one of the following, if true, would most weaken the argument?
- Which one of the following, if true, would most seriously damage the argument?
- Which one of the following, if true, casts the most doubt on the argument?
- Which of the following, if true, would most seriously call into question the plan outlined by the consultant?

Strengthen

- Which one of the following, if true, would most strengthen the argument?
- Which one of the following, if true, would provide the most support for the conclusion in the argument?
- The argument would be more persuasive if which one of the following were found to be true?

To demonstrate how these questions operate, let's use the same stimulus as before but in the context of these other question types:

> Allyson plays volleyball for Central High School. Therefore, Allyson must be over 6 feet tall.

Remember the assumption holding this argument together? It was that all volleyball players for Central High are over 6 feet tall. That's the assumption that makes or breaks the argument. So, if you're asked to *weaken* the argument, you want to attack that assumption:

> Which one of the following, if true, would most weaken the argument?

Prediction: Not all volleyball players at Central High School are over 6 feet tall.

When evaluating answer choices, look for any choice that expresses this idea—even if the wording does not exactly match your prediction. Something like "There is at least one volleyball player who is under 6 feet tall" is a conceptual match to the prediction, even if the language is slightly different.

But what kind of prediction would you make if the question asked you to *strengthen* the argument? Imagine this question stem:

> Which one of the following, if true, would most strengthen the argument?

Prediction: All volleyball players at Central High School are over 6 feet tall.

Again, when evaluating the choices, look for a conceptual match. Something like "At Central High School, there are no volleyball players under 6 feet 2 inches" is absolutely a strengthener.

For the most part, Strengthen and Weaken questions will operate like the examples above: you'll be presented with an argument, and you'll choose an answer that either affirms or casts doubt on the author's assumption. In some situations, though, the correct answer might not focus on an assumption made by the author. Instead, the right answer to a Strengthen question might simply be an independent piece of evidence that, when added to the author's stated evidence, makes the conclusion more likely to be true. Similarly, the correct answer to a Weaken question may merely be a fact that casts doubt upon the conclusion. There may also be occasions in which the author presents no evidence at all to back up her claim; she may simply state that her proposed course of action will lead to a certain outcome. In such a situation, focus on the effect each choice would have on the proposal's likelihood of success.

It's also common for a Strengthen or Weaken question stem to refer explicitly to a specific part of the argument. You might, for example, see the following language:

> Which of the following, if true, casts the most doubt on the author's conclusion that the Brookdale Public Library does not meet the requirements of the new building code?

By reading the question stem first, you learn right away what the author's conclusion is, making your reading of the stimulus much easier to manage.

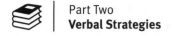

Inference Questions

To make an inference means to consider one or more statements as evidence and then draw a reasonable conclusion from them. On the GMAT, a valid inference is something that must be true if the statements in the stimulus are true. Not *might* be true, not *probably* is true, but *must* be true. Think of an inference as a conclusion that requires no assumption whatsoever.

The answer to an Inference question is just as likely to be drawn from only one or two details as to take into account the stimulus as a whole. For this reason, it can be very difficult to predict an exact answer. Nevertheless, you can make a general prediction: the answer is the one that *must* be true based on the facts in the stimulus. You can use this prediction to help eliminate choices one by one, ruling out options that clearly don't match the facts as you paraphrased them. This is the beauty of a multiple-choice test—once you have identified the four wrong answers, you have also found the right one!

On Test Day, you'll know you're tackling an Inference question when the question stem asks you to take the stimulus as fact and to find something that must be true based on the information presented. Here are some Inference question stems that you may see on your test:

- Which one of the following can be inferred from the argument above?
- Which one of the following is implied by the argument above?
- If all the statements above are true, which one of the following must also be true?
- The statements above, if true, best support the argument that _____.
- Which of the following is the conclusion toward which the author is probably moving?
- The statements above best support which of the following conclusions?

To see how to tackle one of these questions—and how *not* to tackle one of these questions—examine a somewhat expanded version of the volleyball team argument:

> Allyson plays volleyball for Central High School, despite the team's rule against participation by nonstudents. Therefore, Allyson must be over 6 feet tall.

What can be inferred based on this information? Well, one thing you can't infer is this: Allyson must be the best player on the Central High School volleyball team.

Certainly, Allyson *might* be the best player on the team. It's tempting to think that this would *probably* be true—otherwise, the team would not risk whatever penalties violating the rule might entail. But *must* it be true? No. Allyson could be the second best. Or the third best. Or perhaps the coach owed Allyson's dad a favor. There is no support for the idea that she's the best on the team.

But what sort of valid inference can be drawn from the information presented? Something like this: Allyson is not a student at Central High School.

Clearly, if Allyson plays volleyball *despite* the team's rule against participation by nonstudents, she must not be a student. Otherwise, she wouldn't be playing despite the rule; she'd be playing in accordance with the rule. But note that this inference is not an essential assumption of the argument because the conclusion about Allyson's height doesn't depend on it.

So be careful: unlike an assumption, an inference need not have anything to do with the author's conclusion. In fact, the stimuli for many Inference questions aren't even arguments and don't have conclusions—they consist solely of individual facts. Make sure you are prepared for Inference questions, as they require a different approach than do other Critical Reasoning questions. Remember, everything that you'll need will be contained in the stimulus, so focus on the information as it's presented and avoid answers that twist the facts (or make up new ones).

Other Question Types

While Assumption, Strengthen, Weaken, and Inference make up about 85 percent of all Critical Reasoning questions, you might run into other question types as well.

Evaluate Questions

In these questions, you're asked to determine what additional evidence would let you evaluate the validity of an argument. These are sometimes categorized as "Strengthen/Weaken" questions, because the type of evidence in the correct answer might strengthen or weaken the argument, depending on what it revealed. Just as for a Strengthen or Weaken question, therefore, your task is first to identify the author's conclusion and evidence and then to consider the assumptions the author is making. Finally, you'll think about the sort of information that would address one or more of those assumptions.

Here are some example question stems:

- Which of the following would it be most useful to know in order to evaluate the argument?
- The answer to which of the following questions would be most important in evaluating the proposal?
- To assess the likelihood that the plan will achieve its objective, it would be most useful to determine which of the following?
- To evaluate the author's reasoning, it would be most useful to compare . . .
- Which of the following must be studied in order to evaluate the argument presented above?

Flaw Questions

These are similar to Assumption questions in that they ask about what's wrong with the argument. What's wrong is that there's a gap in the author's reasoning. Don't confuse Flaw questions with Weaken questions: instead of asking you for some new fact that, if true, would make the argument questionable, flaw questions ask what's already wrong. Your prediction should focus on reasoning errors in the argument. Expect the answer choices to be worded more abstractly than those for Assumption questions. They might say things like "The author assumes that correlation signifies causality," for instance.

Here are some example question stems:

- Which of the following is a flaw in the reasoning above?
- The argument above is vulnerable to which of the following criticisms?

Fill-in-the-Blank Questions

These questions present you with a short passage that ends with a blank, and you have to pick the choice that best completes the passage. The key to these questions is to pay attention to the key word before the blank, which will indicate what kind of information is missing. If it's "since" or "because," then you'll need to provide missing evidence, which means you can treat this as an Assumption or a Strengthen question. If the key word before the blank is a conclusion key word, such as "therefore," then your task is to mentally compile the evidence and draw a well-supported deduction, much as you would for an Inference question.

Explain Questions

These ask you to find an explanation for a seeming discrepancy in the question stem. Your paraphrasing skills are the key to this problem type: in your own words, restate not only the details in the stimulus but also the nature of the apparent inconsistency. Then, look for an answer that explains how the apparently contradictory facts in the stimulus could both be true.

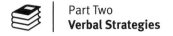

Here are some example question stems:

- Which of the following, if true, would best explain the discrepancy between customer satisfaction and sales?
- Which of the following, if true, would best resolve the paradox described above?

Bolded Statement Questions

Easily recognizable due to the bold text in the stimulus, these questions ask you to identify the role played by one or more statements. They are just like Logic questions in Reading Comprehension, in that they're not asking about what the author says but rather the author's reason for including the statement. Common roles played by statements in Critical Reasoning stimuli are author's conclusion, evidence for the author's conclusion, someone else's conclusion (which the author may agree or disagree with), and evidence for someone else's conclusion.

If more than one statement is bold, it's often helpful to identify the role of one statement first, eliminate all the choices that don't describe that statement accurately, and then see which of the remaining choices describes the second bolded statement correctly.

The Kaplan Method for Critical Reasoning

Critical Reasoning questions on the GMAT are all structured similarly: there will be a paragraph, followed by a question stem, followed by five possible answer choices. But it's a mistake to read these questions from the top of the paragraph down to the bottom of the answer choices. As you've seen in the preceding sections, different Critical Reasoning question types ask you to perform different tasks. That means it will be to your advantage to develop a systematic approach to these types of questions that focuses on identifying the type of question you're dealing with first, then reading the stimulus strategically and with purpose.

> **THE KAPLAN METHOD FOR CRITICAL REASONING**
>
> 1. Identify the question type.
> 2. Untangle the stimulus.
> 3. Predict the answer.
> 4. Evaluate the answer choices.

STEP 1: IDENTIFY THE QUESTION TYPE

Reading the question stem is a great way to focus your reading of the stimulus. Determine the question type, and you'll know exactly what you're looking for. There may be other important information in the question stem as well—possibly even the conclusion itself.

STEP 2: UNTANGLE THE STIMULUS

With the question stem in mind, read the stimulus. Read actively, paraphrasing to make sure you understand the argument's construction and hunting for any potential problems.

STEP 3: PREDICT THE ANSWER

This step is key. Far too many students jump to the answer choices too soon, before they've considered what the correct choice should say or do. Without a prediction, wrong answer choices can look much too enticing.

STEP 4: EVALUATE THE ANSWER CHOICES

Attack each choice critically. Keep your prediction in mind and test the choices one by one to see whether they match it. If you don't find a "clear winner," start looking through the choices that you haven't eliminated. You know what you *like* about each; now focus on what might be *wrong*.

Here's how your prediction and evaluation steps will work for the major question types:

- **Assumption:** Your prediction is the evidence that the author has left out in moving from evidence to conclusion—in other words, the assumption. Depending on the argument, this might be specific (e.g., "The company will not go bankrupt before the end of the year") or general (e.g., "Nothing bad will happen to interfere with the company's plans for next year"). Now hunt for the answer that matches your prediction. If that fails, look for the choice that needs to be true in order for the conclusion to be valid.

- **Strengthen/Weaken:** Identify the author's assumption(s) and predict an answer explaining why that assumption is more (for a Strengthen question) or less (for a Weaken question) likely to be true. Or, if there's no argument in the stimulus, think about what kind of evidence would make the author's claim more or less likely to be true.

- **Inference:** Catalog the most concrete statements in the stimulus. Since the right answer *must* be true, it will align closely with one or more of the author's most definite assertions. Your prediction is thus a mental catalog of these statements. Work through the choices one by one, eliminating those that are not entirely supported by what you know to be true from the text.

Let's apply the Kaplan Method to a Critical Reasoning question:

A study of 20 overweight males revealed that each man experienced significant weight loss after adding SlimDown, an artificial food supplement, to his daily diet. For three months, each man consumed one SlimDown portion every morning after exercising and then followed his normal diet for the rest of the day. Clearly, any adult male who consumes one portion of SlimDown every day for at least three months will lose weight.

Which one of the following is an assumption on which the argument depends?

- ◯ The men in the study will gain back the weight if they discontinue the SlimDown program.
- ◯ No other dietary supplement will have the same effect on overweight men.
- ◯ The daily exercise regimen was not responsible for the effects noted in the study.
- ◯ Women will not experience similar weight reductions if they adhere to the SlimDown program for three months.
- ◯ Overweight men will achieve only partial weight loss if they do not remain on the SlimDown program for a full three months.

STEP 1: IDENTIFY THE QUESTION TYPE

This is an Assumption question, as the stem asks for "an assumption on which the argument depends." Now you are armed with a valuable piece of information: you know that the stimulus will contain an argument that contains some missing link in the chain of reasoning—a missing piece of support without which the conclusion wouldn't be valid.

STEP 2: UNTANGLE THE STIMULUS

Sentence 1 introduces a study of 20 men using a nutritional supplement. All experienced weight loss. Sentence 2 describes how they used it: once a day, for three months, after morning exercise. So far so good—it feels as if the author's building up to something. The key word *clearly* usually indicates that a conclusion follows, and in fact it does: sentence 3 says that anyone who has one portion of the product daily for three months will lose weight, too.

Paraphrase the argument like this:

> Each of 20 overweight men lost weight by consuming some SlimDown every morning after exercise, then eating normally. So, anyone who consumes SlimDown will lose weight.

Reading critically, do you see any scope shifts or other potential problems? Sure—what happened to the exercise? It's in the evidence as part of the study regimen but is totally dropped from the conclusion. That's a pretty significant change in scope, and you can use that as the basis of your prediction in step 3. In fact, you could even look at the argument more abstractly: a bunch of guys did A and B and had x result. So, if someone else does A, they'll get x result, too.

Sounds pretty fishy—who says A (SlimDown) caused x (weight loss)? Why couldn't it have been B (exercise)? Use this insight to make a prediction in step 3. Notice that no matter how abstractly or concretely you analyze the question stem, you'll arrive at the same basic issue—that the author isn't accounting for the exercise.

STEP 3: PREDICT THE ANSWER

Once you realize that the author forgot to consider the exercise, predict something like "The author assumes exercise doesn't matter." That's it. There's no need to come up with a fancy paraphrase. The GMAT will provide plenty of dense language; your job is to rephrase things in simpler terms.

STEP 4: EVALUATE THE ANSWER CHOICES

Judge the choices based on how well they fulfill the requirements of your prediction. And sure enough, only **(C)** even mentions the exercise regimen! Reading it closely, you see it fits the prediction perfectly, clearing up the question of whether the exercise caused the weight loss. Since the difficulty of Critical Reasoning is often in the answer choices (rather than the stimulus), you can't let them make you indecisive. Pick (C) with confidence and move on.

Practice Questions

Having now examined the Kaplan Method and all the most common Critical Reasoning question types, you should be ready to try out what you've learned on the following practice questions. If you encounter a question type you haven't seen before, fear not. Identifying the conclusion, evidence, and underlying assumptions of the argument will most likely be the key to solving the question. If you can't ascertain the correct answer, eliminate as many wrong answer choices as you can, make your best guess, and move on. Answers and explanations follow.

1. Enrollment in graduate and professional programs tends to be high in a strong economy and much lower during recessions. The perceived likelihood of future job availability, therefore, affects people's willingness to pass up immediate earning potential in order to invest in career-related training.

   The argument above assumes that

   O   the perceived likelihood of job availability has decreased in recent years

   O   all those who avoid graduate and professional school during an economic slump do so because of the perceived lack of future jobs

   O   perceptions of the likelihood of job availability are related to the state of the economy

   O   those who enroll in graduate and professional schools during a strong economy help increase the economy's strength

   O   graduate and professional programs admit fewer students during recessions

2. **The university's decision to significantly scale back its teaching of the literary and philosophical classics of the Western Tradition is misguided.** Proponents of the move argue that today's students are not interested in these works and desire more practical business-related courses that will help them in their future careers. But any student lacking a sufficient grounding in the thought and tradition that underlie the present civilization cannot be said to be fully educated. **The classics are the primary vehicle for instilling such knowledge.**

   Which of the following best expresses the relationship between the two bolded statements above?

   O   The first statement offers a hypothesis, and the second statement offers conflicting evidence.

   O   The first statement suggests an alternative explanation for the phenomenon described in the second statement.

   O   The second statement provides evidence for a conclusion drawn in the first statement.

   O   The second statement must be true for the first statement to be true.

   O   The second statement is an inference drawn from the first statement.

3. Due to a string of dismal performances, a touring band has begun to lose its audience. News of the disappointing concerts has traveled quickly via the internet and has negatively influenced ticket sales for future performances. Due to the poor ticket sales, a number of promoters have canceled the band's upcoming shows, forcing the band to attempt to recoup its touring and recording expenses from fewer total performances.

    Which of the following, if true, taken together with the information above, best supports the prediction that more of the band's shows will be canceled?

    ○   The promoters who canceled shows did so with the promise that they would monitor the band's reception in other cities before deciding whether or not to reschedule the canceled shows.

    ○   The pressure to restore its diminishing fan base and recoup its overall expenses from a decreased number of performing opportunities is likely to cause the band to perform poorly in future concerts.

    ○   Because of the canceled shows, it will be impossible for the band to earn a profit on the current tour.

    ○   If the band cannot salvage the tour, its next album will likely fail economically unless the band can restore its image through online videos.

    ○   It is impossible for the management of a rock band to predict accurately the success of a tour because fans of rock bands are notoriously fickle in their tastes.

4. Over the past several years, Running River Water Park has experienced a serious decline in attendance and sales despite the addition of several state-of-the-art water slides. This year, the board of directors lowered the park's weekday admission prices in order to attract more customers. Attendance during the first two months of this year's season has been 30 percent higher than the attendance during the same two months last year. Clearly, the price cut has had the desired effect.

    Each of the following, if true, weakens the conclusion above EXCEPT:

    ○   Nationwide, the number of people attending amusement parks has increased by 30 percent this year over last year.

    ○   Grand Excursions Amusement Park, located 10 miles from Running River, has been closed during most of this year's season due to unexpected equipment problems.

    ○   The most popular movie released this summer, *The Big Chase*, features a long action sequence that was filmed at Running River.

    ○   Several large businesses relocated near Running River during the past year, bringing with them many employees and their families.

    ○   Most amusement park visitors are aware of the admission prices before they arrive at an amusement park.

5. Staff members at the Willard Dodd Academy typically oversee students' schedules and make all final decisions regarding the required activities in which students participate. Students are permitted, however, to make their own decisions regarding how they spend their free time. Therefore, students should be permitted to make their own decisions regarding the elective courses that they wish to take.

The conclusion above would be more reasonably drawn if which of the following were inserted into the argument as an additional premise?

- O Decisions regarding required activities are more important than decisions regarding the elective courses that students take.
- O Students are more willing to take elective courses than to participate in required activities at Willard Dodd.
- O Required activities contribute more to the students' personal growth than do their free-time activities.
- O Staff members at Willard Dodd have found that elective courses are more beneficial for students than the available free-time activities.
- O When compared for decision-making purposes, elective courses are more like free-time activities than required activities.

6. The average math score on a statewide proficiency exam for students attending Middlebury High School last year was 20 points higher than the average math score for students attending nearby Ellingsford High School. Therefore, any student at Ellingsford High School wishing to achieve a better math score on next September's proficiency exam should transfer to Middlebury High School over the summer.

Which of the following statements, if true, would most significantly strengthen the conclusion drawn in the passage?

- O Middlebury High School offers its students a unique, week-long course just before they take the proficiency exam that has consistently proven effective in raising student scores.
- O One-third of all the students who have transferred to Middlebury High School the summer before taking the test got scores that are at least 20 points higher than the average score at Ellingsford High School.
- O Middlebury High School students who transfer to Ellingsford High School in the summer before they take the proficiency exam get average scores that are comparable to the average scores of students who remain at Middlebury.
- O In the past five years, the average score at Ellingsford High School has been rising at a faster rate than has the average score at Middlebury High School.
- O Students wanting better proficiency exam scores are transferring to Middlebury High School at a high rate, which will ultimately result in a lowering of the school's average score.

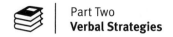

7. For the third year in a row, the town of Springdale is experiencing a shortfall in its school budget. The town council has proposed raising the funds to meet this year's needs by increasing the meals tax charged by local restaurants from 5 to 7.5 percent.

    Which of the following, if true, would cast the most doubt on the effectiveness of the town council's plan to address the Springdale school budget shortfall by raising the local meals tax?

    O   According to the town's bylaws, any proposed tax increase must be put to a public vote during a general election, which could delay the implementation of the new tax by several months.

    O   To ensure compliance with the new rate, the town will have to employ additional auditors to review restaurants' quarterly tax filings.

    O   Managers of local chain and franchise restaurants cannot revise menu prices without permission from their parent companies.

    O   The last time the meals tax was raised in Springdale, restaurants reported a 15 percent decrease in revenues during the first year following the increase, while those in neighboring towns experienced increases of as much as 25 percent.

    O   The Springdale Merchant's Association, to which most local restaurant owners belong, is strongly opposed to the increase.

8. Only city-registered cab drivers are permitted to pick up passengers at the airport. Therefore, if the city eliminates some of its current regulations, such as the requirement that a cab driver have five years of experience before applying for city registration, passengers will not be forced to wait as long for cabs at the airport as they are currently, because _____.

    Which of the following most logically completes the passage above?

    O   increased competition for fares will cause some city-registered cab drivers to stop picking up passengers at the airport

    O   more people will ride in cabs if there are fewer regulations imposed on city-registered cab drivers

    O   more cab drivers will apply for city registration if this requirement is removed

    O   non-city-registered cab drivers will be forced to reduce their fares in order to compete

    O   most cab drivers would apply for city registration if the only regulations imposed on city-registered cab drivers were those required by the state for all cab drivers

9. Country X complains that Country Y's high tariffs on imported goods have artificially inflated the price of cars imported from Country X into Country Y, and that this is the reason that few of Country X's cars are sold in Country Y. On the other hand, Country X's very low tariffs allow Country Y to sell many cars there at relatively low prices. Country X says that if Country Y would lower its tariffs, then Country X's cars would be able to compete in Country Y and an equitable balance of trade would be achieved.

   Which of the following, if true, would most undermine the validity of Country X's explanation for the poor sales of its cars in Country Y?

   O   In places where the tariffs on goods from both countries are equal, Country Y's cars far outsell cars from Country X.

   O   Cars imported from Country Z sell poorly in Country Y.

   O   In countries where tariffs on imported goods are higher than in Country Y, Country X sells more cars than does Country Y.

   O   Other goods from Country X sell poorly in Country Y.

   O   Cars imported from Country X sell well in Country Z.

10. Many adults, no matter what their age, respond to adversity by seeking advice only from their parents. Consciously or not, they regress to a psychological state of childhood dependence in which the parent is seen as the only source of wisdom and comfort. Adults who do not regress to this childhood mode turn for advice in adversity only to other loved ones—a spouse or a best friend—whom they perceive and relate to as peers.

    If all of the above statements are true, which of the following must also be true?

    O   One's parents offer more wisdom in adversity than those whom one perceives as peers.

    O   Adults who do not suffer adversity look only to their parents for advice.

    O   No adults seek advice in adversity from total strangers.

    O   Adults who seek advice in adversity from their parents do not expect to receive wisdom and comfort.

    O   Adults who regress to a state of childhood dependence lose touch with their peers.

Answers and Explanations

1. C	4. E	7. D	9. A
2. C	5. E	8. C	10. C
3. B	6. A		

1. C

The Conclusion: People are more likely to go to graduate school when they think it will help them get a job in the future.

The Evidence: Graduate school enrollment is high in a strong economy and low during recessions.

This question asks for an assumption, and the argument involves a question of cause and effect. Since enrollment in graduate and professional programs tends to be high when the economy is strong and low when it is weak, the reason must be, according to the author, a matter of people's perceptions of job availability. Sounds reasonable, but check to see if all the terms match up with those in this conclusion. The evidence pertains to the state of the economy, but the conclusion strays into the area of psychology—people's perceptions. Are these the same things? The author treats them as such by arguing from evidence regarding the state of the economy to a conclusion based on people's *perceptions* of the economy. The author takes the relationship between these for granted, but technically, in order for the argument to work, this must be established. (C) reveals this basic assumption.

2. C

The Conclusion: It's a bad idea to stop teaching philosophical classics at university.

The Evidence: Students need an understanding of the thought that underlies their civilization, and the philosophical classics are the best way to teach that.

This question asks about the functions played by the bolded sentences in an argument. Once again, your primary task is to break down the argument and identify its parts. Here, the conclusion is in fact the first sentence of the passage; the rest of the passage goes on to explain why the university's decision is

misguided. The first sentence, when it is phrased as an assertion as it is here, is often the conclusion of the passage. So why is the university's decision misguided? (1) Students lacking a certain grounding cannot be considered fully educated. (2) The classics are the primary vehicle for instilling such knowledge. So, the final sentence (second statement) provides evidence for the conclusion drawn in the first sentence (first statement), which is exactly what (C) says. You can also use the process of elimination. (A) is out because the second statement offers no *conflicting* evidence. (B) is out because the second statement does not describe a *phenomenon*, and the first statement suggests no *alternative* explanation. (D) is out because the second statement does not have to be true in order for the first statement to be true, nor is the second statement an inference, or logically drawn conclusion, of the first statement, as (E) states.

3. B

The Conclusion: More of a band's future performances will be cancelled.

The Evidence: Bad performances have led to lower ticket sales and cancelled concerts, so the band has to recoup its expenses from fewer shows.

In this question, the conclusion—more of the band's shows will be canceled—appears in the actual question. You already know the argument's conclusion, so read the passage carefully and follow the flow of the evidence presented. Dismal performances led to a drop in ticket sales for future concerts, which in turn led concert promoters to cancel concerts, putting additional pressure on the band to make up the lost money from fewer shows. You're looking for the choice that leads to more canceled shows, and it's not easy to predict the answer here. But you can test each choice to see where it fits into this chain of events, if at all.

Canceled concerts must now lead to a result that will trigger additional canceled concerts. What do you already know leads to canceled concerts? Dismal performances and lower ticket sales. Keep this in mind while testing out the choices. (B) works by turning the chain of events into a vicious cycle. If (B) were true, you would expect the events to follow the same course, culminating in the cancellation of more shows. Of the wrong choices, (A) indicates that some of the shows that have already been canceled might be rescheduled. Optimally, the band would get to perform the original number of shows, and at worst, the band will perform the current reduced number of concerts. But there is nothing here to indicate that even more shows will be canceled. (C) begins with the canceled concerts but then jumps to the irrelevant issue of "profit." The impossibility of earning a profit under the current circumstances is an effect of the canceled shows—but it does nothing to suggest that more shows will be canceled. (D) discusses the long-term prospects for the band, but nothing here suggests that more shows on the current tour will be canceled. The effect that this tour ultimately has on the band's next album does not directly influence what happens now. (E) goes beyond the scope of the evidence. The accuracy of the management's predictions is not at issue.

4. E

The Conclusion: A lower ticket price led to an increase in visitors at a certain water park.

The Evidence: Attendance increased after the ticket price was lowered.

This is a Weaken "EXCEPT" question, so you're looking for the one choice that would *not* weaken the conclusion. This is a classic causal argument. The author concludes that the water park's admissions price cut is responsible for the increase in attendance over the same period last year. Of course, to weaken a causal argument, one needs only to point out another plausible explanation for the increase in attendance. (A), which notes an increase in park attendance nationally, (B), which notes the closing of a competitor, (C), which notes favorable publicity in a popular movie for the park, and (D), which notes an increase in the

size of the local population, all offer other plausible reasons for the increase in attendance. Only (E), which notes that most people are aware of admission prices, would strengthen, rather than weaken, the conclusion, since public awareness of the price cut would be necessary for the price cut to have a positive effect on attendance.

5. E

The Conclusion: Students should be able to pick their own elective courses.

The Evidence: Although staff members decide what required activities a student must participate in, students can choose how they spend their free time.

The argument here is as follows: since students at the Willard Dodd Academy make their own decisions about free time, they should also make their own decisions about elective courses. The argument assumes that, for these students, decisions about what to do with free time are similar to decisions about what electives to take in school. Since you're looking for a premise to complete the argument, look for a choice that provides evidence that these things are similar. (E) provides the evidence you need. If it is true that elective courses are more akin to free time than to required activities, then the conclusion that students should be able to choose their own electives is more reasonable. You could have eliminated as follows: (A) is irrelevant to the argument; it's not the *importance* of the decision that's at issue here, it's who should have the power to make the decision. (B) is irrelevant; students' relative willingness to take the different types of courses doesn't matter. The argument concerns only who should make the decisions regarding activities. (C) may explain why staff members oversee decisions about required activities, but it tells you nothing about why students should be allowed to choose their own elective courses. In fact, it doesn't refer to elective courses at all. (D) follows the same general pattern of the other wrong choices, focusing on an irrelevant issue (in this case, the relative benefits of electives versus free-time activities), rather than the issue at hand: who should make the decisions.

6. A

The Conclusion: Ellingsford students who wish to do well on a statewide math test this year should transfer to Middlebury.

The Evidence: Last year, Middlebury students scored higher on the test than did Ellingsford students.

As you read the stimulus, you should have tried to identify the evidence and conclusion and think about the assumption that glues the two together. An answer choice that validates that assumption will strengthen the author's argument. The author argues that since Middlebury High School students tend to get better math scores on the test, Ellingsford High School students who want better math scores should transfer to Middlebury the summer before they take the test. Think about the time frame employed here. The author assumes that former Ellingsford High School students will learn what they need to improve their math scores almost immediately after transferring to Middlebury. The correct answer will most likely offer a plausible reason why this might be the case. (A) provides a plausible reason to expect that students who transfer to Middlebury during the summer can significantly benefit before taking the test in September by taking advantage of the unique, week-long course offered just before the test. If (A) is true, then a major stumbling block to the potential efficacy of the proposal is removed, and the argument would be strengthened.

As to the wrong choices: (B) tells you nothing. The average score of only part of a group cannot be fairly compared to the average score of an entire group. A third of the students who remained at Ellingsford High School may also have scored at least 20 points higher than their school's average. (C) weakens the argument's conclusion. If Middlebury students who transfer to Ellingsford during the summer before they take the test still get higher math scores, then the notion that transferring the summer before is a cure-all seems less plausible. (D) presents an irrelevant comparison. The scores at Ellingsford High School may be rising faster than those at Middlebury High School, but the average score at Middlebury is still 20 points higher than the average score at Ellingsford. (E) is irrelevant because the argument does not concern itself with what will happen *ultimately*. The main issue is whether Ellingsford students can raise their scores by transferring. Even if (E) is true, and many students transfer and Middlebury's test score average drops, it's impossible for you to tell whether the transferees' scores are higher or lower than they would have been had they remained at Ellingsford.

7. D

The Conclusion: The town council's plan to raise the meals tax will raise enough money to address the shortfall in the school budget.

From the key words "cast doubt," you know you're dealing with a Weaken question. Specifically, you're weakening the effectiveness of a plan presented by the town council of Springdale. So be sure to look for the details of that plan in the stimulus. The town council of Springdale plans to raise money for schools by increasing the meals tax by 2.5 percent. To weaken the effectiveness of a plan like this one, consider the circumstances that would prevent it from achieving its goal. The new tax will generate revenue only if the price hike doesn't deter people from eating at Springdale restaurants. So, you can go to the answer choices seeking a fact that could keep the restaurants from generating sufficient revenue.

If, as choice (D) suggests, there is reason to believe that fewer people will eat in Springdale restaurants if the tax is raised, the viability of the town council's proposal is cast into doubt. If there are also good restaurants in nearby towns, the plan is further weakened. (D) is the therefore the correct answer.

(A) suggests that implementation of the tax may take a while. However, there is no reason not to believe that it would be effective once implemented. (B) presents an extra hassle for the town, but nothing indicates that this hassle would keep the town council from levying the tax to cover the school budget deficit. (C) introduces a hassle for the restaurants, but again, this difficulty by itself does nothing to interfere with the successful collection of tax revenues. And opposition to the new tax, mentioned in (E), has no bearing on whether or not it could raise the necessary funds.

8. C

The Conclusion: If the city eliminates some of its regulations on cab drivers, there will be shorter wait times for taxis at the airport.

This question asks you to fill in the blank; since the blank is preceded by "because," you'll need to fill it in with evidence supporting a claim made by the author. Paraphrase the stimulus: The author states that if the city eliminates some of its regulations—such as the five years of experience required before cab drivers can apply for registration—then passengers will be able to get cabs more quickly at the airport. Now, think about what kind of evidence would support this. For passengers to be able to get cabs more quickly at the airport, the number of cabs allowed to pick up passengers there would have to increase. The number of cabs allowed to pick up passengers at the airport will only increase if more cab drivers apply for city certification. Therefore, for the elimination of the five-year rule to decrease airport wait time, more cab drivers will have to apply for city certification. (C) would certainly have to be true and matches our prediction.

If (A) were true, people might actually experience longer wait times for cabs, not shorter ones. (B) says that cabs might become more popular, but it doesn't establish that there will be more cabs at the airport. (D) brings up fares, which aren't relevant to the stimulus. (E) discusses what would happen if even more regulations were removed, not just the effects of removing the one regulation under discussion.

9. A

The Conclusion: If Country Y lowers its tariffs, Country X's cars would be able to compete with those produced in Country Y.

The Evidence: Country X has low tariffs, and Country Y sells many cars there. Country Y has high tariffs, and Country X sells few cars there.

The argument develops from evidence that Y's high tariffs make X's cars relatively expensive, but X's low tariffs make Y's cars relatively cheap. The argument concludes that if Y lowers its tariffs, then real

competition and an equitable balance of trade would result. Country X assumes that Y sells more cars in X than X sells in Y because of the price difference created by the different tariffs. This suggests a classic case of ignored alternatives. Look for a choice that suggests that there might be an alternative explanation besides the difference in tariffs that could explain the weakness of X's car sales relative to Y's. (A) weakens country X's argument by illustrating that the effect (more Y cars sold than X cars) is possible without the supposed cause (a tariff imbalance favoring Y). This implies that something other than tariffs—the reason offered by X for its poor performance in the car market—could very well explain the difference in sales (maybe X's car's are no good).

For the record, (B), (C), and (D) would strengthen rather than weaken the author's point that the tariffs are causing poor sales in Country Y. The fact that sales of cars from Country Z are also doing poorly in Country Y, (B), supports the idea that Country Y is doing something to affect the sales of cars from other countries. (C) might sound similar to (A) but the logic is reversed—here, cars from Country X outsell cars from Country Y on an equal playing field, which supports the argument. In (D), if other goods from Country X also fare poorly in Country Y, then the culprit might very well be a tariff. (E) is irrelevant, as it offers no comparison to the sales performance of cars from Country Y to those from Country X.

10. C

The Evidence: Under adversity, some adults regress to a child-like state and seek advice only from their parents. Other adults do not regress and seek advice only from other adults they see as peers.

The question stem sends you searching for a valid inference that can be drawn from the statements in the passage. You're looking for a conclusion *that must be true* based upon the statements in this argument. Reading the passage, you learn that adults can be divided into two groups: adults in adversity who seek advice in adversity only from their parents, and the remainder, who seek that advice only from other loved ones. There is not much room here for argument. All adults fall into one or the other of

these categories, but not both. If these statements are true, then adults must turn either to parents or to other loved ones in times of adversity, and to no one else. (C) is a valid inference, given the evidence above. Adults seek advice from parents or other loved ones—not from strangers. Of the wrong answers, (A) introduces a concept foreign to the evidence. The passage tells you nothing about the relative wisdom of parents and peers. (For all you know, everyone gives terrible advice.) (B) introduces another concept foreign to the evidence. The passage tells you nothing about what people do for advice when they are not in adversity. (D) is unsupported by the evidence. Expectations are not discussed in the passage. The issue here is where people in trouble go for advice—not what they expect to find. And (E) goes too far. Adults who regress will seek advice from parents if they face adverse circumstances and wish to get advice. This doesn't mean they will necessarily lose touch with peers.

Practice Sets

CHAPTER 5

Sentence Correction Practice

Sentence Correction Practice Set One

Directions: Each Sentence Correction question presents a sentence, part or all of which is underlined. Below each sentence, you will find five ways to phrase the underlined portion. The first answer choice repeats the original version, while the other four choices are different. If the original seems best, choose the first answer choice. If not, choose one of the revisions.

In choosing an answer, follow the norms of standard written English: grammar, word choice, and sentence construction. Choose the answer that produces the most effective sentence, aiming to eliminate awkwardness, ambiguity, redundancy, and grammatical error.

1. To be a leading producer in the computer industry, a company must operate internationally, achieve a turnover that makes large-scale production efficient, <u>and secure information about technical advances.</u>

    O   and secure information about technical advances

    O   and securing information about technical advances

    O   while secure information about technical advances

    O   and secure information of how to technically advance

    O   and secure information in regard to technical advances

2. Of the people who brought about the Reformation, the religious revolution that grew out of objections to the doctrines of the medieval church, <u>Martin Luther is the best known of them.</u>

    O   Martin Luther is the best known of them

    O   the best known is Martin Luther

    O   the better known of them was Martin Luther

    O   Martin Luther is better known

    O   the best known one was Martin Luther

3. Declining enrollments are forcing smaller private colleges to choose <u>between raising tuition and reduction of the staff</u>.

    ○   between raising tuition and reduction of the staff

    ○   among raising tuition and reducing staff

    ○   between raising tuition or reducing staff

    ○   between raising tuition and reducing staff

    ○   between the rise of tuition and the reduction of the staff

4. Unable to keep up with the new competitors that had recently entered its industry, the company was forced to begin closing plants, laying off workers, and <u>reduced</u> its research and marketing budgets.

    ○   reduced

    ○   it reduced

    ○   reducing

    ○   would reduce

    ○   it had reduced

5. Although it is conceivable that certain electronic devices implanted in the brain may someday correct blindness caused by nerve damage, there is now no clear evidence <u>of their ability to do it</u>.

    ○   of their ability to do it

    ○   of their doing that

    ○   that they can do so

    ○   that they might one day be able to do it

    ○   to do so

6. Setting up a corporation requires more paperwork and legal provision <u>than to establish either a proprietorship or a partnership</u>.

    ○   than to establish either a proprietorship or a partnership

    ○   than what it requires to establish either a proprietorship or a partnership

    ○   than to either establish a proprietorship or a partnership

    ○   than establishing either a proprietorship or a partnership

    ○   than establishing proprietorships and partnerships

7. In the Champagne region of France, <u>wine growers still harvest grapes as they have done</u> for centuries, by carefully handpicking their crop and storing their precious fruit in specially aged casks.

    ○   wine growers still harvest grapes as they have done

    ○   the wine grower still harvests grapes as has been done

    ○   wine growers still harvest grapes as was done

    ○   wine growers still harvest grapes as they were doing

    ○   wine growers still harvest grapes as they did

8. A new generation of sophisticated copy <u>machines, capable of unprecedented detail and accuracy, are</u> prompting the development of more complex currency designs to prevent counterfeiting.

   O machines, capable of unprecedented detail and accuracy, are

   O machines, capable for unprecedented detail and accuracy, is

   O machines, capable of unprecedented detail and accuracy, is

   O machines, capable for unprecedented detail and accuracy, are

   O machines that are capable of unprecedented detail and accuracy are

9. In an unusual move for a member of her party, <u>the president's directive established price controls</u>.

   O the president's directive established price controls

   O the president's directive was to establish price controls

   O the president was successful in the establishment of controls on prices

   O the president had instituted controls on prices

   O the president established price controls

10. The United Automobile Workers returned to the AFL-CIO because <u>of the wish of both groups to strengthen labor's role not only in politics but also industry</u>.

    O of the wish of both groups to strengthen labor's role not only in politics but also industry

    O both groups wished to strengthen labor's role in politics as well as in industry

    O the strengthening of labor's role in politics as well as industry was wished for by both groups

    O it was wished by both groups to strengthen labor's role in politics and industry as well

    O both groups wished to strengthen labor's role in both of the two areas of politics and industry

11. <u>Compiled from documents provided by several government agencies</u>, the investigative commission produced a report clearly indicating that federal officials had frequently authorized expenditures far above statutory limits.

    O Compiled from documents provided by several government agencies

    O Compiling it from several government agencies' documents

    O A compilation of documents from several government agencies

    O Documents provided by several government agencies

    O Compiling documents provided by several government agencies

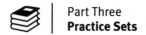
12. Unlike <u>the people whom settled the western states after the passage of the Homestead Act of 1862, the hope of the prospectors and adventurers who came to California during the gold rush was</u> to get rich quickly.

   O   the people whom settled the western states after the passage of the Homestead Act of 1862, the hope of the prospectors and adventurers who came to California during the gold rush was

   O   the people who settled the western states after the passage of the Homestead Act of 1862, the hope of the prospectors and adventurers who came to California during the gold rush was

   O   that of the people who settled the western states after the passage of the Homestead Act of 1862, the prospectors and adventurers who came to California during the gold rush hoped

   O   that of the people whom settled the western states after the passage of the Homestead Act of 1862, the hope of the prospectors and adventurers who came to California during the gold rush was

   O   the people who settled the western states after the passage of the Homestead Act of 1862, the prospectors and adventurers who came to California during the gold rush hoped

13. <u>Just like Congress is the legislative branch of the federal government of the United States, so</u> Parliament is the legislative body of the United Kingdom.

   O   Just like Congress is the legislative branch of the federal government of the United States, so

   O   As Congress is the legislative branch of the federal government of the United States,

   O   As Congress is the legislative branch of the federal government of the United States, in the same way

   O   Just as Congress is the legislative branch of the federal government of the United States, so

   O   Just as the federal government of the United States' legislative branch is Congress,

14. The reason Frances Willard founded the Women's Christian Temperance Union was because she believed that national prohibition of alcohol will empty the poorhouses, jails, and asylums of the United States.

    ○ The reason Frances Willard founded the Women's Christian Temperance Union was because she believed that national prohibition of alcohol will empty the poorhouses, jails, and asylums of the United States.

    ○ Frances Willard founded the Women's Christian Temperance Union, the reason being that she believed that national prohibition of alcohol will empty the poorhouses, jails, and asylums of the United States.

    ○ The reason Frances Willard founded the Women's Christian Temperance Union was she believed that national prohibition of alcohol will empty the poorhouses, jails, and asylums of the United States.

    ○ Because she believed that national prohibition of alcohol would empty the poorhouses, jails, and asylums of the United States, so Frances Willard founded the Women's Christian Temperance Union.

    ○ Frances Willard founded the Women's Christian Temperance Union because she believed that national prohibition of alcohol would empty the poorhouses, jails, and asylums of the United States.

15. The combination of technical expertise, commercial enterprise, and that the government backs them judiciously should ensure Italian firms continuing to innovate and gain competitively in world markets.

    ○ that the government backs them judiciously should ensure Italian firms continuing

    ○ the government backing them judiciously should ensure Italian firms of being about to continue

    ○ judicious government backing should ensure that Italian firms will continue

    ○ the government's judicious backing should ensure Italian firms that they will continue

    ○ the government to back them judiciously should ensure Italian firms of continuing

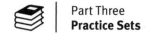
Answers and Explanations

1. A	5. C	9. E	13. D
2. B	6. D	10. B	14. E
3. D	7. A	11. E	15. C
4. C	8. C	12. E	

1. A

All items in a list must be in parallel form. The verb "secure," meaning "to make safe," is in the same form as "operate" and "achieve," so (A) is fine as is. (D) and (E) also use the correct form of "secure" and the connector "and" before the last item in the list. However, "of how to" and "in regard to" are unidiomatic in context.

2. B

After beginning with "Of the people," there's no reason for the author to tack "of them" onto the end of the sentence. This is redundant; eliminate (A). Two choices, (C) and (D), use "better," while three use "best." "Better" is used to compare two people or things. "Best" is used to compare one person or thing to a group. Since you're comparing Martin Luther to all the other people who brought about the Reformation, use "best." Eliminate (E) because "one" is redundant.

3. D

Words linked by "and" must be in similar grammatical form. (A) is wrong because "and" links "raising" and "reduction." The author is comparing two things, so use "between," not "among" in (B). (C) uses "or" when it should use "and." (You choose *between X and Y*, not *between X or Y*.) In (E), the insertions of "the" are unidiomatic.

4. C

When you see items in a list, consider whether there is a problem with parallelism. Here you have a list of three things the company was forced to do: close plants, lay off workers, and reduce budgets. In the original sentence, the first two items have the gerund *-ing* form ("closing," "laying"), so the third item must be "reducing." (C) is correct.

5. C

In (A), (B), and (D), "it" and "that" are ambiguous. That is, these pronouns don't clearly refer to a specific noun. By using "to" as a connecting word, (E) implies that the evidence is going to correct blindness, which is illogical. (C) forms the idiomatically correct "evidence that" and uses the adverb "so" (instead of a pronoun that requires a noun) to indicate action the devices are unable to do.

6. D

"Than" must compare grammatically similar terms: for instance, *cooking chickens* is harder than *cooking eggs*, not *cooking chickens* is harder than *eggs*. Since "setting" is not underlined, you'll have to make the underlined portion agree with it. (D) and (E) have a matching *-ing* form. The beginning of the comparison discusses setting up "a corporation," not multiple entities, so the connector "or" between singular nouns, in (D), is correct.

7. A

If you can't spot an error in the original but aren't sure it's error-free, scan the choices and look for reasons to cross them out. (B) uses the singular "wine grower," but you need the plural to go with "their crop" and "their fruit" in the nonunderlined part of the sentence. By deleting "they," (C) switches to passive voice and makes it sounds as though the grape harvesting might have been done by someone other than wine growers. (D) incorrectly uses a progressive tense with "were doing." In (E), "did" implies that the wine growers have stopped harvesting. You need "have done" in (A) to match the fact that harvesting happened in the past and still happens today.

8. C

As soon as you see a subject ("a generation") followed by a long phrase ("of sophisticated copy machines capable of unprecedented detail and accuracy") beware! GMAT Sentence Correction questions often separate subjects and verbs. The verb "are" here is separated from the subject "generation," but they still need to agree. "Generation" is singular, so the sentence should read "a new generation . . . is prompting." This makes (A), (D), and (E) incorrect. In (B), it's unidiomatic to say "capable for." You need to say "capable of" detail.

9. E

When an introductory phrase is followed by a comma, check whether the phrase correctly modifies what follows it. You can't say that a directive is making "an unusual move." It's a person, the president, who's making the move. This makes (A) incorrect. (B) is wordy and makes it sound as though the president was directing someone else to establish the price controls. (C) is in the passive voice, and (D) is in the wrong tense. (E) says what the author of the sentence wants to say, clearly and simply.

10. B

Connectors like "as well as" or "not only . . . but also" must link like terms. Therefore, "in politics" must be paired with "in industry." Choices (A), (C), (D), and (E) do not use "in industry," so they are incorrect. Also, (E) is unnecessarily wordy.

11. E

The sentence begins with a descriptive phrase, which should modify the noun that immediately follows it, which in this case is "the investigative commission." But the commission itself was not compiled from government documents; its report was. Look for an opening phrase that correctly modifies "commission." (C) and (D) commit the same error as the original, describing the commission as "a compilation" and as "documents," respectively. (B) uses the pronoun "it," and "report" is too far away for the relationship to be clear. (E) changes the phrase so that it modifies "commission"; the commission worked with the documents to produce the report. (E) is correct.

12. E

"Like" or "unlike" signals a comparison, one of the test maker's favorite places to introduce errors. Make sure this sentence compares similar things—things that can be logically compared and things that are in the same grammatical form. Here, "the people whom settled the Western states . . . " and "the hope of the prospectors . . ." are both nouns, but it's illogical to compare people to "hope," a feeling. You have to compare people to people, and that's what choice (E) does. In (E), "the people who settled the Western states" are compared to "the prospectors and adventurers." Also note that you need "who" instead of "whom" when referring to the subject of a clause.

13. D

Be on the lookout for connectors such as "like" and as." Use "like" to compare things and "as" to compare actions. This author isn't directly saying Congress is like Parliament. Instead, the author compares how Congress "is" one thing and Parliament "is" another thing. "Just like" is incorrect, so eliminate (A). (D) and (E) start with "just as." (E) reverses the order of ideas in the first part of the comparison, causing unparallel structure. (D) is correct.

14. E

The correct phrasing is "the reason . . . was *that*," not "the reason . . . was *because*." You can think of the word *reason* as already including the meaning of *because*, so adding that meaning again is just redundant. The original sentence also uses the future tense "will empty" for a situation in the past. Eliminate (A). (B)'s "the reason being that" is too informal for the GMAT. This choice also uses the future tense, as does (C). (D) would be okay if "so" were eliminated. (E) is logical and direct.

15. C

When you see a list or series, ask yourself: Are all the listed items similar grammatically and logically? The phrase that matches "technical expertise" and "commercial enterprise" is "judicious government backing," in (C). (D)'s movement of the word "that" garbles the meaning of the sentence.

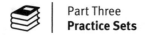
Sentence Correction Practice Set Two

Directions: Each Sentence Correction question presents a sentence, part or all of which is underlined. Below each sentence, you will find five ways to phrase the underlined portion. The first answer choice repeats the original version, while the other four choices are different. If the original seems best, choose the first answer choice. If not, choose one of the revisions.

In choosing an answer, follow the norms of standard written English: grammar, word choice, and sentence construction. Choose the answer that produces the most effective sentence, aiming to eliminate awkwardness, ambiguity, redundancy, and grammatical error.

1. The executive officer of the board of directors <u>have decided that this year's profits will be used</u> for research and development rather than for a shareholder dividend.

    ○ have decided that this year's profits will be used

    ○ has decided that this year's profits will be used

    ○ have decided on using this year's profits

    ○ has decided on using this year's profits

    ○ decided this year's profits will have been used

2. <u>Not only do deep-sea divers risk nitrogen narcosis, often called "raptures of the deep," if they descend below 200 feet, but</u> they may also fall prey to decompression sickness, commonly known as "the bends," if they ascend too quickly.

    ○ Not only do deep-sea divers risk nitrogen narcosis, often called "raptures of the deep," if they descend below 200 feet, but

    ○ Deep-sea divers risk nitrogen narcosis, often called "raptures of the deep," if they descend below 200 feet, but

    ○ Nitrogen narcosis, often called "raptures of the deep," is risked by deep-sea divers if they descend below 200 feet, in addition

    ○ The descending of deep-sea divers to below 200 feet causes them risking nitrogen narcosis, often called "raptures of the deep," and

    ○ Not only do deep-sea divers risk nitrogen narcosis, often called "raptures of the deep," if they have descended below 200 feet, but

3. A 32 percent wage hike, working four days a week, and above all a higher standard of factory safety is a demand that management must meet if it wishes to avoid a crippling strike.

    O   A 32 percent wage hike, working four days a week, and above all a higher standard of factory safety is a demand

    O   A 32 percent wage hike, a four-day workweek, and above all a higher standard of factory safety is a demand

    O   A 32 percent wage hike, a four-day workweek, and above all a higher standard of safety in the factory are demands

    O   A 32 percent wage hike, working four days a week, and above all a higher standard of factory safety are demands

    O   Hiking wages 32 percent, working four days a week, and above all heighten the standard of factory safety are demands

4. As evidence of sushi's dramatically increasing popularity, recent studies show that the number of sushi restaurants in the state increased by more than three times in the past five years.

    O   increased by more than three times

    O   increased by more than triple

    O   was increased more than three times

    O   has more than tripled

    O   was more than tripled

5. At a recent conference, the Transit Authority has stated that the provisions in the Clean Air Act fail to promote mass transit as an alternative to private transportation.

    O   has stated that the provisions in the Clean Air Act fail

    O   stated that the provisions of the Clean Air Act fail

    O   has stated that the provisions of the Clean Air Act will fail

    O   stated that the provisions in the Clean Air Act are a failure

    O   has stated the provisions in the Clean Air Act failed

6. A revolution has taken place in medical science as a result of the introduction of new methods of surgically implanting artificial and human organs.

    O   introduction of new methods of surgically implanting artificial and human organs

    O   introduction of new surgical implantation methods of human and artificial organs

    O   surgical introduction of new artificial and human organ implantation methods

    O   introduction of implantation methods of new artificial and human organs

    O   introduction of methods of surgically implanting new artificial and human organs

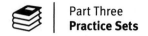
7. <u>Added to worries about budget cuts and cost of living increases</u>, the administrators of public healthcare facilities must contend with the possibility of a strike by employees.

    ○   Added to worries about budget cuts and cost of living increases

    ○   Added to budget cuts and increases in the cost of living

    ○   In addition to worry about cuts in the budget and as the cost of living increases

    ○   Added to their worrying about budget cuts and cost of living increases

    ○   In addition to worrying about budget cuts and increases in the cost of living

8. The Renaissance scientist Copernicus found that his rejection of the Ptolemaic system placed him at odds <u>not only with the Church and the scientific community of his day, but also with ship captains, who navigated according to a geocentric universe</u>.

    ○   not only with the Church and the scientific community of his day, but also with ship captains, who navigated according to a geocentric universe

    ○   opposing the Church and the scientific community of his day, and also the ship captains, who navigated according to a geocentric universe

    ○   not only in opposition to the Church and the scientific community of his day, but with ship captains, who navigated according to a geocentric universe

    ○   not only with the Church and the scientific community of his day, but with ship captains, who calculated their navigations on a geocentric basis

    ○   opposing not only churchmen and scientists, but the ship captains, who navigated according to a geocentric universe

9. Despite <u>them attempting to do it</u>, doctors have not yet found a cure for the common cold.

    ○   them attempting to do it

    ○   their attempts to do so

    ○   them attempting to do so

    ○   the fact that they have attempted to do it

    ○   their attempts to do it

10. Unlike the Pulitzer, which is given for a specific work, <u>an author receives the Nobel Prize for a lifetime's achievement in literature</u>.

    ○   an author receives the Nobel Prize for a lifetime's achievement in literature

    ○   an author's lifetime achievement in literature receives the Nobel Prize

    ○   the Nobel Prize is awarded to an author's lifetime's achievement in literature

    ○   the Nobel Prize is awarded to an author for a lifetime of achievement in literature

    ○   the Nobel Prize is awarded for a lifetime of achievement in literature by an author

11. The crew of Apollo 13, following a set of instructions hastily cobbled together by a team of NASA engineers, <u>were able to adapt a square air filter to fit a round filter barrel, thus enabling the three astronauts</u> to survive in a vehicle designed for two.

    O were able to adapt a square air filter to fit a round filter barrel, thus enabling the three astronauts

    O were able to adapt a square air filter to fit a round filter barrel, thus making the three astronauts able

    O had been able to adapt a square air filter to fit a round filter barrel, thus enabling the three astronauts

    O was able to adapt a square air filter to fit a round filter barrel, thus enabling the three astronauts

    O were able to adapt a square air filter to fit a round filter barrel, so the three astronauts were enabled

12. Unable to walk without assistance, <u>radio provided Franklin Roosevelt with a medium for conveying</u> a message of vigor and confidence that would have been belied by the visual image presented on television.

    O radio provided Franklin Roosevelt with a medium for conveying

    O Franklin Roosevelt conveyed in the radio

    O Franklin Roosevelt used radio to convey

    O radio allowed Franklin Roosevelt to convey

    O through radio it was possible for Franklin Roosevelt to convey

13. Modern inventions such as the pneumatic drill may seem to have improved the work conditions of manual laborers, but in fact <u>have increased the incidence of health hazards such as silicosis because it has aggravated the dust hazard</u> involved in excavation and demolition.

    O have increased the incidence of health hazards such as silicosis because it has aggravated

    O has increased the incidence of health hazards such as silicosis because it has aggravated

    O have increased the incidence of health hazards such as silicosis because they have aggravated

    O increased the incidence of health hazards such as silicosis because they aggravated

    O increased the incidence of health hazards such as silicosis because of aggravating

14. The Federal Reserve <u>Board assumes primary responsibility of the regulation for</u> this nation's commercial banks and savings institutions.

    O Board assumes primary responsibility of the regulation for

    O Board's assumption of primary responsibility for the regulation of

    O Board's assuming primary responsibility to regulate

    O Board assumes primary responsibility for the regulation of

    O Board regulates primary responsibility for

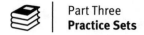
15. Though caterpillars transform large amounts of plant matter into animal tissue and wastes, and therefore hold an important place in the food chain, they are so voracious that they have become an economic threat to the farmers whose crops they eat.

   ○ they are so voracious that they have become an economic

   ○ they are of such voracity, they have become an economical

   ○ so voracious are they as to become an economical

   ○ such is their voracity, they become an economic

   ○ there is so much voracity that it has become an economical

Answers and explanations follow on the next page. ▶ ▶ ▶

Answers and Explanations

1.	B	5.	B	9.	B	13.	C
2.	A	6.	A	10.	D	14.	D
3.	C	7.	E	11.	D	15.	A
4.	D	8.	A	12.	C		

1. B

The GMAT test makers like to make subject-verb agreement errors harder to spot by putting a lot of words between the subject and verb. Learn to anticipate and ignore prepositional phrases like "of the board of directors." The verb has to agree with the singular subject "officer," rather than with the plural "directors." Only (B) and (D) use "has." (B) is correct because the idiom is "decided that" (or "decided to"), not "decided on."

2. A

"Not only . . . but also" must connect similar terms. "Deep-sea divers not only risk" and "but also fall prey" are correctly parallel in (A). In addition, the underlined pronoun "they" unambiguously refers to "divers." (B) would work if "and" were substituted for "but." There are two problems with (C): "nitrogen narcosis . . . is risked" is unnecessarily in the passive voice, and (C) is actually two complete sentences incorrectly linked with a comma. "In addition" cannot be used with a comma to join two clauses. In (D), the beginning is awkward and "causes them risking . . . " is unidiomatic. The infinitive "to risk" is needed in place of "risking." (E) incorrectly introduces "have descended"; the simple present tense, used in the rest of this sentence, is correct here.

3. C

Whenever you see a list on the GMAT, check that the items in it are in grammatically similar form. Only (B) and (C) put the three listed items in similar form: "wage hike," "workweek," and "standard." The three things listed in the sentence *are* demands the management must meet, so "is" in (B) doesn't work.

4. D

The answer choices have a 2-2-1 split among verb tenses: increased/was/has. Immediately after the underlined portion is the critical clue letting you know what tense to use: "in the past five years." Clearly, the increase started in the past and is still in force in the present. That's what the present perfect "has" form is for, so (D) is correct. Also note that "increased by more than three times" is unidiomatic; the proper way to express the idea is "more than tripled." (C), "was increased more than three times," changes the meaning to imply that there were more than three increases.

5. B

When you scan the choices, notice you have to choose between three that begin with "has stated" and two that begin with "stated." Begin by deciding which of the two forms, "has stated" or "stated," is correct. The Transit Authority made its statement and it was over. The action didn't continue. So, the correct choice will say "the Transit Authority *stated*." (D) results in "are a failure to promote," which is awkward. (B), which results in "fail to promote," is idiomatically correct.

6. A

This sentence is written in the passive voice. Although there aren't any errors, check whether a choice offers a more direct way of expressing the same idea. As it happens, the rearrangements of words in (B)–(E) all result in illogical sentences. (B) makes it sound like the organs are somehow related to the methods rather than being implanted, while (C) uses "surgical" to modify "introduction" instead of "implantation." (D) and (E) say that the artificial and human organs are new, but it's *the methods* that are new.

7. E

An introductory phrase set off by a comma is your signal to watch out for modification errors. Simply put, that means you should make sure the sentence is logical. Here, it's not "the administrators" who are added to worries, budget cuts, or worrying, so (A), (B), and (D) are out. (C) may seem to make sense, but look at it closely: "worry" is wrong, and the insertion of "as" after "and" results in an illogical relationship of ideas. (E) clearly states what else the administrators are worrying about.

8. A

The correct phrase is "at odds with," not "at odds . . . opposing," in (B) and (E), or "at odds . . . in opposition," in (C). It's more concise to say "navigated according to a geocentric universe" than "calculated their navigations on a geocentric basis," in (D).

9. B

In the choices, there's a "3-2 split" at the ends, between "to do it" and "to do so." "It" is an ambiguous pronoun. You might assume "it" stands for "cure," but if you substitute "cure" for "it" in the sentence, you get the unidiomatic "despite them attempting to do a cure." This rules out (A), (D), and (E). "Doctors" is the subject, so the author should use the pronoun "their," not "them," (C), to stand for "doctors."

10. D

The Pulitzer Prize must be compared to some other prize. Hence, (A) and (B) are incorrect. In (C), the prize isn't awarded to an author's achievement; it's awarded to an author. In (E), "author" incorrectly follows "literature" ("literature by an author"), making it unclear who exactly is doing the achieving. (D) makes it clear whose achievement is being awarded.

11. D

Notice that the underlined portion begins with the verb "were." Check this verb to make sure it agrees with the subject of the sentence, "crew." Don't let the intervening phrase "following a set of instructions . . ." distract you. Even though a crew typically consists of more than one person, the noun itself is grammatically

singular and requires a singular verb form, since the crew acts as a unit in this sentence. (A), (B), and (E) all begin with "were," so eliminate these choices. (D) begins with the singular verb "was," while (C) begins with "had been able," a past perfect verb form. Here, this verb tense is inappropriate; the past perfect indicates a past action completed prior to another past action, but the filter could not have been adapted before the instructions were developed. (D) properly replaces the plural "were" with the correct singular form "was" and does not introduce any new errors.

12. C

The opening phrase describes Franklin Roosevelt, so his name must immediately follow that phrase, as it does in (B) and (C). In (B), it's illogical to say that Roosevelt "conveyed in the radio a message." That would be correct only if there were a single radio and it functioned like a bucket.

13. C

The original sentence uses the pronoun "it," which would have to refer to "silicosis," but logically the disease comes about because the dust is made worse; the disease doesn't "aggravate" the dust. Eliminate (A). The subject of this sentence is "inventions." It's not "drill," which is just offered as one example of the problematic inventions. Therefore, the verb needs to be plural, and "has" in (B) is incorrect. The simple past "increased" of (D) and (E) is incorrect, since the inventions still cause health problems today. That leaves (C).

14. D

The correct phrasing is "assumes responsibility for." You don't take responsibility *of* (A) or *to* (C) completing your work; you take responsibility *for* completing it. If you plug in (B), you get an incomplete sentence. You need a noun, "Board," and a verb, "assumes." In (E), the Board isn't regulating responsibility. That leaves (D), which corrects the error and introduces no new issues.

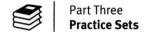
15. A

The pronoun "they" correctly refers to "caterpillars." The phrasing "so voracious that" is idiomatically correct. And the adjective "economic" correctly modifies the noun "threat." This sentence is correct as written, (A). (B), (C), and (E) can all be eliminated for using the adverb "economical" at the end, as well as for committing other errors. (D) switches to the present tense "become," subtly changing the meaning of the sentence.

Sentence Correction Practice Set Three

Directions: Each Sentence Correction question presents a sentence, part or all of which is underlined. Below each sentence, you will find five ways to phrase the underlined portion. The first answer choice repeats the original version, while the other four choices are different. If the original seems best, choose the first answer choice. If not, choose one of the revisions.

In choosing an answer, follow the norms of standard written English: grammar, word choice, and sentence construction. Choose the answer that produces the most effective sentence, aiming to eliminate awkwardness, ambiguity, redundancy, and grammatical error.

1. One student at the school was not yet 15, yet he was already a master in both chess and in bridge.

   ○ in both chess and in
   ○ of both chess and in
   ○ of both chess and of
   ○ both over chess and
   ○ of both chess and

2. It has been demonstrated that individuals who participated in competitive sports when they are in college tend toward remaining physically active in their later years.

   ○ are in college tend toward remaining
   ○ were in college tend to remain
   ○ were in college tended to remain
   ○ are in college tend to remain
   ○ were in college tend at remaining

3. The customer will not be responsible for transactions made with lost or stolen credit cards after issuing replacement cards.

   ○ The customer will not be responsible for transactions made with lost or stolen credit cards after issuing replacement cards.
   ○ No customer after receiving replacement cards will be responsible for transactions made with lost or stolen credit cards after they are issued.
   ○ The customer will not be responsible for transactions made with lost or stolen credit cards after replacement cards have been issued.
   ○ Responsibility for transactions made with lost or stolen credit cards will not be the customer's after being issued replacement cards.
   ○ The customer will not be responsible for transactions made with lost or stolen credit cards after such time as replacement cards will have been issued.

4. <u>Despite that they were able to calculate faster than ever before possible</u>, the earliest computers, built with tubes instead of transistors, were too bulky, expensive, and unreliable to be useful to businesses.

- O Despite that they were able to calculate faster than ever before possible
- O Even though it could calculate faster than previously possible
- O Although faster in its calculating than ever before possible
- O Despite their calculations being faster than ever before possible
- O Despite calculating faster than ever

5. As genetics researchers achieve greater success in their attempt to map the exact locations and functions of human genes, the <u>close connection between genes and birth defects has become</u> increasingly clear.

- O close connection between genes and birth defects has become
- O closeness of the connection between genes and birth defects has become
- O close connection genes have with birth defects has been becoming
- O close connection between genes and birth defects has been becoming
- O close connection between genes and birth defects becomes

6. At Agincourt, Charles D'Albret's battle plan was thwarted <u>as a direct result of the irrepressible desire the French nobility under his command had to</u> charge headlong into any enemy offering a challenge.

- O as a direct result of the irrepressible desire the French nobility under his command had to
- O because the French nobility under his command had an irrepressible desire to
- O insofar as the French nobility under his command desired to
- O because the French nobility under his command would have an irrepressible desire to
- O by the desire of the French nobility under his command to irrepressibly

7. <u>That students in our public schools score as well if not better than students in private schools on standardized tests disprove</u> one prevalent education myth.

- O That students in our public schools score as well if not better than students in private schools on standardized tests disprove
- O That students in our public schools score as well if not better than students in private schools on standardized tests disproves
- O That students in our public schools score as well as if not better than students in private schools on standardized tests disproves
- O That students in our public schools score as well as if not better than students in private schools on standardized tests disprove
- O The fact of public school students' scoring as well if not better than private school students on standardized tests disproves

8. A common social problem in the workplace occurs <u>when workers accept supervisory positions, and it causes them to lose</u> the trust of their former coworkers.

    O   when workers accept supervisory positions, and it causes them to lose

    O   by workers' accepting supervisory positions, which causes them to lose

    O   when workers accept supervisory positions and so lose

    O   when workers who accept supervisory positions, thereby losing

    O   if workers accept supervisory positions, they would lose

9. To restore fishing grounds damaged by pollution, marine engineers can create an artificial reef by towing old barges to an offshore location <u>and sinking</u> to the sandy bottom.

    O   and sinking

    O   and sinking them

    O   and sinking it

    O   where it sinks

    O   having sunk them

10. Popular industrial psychologists have advocated that managers discipline supervisory staff <u>similarly to the fashion in which they discipline</u> blue-collar employees.

    O   similarly to the fashion in which they discipline

    O   in the same manner that they would use with

    O   like they would handle

    O   as they discipline

    O   as they would

11. In the Middle Ages, philosophers <u>were so devoted to Aristotle that they neglected</u> the evidence of their own senses and accepted whatever he wrote.

    O   were so devoted to Aristotle that they neglected

    O   were so devoted to Aristotle as to neglect

    O   were devoted to Aristotle to such a degree that they were to neglect

    O   were so devoted to Aristotle that they had to neglect

    O   were as devoted to Aristotle as to neglect

12. <u>To rely on anecdotal evidence of social phenomena is ignoring</u> decades of increasing sophistication in the use of statistics in sociology.

    O   To rely on anecdotal evidence of social phenomena is ignoring

    O   To rely on anecdotal evidence of social phenomena is to ignore

    O   To rely on anecdotes for demonstration of social phenomena is ignoring

    O   Relying on anecdotal evidence of social phenomena is to ignore

    O   Relying on anecdotal evidence of social phenomena amounts to the ignoring of

13. The team members streamed into the locker room, donned their uniforms, <u>and, before commencing their first practice, they joined in a brief strategy session</u>.

   ○   and, before commencing their first practice, they joined in a brief strategy session

   ○   and their first practice was preceded by a brief strategy session

   ○   and a brief strategy session preceded their first practice

   ○   and, before commencing their first practice, they joined in a brief strategy session

   ○   and, before commencing their first practice, joined in a brief strategy session

14. Records of the first 736 British convicts deported to Australia reveal <u>convictions for crimes against property, and they ranged</u> from highway robbery to forgery.

   ○   convictions for crimes against property, and they ranged

   ○   that the convictions were for crimes against property and ranging

   ○   a range of convictions for crimes against property

   ○   that they were convicted of crimes against property ranging

   ○   that they had convictions for crimes that were against property, with the range being

15. A turning point in U.S. labor history was reached when most of the nation's air traffic controllers supported their union's strike and ignored President Reagan's demand <u>that they</u> go back to work.

   ○   that they

   ○   to them that they

   ○   for them to

   ○   that they would

   ○   they should

Answers and explanations follow on the next page. ▶ ▶ ▶

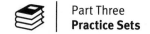

Answers and Explanations

1.	E	5.	E	9.	B	13.	E
2.	B	6.	B	10.	E	14.	D
3.	C	7.	C	11.	A	15.	A
4.	E	8.	C	12.	B		

1. E

In the "both . . . and" construction, the things being linked have to be grammatically parallel. If you say "*both* of chess," you have to follow with "*and* of bridge." If you say "of *both* chess," you have to follow it with "*and* bridge." And idiomatically, one speaks of a master *of* chess or bridge, not a master *in* or *over* chess or bridge. So (E) is correct.

2. B

The phrase "tend toward remaining" is unidiomatic. The correct phrasing is "tend to remain." Eliminate (A). Also, this sentence discusses two time frames. One, when people played sports, is in the past, as signaled by "participated." People were in college when they played sports, so eliminate (A) (if you haven't already) and (D) for using "are" here. The other time frame is that of a general, eternal truth (these people stay active), for which the present tense is correct. Eliminate (C) for using "tended." "Tend at remaining" in (E) is unidiomatic. (B) is the winner.

3. C

The problem here has to do with modification. Who or what will issue replacement cards? Not the customer, certainly, but that's what (A) seems to be saying. (B) has a pronoun problem, since "they" seems to refer to the missing cards instead of the replacement cards. The "being issued" in (D) is weak and vague, and the "will have been issued" of (E) is an unnecessarily complicated verb tense. That leaves (C), which is clear and logical.

4. E

This question presents problems of idiom. "Despite that" in (A) is unidiomatic, and "than ever before possible" in (A), (C), and (D) is wordy. Choice (B) has a pronoun reference problem: the singular "it" is used to refer to the plural "computers."

5. E

Logically, both things must be going on in the present. The genetics researchers are achieving success, and the connection between genes and birth defects is becoming clear. So, there's no need to switch to the past "has become" or "has been becoming" as (A), (B), (C), and (D) do.

6. B

In the original, both "as a direct result of" and "of the . . . desire the French nobility . . . had" are wordy. Look for a more direct expression of the author's thought. "Insofar" in (C) does not connect the ideas in the sentence logically. There's no need for the subjunctive "would have" in (D). The shift from "irrepressible" to "irrepressibly" in (E) changes the meaning of the sentence. (B) is clear and correct.

7. C

This question tests your knowledge of a common idiom. The correct expression is "as well as . . . if not better than." Choices (A), (B), and (E) lack the "as." Then the subject of this sentence is a bit unusual: it's the entire phrase "That students . . . on standardized tests." This is a singular fact, so the verb "disproves" in (C) is correct.

8.   C

The pronoun "it" is meant to refer to "workers' accept[ing] supervisory positions." But that noun phrase does not appear in the sentence, so the pronoun has no antecedent. Eliminate (A).

Scanning the beginning of the choices, you see a 3-1-1 split among "when," by," and "if." In context, "occurs by" is unidiomatic, so eliminate (B). By adding "who," (D) places the verb "accept" into a subordinate clause, stealing it away from "workers" and resulting in an incomplete sentence. In (E), the shift from the simple present tense "problem . . . occurs" to the subjunctive "if . . . would lose" is incorrect. (C) is left, and with "and so lose," it establishes the correct relationship between ideas.

9.   B

(A) seems to say that the engineers sink to the bottom. You need a choice that says the barges sink. The pronoun "it" in (C) and (D) is singular and so cannot stand for "barges." Look at (B) and (E), which use "them." "Having sunk," in (E), illogically suggests that the engineers sunk the barges before towing them into position. The correct answer is (B).

10.   E

Here, the main things to look for are clarity and brevity. The shortest choice, (E), is best: none of the other, longer choices are any clearer. Choices (A) and (B) use other, wordier grammatical constructions. (C) adds the redundant word "handle" to the phrasing, which is not needed because managers handling the situation is implied by the rest of the sentence. Additionally, only use "like" when there is no implied or stated verb in the second half of a comparison. (D) changes the sentence's meaning, suggesting that managers discipline supervisory and non-supervisory employees simultaneously.

11.   A

The "so . . . that" construction, the past tense "were" and "neglected," and the plural pronoun "they" are all correct. Choose (A). "So . . . as to" in (B) and "as . . . as to" in (E) are unidiomatic. "To such a degree that they were to neglect" in (C) and "they had to neglect" in (D) introduce unnecessary verbiage.

12.   B

Elements joined by "is" have to be parallel. You can join an infinitive (*to rely*) with an infinitive (*to ignore*), or a participle (*relying*) with a participle (*ignoring*), but not a participle with an infinitive or an infinitive with a participle. Hence, (B) is correct.

13.   E

The question tests parallelism: the three things that the team did have to be expressed in the same form. To match "streamed" and "donned," you need "joined." This eliminates (B) and (C). You just say "the team streamed, donned, and joined . . . ." There's no need to say "and they joined," in (A) and (D). This leaves (E) as the correct answer.

14.   D

The pronoun "they" is somewhat ambiguous, as it logically refers to "crimes" but grammatically could refer to "convictions" or "convicts." Also troubling is the use of a co-equal independent clause to present a supporting detail about the crimes. Look for a more elegant, clearer version. (B)'s "and ranging" is not parallel with "convictions were." (C) inappropriately puts intervening phrases between "range of convictions and "from highway robbery to forgery," making it sound as though the *property* ranged from robbery to forgery. In (E), it's unidiomatic to say they "had convictions," and "with the range being" is weak. (D) is correct.

15.   A

Verbs such as *demand*, *suggest*, and *request* invoke the subjunctive mood, which is correctly constructed here with "demand that they go."

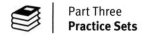
Sentence Correction Practice Set Four

Directions: Each Sentence Correction question presents a sentence, part or all of which is underlined. Below each sentence, you will find five ways to phrase the underlined portion. The first answer choice repeats the original version, while the other four choices are different. If the original seems best, choose the first answer choice. If not, choose one of the revisions.

In choosing an answer, follow the norms of standard written English: grammar, word choice, and sentence construction. Choose the answer that produces the most effective sentence, aiming to eliminate awkwardness, ambiguity, redundancy, and grammatical error.

1. The sloth, <u>which is a South American mammal related to armadillos and anteaters, live in tropical forests where they travel</u> through the trees upside down.

    ○ which is a South American mammal related to armadillos and anteaters, live in tropical forests where they travel

    ○ a South American mammal related to armadillos and anteaters, live in tropical forests where they travel

    ○ a South American mammal related to the armadillo and the anteater, lives in tropical forests where it travels

    ○ a South American mammal related to the armadillo and the anteater, lives in tropical forests where they travel

    ○ a South American mammal in relation to the armadillo and the anteater, lives in tropical forests where it travels

2. Early derisive reactions from art critics and established painters did not discourage the Primitivist painter Henri Rousseau <u>to exhibit repeatedly, despite him completely lacking formal training and starting late</u> as a professional artist.

    ○ to exhibit repeatedly, despite him completely lacking formal training and starting late

    ○ exhibiting repeatedly, completely lacking formal training though he was, and starting late

    ○ to exhibit repeatedly, despite their complete lack of formal training and late start

    ○ in exhibiting repeatedly, despite his complete lack of formal training and late start

    ○ from exhibiting repeatedly, despite his complete lack of formal training and late start

3. The poll taxes enacted in the Southern states between 1889 <u>and 1910 disenfranchised many citizens, since</u> payment of the tax was a prerequisite for voting.

   O   and 1910 disenfranchised many citizens, since

   O   to 1910 disenfranchised many citizens, since

   O   and 1910 have disenfranchised many citizens since

   O   to 1910 has been disenfranchising many citizens because

   O   and 1910 had the effect of disenfranchising many citizens, inasmuch as

4. <u>With a population equal to Kansas in an area one three-hundredth its size, Singapore is the most densely populated nation in the world, averaging</u> almost ten thousand people per square mile.

   O   With a population equal to Kansas in an area one three-hundredth its size, Singapore is the most densely populated nation in the world, averaging

   O   With a population equal to that of Kansas in an area one three-hundredth its size, Singapore is the most densely populated nation in the world, averaging

   O   With Kansas's population in one three-hundredth of its area, the densest population in the world is that of Singapore, with an average of

   O   Singapore has the same population as Kansas but only one three-hundredth of its area, and makes it the most densely populated nation in the world, averaging

   O   Singapore is the most densely populated nation in the world, with Kansas's population in one three-hundredth of its area, or an average of

5. Many medical schools offer courses in the ethics of treating terminal patients, partly to alert students to the legal implications involved in such treatment, but primarily <u>to prepare students, through discussion and forethought, to make responsible decisions that respect terminal patients' dignity</u>.

   O   to prepare students, through discussion and forethought, to make responsible decisions that respect terminal patients' dignity

   O   so as to prepare students, by discussing and by thinking ahead, for responsible decision making that respects terminal patients' dignity

   O   for the purpose of preparing them, with discussion and forethought, to make responsible decisions that respect terminal patients' dignity

   O   for preparing them, through discussion and forethought, for deciding responsibly so that they respect terminal patients' dignity

   O   to prepare them, by discussing and thinking ahead, to responsibly decide so as to respect the dignity of terminal patients

6. The nations with nuclear capabilities have restrained the proliferation of nuclear weapons less by reaching diplomatic understandings with other countries than <u>by the refusal to sell</u> associated technologies.

   O   by the refusal to sell

   O   not selling

   O   the refusal to sell

   O   refusing to sell

   O   by refusing to sell

7. At 60 inmates per 100,000 citizens, Norway has one of the lowest incarceration rates of all Western countries, <u>reflecting their long</u> humanitarian tradition.

    O   reflecting their long

    O   being a reflection of its long

    O   reflection of their long

    O   reflecting its long

    O   reflecting its longer

8. <u>Compared with the time period of John Steinbeck's *The Grapes of Wrath*,</u> the poor of today would be considered wealthy.

    O   Compared with the time period of John Steinbeck's *The Grapes of Wrath*

    O   Compared with the time period during which John Steinbeck's *The Grapes of Wrath* took place

    O   Compared with the characters in John Steinbeck's *The Grapes of Wrath*

    O   In comparison to the time of John Steinbeck's *The Grapes of Wrath*

    O   In comparison to John Steinbeck's *The Grapes of Wrath*

9. According to the teachings of the Buddhist and Hindu religions, <u>attaining nirvana is to enter</u> a state of supreme liberation, leaving behind the desires that perpetuate the cycle of death and rebirth.

    O   attaining nirvana is to enter

    O   to attain nirvana is entering

    O   to attain nirvana is having entered

    O   to attain nirvana is to enter

    O   attaining nirvana is to be entering

10. Uninformed about students' experience in urban classrooms, critics often condemn schools' performance as gauged by <u>an index, such as standardized test scores, that are called objective and can be quantified and overlook less measurable progress, such as that</u> in higher-level reasoning.

    O   an index, such as standardized test scores, that are called objective and can be quantified and overlook less measurable progress, such as that

    O   an index, such as standardized test scores, that are called objective and can be quantified and overlook less measurable progress, such as what is made

    O   an index, such as standardized test scores, that is called objective and can be quantified and overlook less measurable progress, such as what is made

    O   a so-called objective index, such as standardized test scores, that can be quantified and overlook less measurable progress, such as what is made

    O   a so-called objective index, such as standardized test scores, that can be quantified and overlook less measurable progress, such as that

11. One of the informants eventually professed <u>ignorant of the crime, having</u> fear that his testimony would lead to reprisals against him by his former confederates.

    O   ignorant of the crime, having

    O   ignorantly to the crime, with

    O   ignorance of the crime, since

    O   ignorance of the crime, for

    O   to have ignorance of the crime, since

12. The 19th-century Russian composers known as "The Five" <u>were united by their holding</u> a shared ideal of a national music based on folk melodies and themes.

    O   were united by their holding

    O   had as their uniting ideal

    O   united with each other through

    O   united by

    O   were united with

13. The symphonies of Mahler are characterized by <u>a much freer use of dissonance than Haydn</u>.

    O   a much freer use of dissonance than Haydn

    O   a much freer use than Haydn of dissonance

    O   a much freer use of dissonance than are those of Haydn

    O   a use much freer than the dissonance of Haydn

    O   a use of dissonance that is much freer than Haydn

14. King James I of England tried unsuccessfully to merge the legislature of Scotland—his original kingdom—<u>with England</u>.

    O   with England

    O   and England

    O   with that of England

    O   and England's

    O   and England's legislature

15. In a convincing demonstration of Newtonian physics, <u>it was anomalies in the orbit of Uranus that</u> led astronomers to predict the discovery of Neptune.

    O   it was anomalies in the orbit of Uranus that

    O   it was the orbit of Uranus showing anomalies that

    O   the orbit of Uranus showing anomalies was what

    O   the orbit of Uranus being anomalous was what

    O   anomalies in the orbit of Uranus

Answers and Explanations

1. C
2. E
3. A
4. B

5. A
6. E
7. D
8. C

9. D
10. E
11. D
12. D

13. C
14. C
15. E

1. C

This sentence is about "the sloth," which is singular. To be correct, the sentence must read "The sloth . . . *lives* . . . where *it travels* . . ." (C) and (E) meet these requirements, but (E) uses the phrase "in relation to," which is unidiomatic in this context. You say *X is related to Y*, not *X is in relation to Y*. (C) is correct.

2. E

The correct idiom is "discourage from exhibiting." Also, "despite him completely lacking . . . and starting" in the original is incorrect. You have to say "despite his complete lack of . . . and late start."

3. A

Here's another connector you should know: "between . . . and" (as in "Between me and you . . ."). When you scan the choices, quickly eliminate those with incorrect idioms like "between . . . to." In (C), you could use "have" only to discuss an action still taking place. You could say "the *recent* poll taxes have disenfranchised many citizens," but here the author is discussing an action that ended in 1910, so the sentence should simply say "the taxes disenfranchised many citizens." In (E), "had the effect of" and "inasmuch as" are unnecessarily wordy.

4. B

When scanning the answer choices here, you may have noticed that each plays with the wording of "population equal to Kansas." It's not logical to compare a population to a state, so (A) is incorrect. In (B), "that" stands for "population": "With a population equal to that of Kansas" is just a more elegant way of saying "With a population equal to the population of Kansas." This comparison is logical and correct. In (C), the population isn't "with an average" of ten thousand people per square mile. (D) introduces a comma

splice—a new error—and is thus another wrong answer. In (E), the pronoun "it" has to refer to the noun "population," but the population doesn't have an area.

5. A

In (A), "but" connects two phrases in parallel form: "to alert . . . " and "to prepare." Choices (B), "so as to prepare," (C), "for the purpose of preparing," and (D), "for preparing," break this parallel construction. (E) has "to prepare," but the "so as to" is wordy, and "by discussing and thinking ahead" doesn't correctly relate these activities to the academic preparation under discussion.

6. E

The phrase "less by . . . than by" must link similar terms. What follows the first "by"? "Reaching." So, what must follow the second "by"? "Refusing." Only (D) and (E) use the gerund "refusing." (D) won't work. It takes out the second "by," which is needed to complete the comparison.

7. D

The plural pronoun "their" incorrectly refers to the singular noun "Norway." "Their" should be "its." So (A) and (C) are out. (B) corrects the pronoun error but changes "reflecting" to the awkward "being a reflection of" ("reflection of," in (C), is also incorrect). (E), too, uses the correct pronoun, but the comparison word "longer" changes the meaning of the sentence; Norway's humanitarian tradition isn't being compared to that of any other country. That leaves (D).

8. C

Notice that the very first word you read is "Compared." Start hunting for comparison errors as you read. Only similar things can be compared. So, "the poor" can be compared only with other people, real or fictional, (C). People cannot be compared with a "time period," as in (A) and (B); or with a "time," as in (D); or with a book, as in (E). Only (C) presents a valid comparison.

9. D

"Attaining" and "to enter" must be made parallel. (D) fixes the problem, with "to attain" and "to enter." The other choices are not parallel.

10. E

To evaluate this relatively lengthy underlined portion, first ignore the descriptive clause "such as standardized test scores" that is set off by commas. Now read the remaining parts of the underlined portion together: "an index that are called objective and can be quantified and overlook less measurable progress, such as that." Since "index" is singular, the verb should be "is called." Eliminate (A) and (B). The phrase "such as what is made" is unnecessarily wordy, so eliminate (C) and (D). The remaining choice, (E), fixes the verb issue and the wordiness issue. In addition, it changes "that are called objective" to the more concise "so-called objective" and places that descriptor in a more appropriate place.

11. D

The idiom is "professed ignorance of." Therefore, "ignorant" in (A) is incorrect. It's also not correct to say one *has* either ignorance or fear, so "having fear" in (A) and "to have ignorance" in (E) are both wrong. It doesn't make sense to say the informant was professing "ignorantly," in (B), because in fact the informant is knowledgeable (although choosing not to share that knowledge). (C) and (D) both correctly begin with "ignorance," but "since" is the wrong connecting word. The correct phrasing is "for fear that," and that's (D).

12. D

The composers were united by a shared ideal; the words "their holding" are superfluous, so eliminate (A). (B) unnecessarily repeats "ideal." In (C), it's redundant to say the composers "were united with each other." In (E), the composers didn't unite *with* the ideal. (D) makes sense and doesn't use any unnecessary words.

13. C

The word "than" indicates a comparison, so make sure that like things are being compared. Here Mahler's symphonies are compared to Haydn. That's no good. Eliminate (A). (E) repeats the mistake of (A). (B) compares "use" to "Haydn," and (D) compares "use" to "dissonance"; neither is correct. Only (C) is left standing. By adding the pronoun "those" to represent "symphonies," this choice compares how Mahler's symphonies are characterized with how Haydn's symphonies are characterized.

14. C

Logically, King James was trying to merge one country's legislature with another country's legislature. However, the sentence as written says he was trying to merge the legislature of Scotland with the country of England. Eliminate (A). By adding the pronoun "that," (C) completes the thought logically and is correct. Note that the idiom is "merge [one thing] *with* [another thing]," so "and" in the other choices is incorrect.

15. E

The underlined portion after the introductory phrase should start with the thing that made a convincing demonstration of physics. "It was anomalies" uses both a pronoun and a noun when only the noun is needed. By beginning with "anomalies," (E) is correct. (B), (C), and (D) use weak phrasing with "showing" and "being" and require an extra pronoun, either "that" or "what."

CHAPTER 6

Reading Comprehension Practice

Reading Comprehension Practice Set One

Directions: The questions in this group are based on the content of a passage. After reading the passage, choose the best answer to each question. Base your answers only according to what is stated or implied in the text.

Questions 1–6 refer to the following passage.

A basic principle of ecology is that population size is partly a reflection of available food resources. Recent experiments suggest that the relationship is more complex than
5   formerly thought. Specifically, the browsing of certain rodents appears to trigger chemical reactions in food plants that, in turn, affect the size of the rodent populations. Two examples of such
10 regulation have been reported.

Berger has demonstrated the power of a naturally occurring chemical called 6-MBOA to stimulate reproductive behavior in the mountain vole, a small, mouse-like rodent.
15 6-MBOA forms in young grass in response to browsing by voles. Berger experimented by feeding oats coated with 6-MBOA to nonbreeding winter populations of voles. After three weeks, she found a high
20 incidence of pregnancy among females. Since the timing of reproduction is crucial to the short-lived vole in an environment in which the onset of vegetative growth may be considerably delayed, the phytochemical
25 triggering of reproductive behavior represents a significant biological adaptation.

In an example reported by Bryant, plants appear to have developed a phytochemical defense against the depredations of
30 snowshoe hares in Canada. Every 10 years, for reasons that are unclear, the hare population swells. The result is overbrowsing of certain deciduous trees and shrubs. Bryant found that trees favored by the hare produce
35 young shoots high in terpene and phenolic resins, which discourage hare browsing. After treating non-resinous willow twigs with resinous extracts and placing treated and untreated samples at hare feeding stations,
40 Bryant found that samples containing at least half of the resin concentration of natural twigs were untouched. The avoidance of resinous shoots, he concludes, may play a role in the decline of the hare population to
45 normal levels.

Both of these reports suggest areas for further research. For example, data should be reviewed to determine if periodic population explosions among lemmings
50 (another small rodent living in a northern environment) occur during years in which there is an early onset of vegetative growth; if so, a triggering mechanism similar to that prompted by the vole may be involved.

1. The author provides specific information to answer which of the following questions?

    ○ What factors other than food supply affect the population size of rodents?

    ○ Why is the timing of the voles' reproductive effort important?

    ○ Are phytochemical reactions found only in northern environments?

    ○ How does 6-MBOA trigger reproductive activity in the mountain vole?

    ○ What are the causes of the periodic increase in the snowshoe hare population?

2. The passage describes the effect of 6-MBOA on voles as a "significant biological adaptation" (line 26) because it

    ○ limits reproductive behavior in times of food scarcity

    ○ prompts the vole population to seek new food sources

    ○ supports species survival during periods of fluctuating food supply

    ○ maximizes the number of offspring in individual litters

    ○ minimizes territorial competition

3. It can be inferred that the study of lemmings proposed by the author would probably

    ○ strengthen the conclusions of Bryant

    ○ cast doubt on the conclusions of Bryant

    ○ support the specific findings of Berger

    ○ provide evidence as to whether Berger's conclusions can be applied to other species

    ○ disprove common beliefs about the relationship between population size and food supply

4. The author of the passage is primarily concerned with

    ○ reviewing findings about phytochemical regulation of rodent populations

    ○ outlining the role of 6-MBOA in regulating population size

    ○ summarizing knowledge on population size of rodents

    ○ explaining why earlier studies of population size were wrong

    ○ describing mechanisms used by plants to protect themselves

5. Bryant's interpretation of the results of the experiment described in lines 42–45 depends on which of the following assumptions?

    ○ The response of hares to resinous substances may be different in nature than under experimental conditions.

    ○ The periodic rise in the hare population is triggered by an unknown phytochemical response.

    ○ Many hares will starve to death rather than eat resinous shoots.

    ○ Hares alter their breeding behavior in response to the declining availability of food.

    ○ Significant numbers of hares die from ingesting the resins in shoots.

6. Both experiments described in the passage did each of the following EXCEPT

    ○ measure changes in the behavior of test animals

    ○ measure changes in the populations of experimental animals

    ○ simulate a hypothesized phytochemical effect in nature

    ○ measure the consumption of foods by test animals

    ○ analyze the effects of food on breeding behavior

Questions 7–12 are based on the following passage.

In many underdeveloped countries, the state plays an important and increasingly varied role in economic development today. There are four general arguments, all of them related, for state
5 participation in economic development. First, the entrance requirements in terms of financial capital and capital equipment are very large in certain industries, and the size of these obstacles will serve as barriers to entry on the
10 part of private investors. One can imagine that these obstacles are imposing in industries such as steel production, automobiles, electronics, and parts of the textile industry. In addition, there are what Myint calls "technical
15 indivisibilities in social overhead capital." Public utilities, transport, and communications facilities must be in place before industrial development can occur, and they do not lend themselves to small-scale improvements.

20 A related argument centers on the demand side of the economy. This part of the economy is seen as fragmented, disconnected, and incapable of using inputs from other parts of the economy. Consequently, economic activity in one
25 part of the economy does not generate the dynamism in other sectors that is expected in more cohesive economies. Industrialization necessarily involves many different sectors; economic enterprises will thrive best in an
30 environment in which they draw on inputs from related economic sectors and, in turn, release their own goods for industrial utilization within their own economies.

A third argument concerns the low-level
35 equilibrium trap in which less developed countries find themselves. At subsistence levels, societies consume exactly what they produce. There is no remaining surplus for reinvestment. As per capita income rises, however, the
40 additional income will not be used for savings and investment. Instead, it will have the effect of increasing the population, which will eat up the surplus and force the society to its former subsistence position. Fortunately, after a certain
45 point, the rate of population growth will decrease; economic growth will intersect with and eventually outstrip population growth. The private sector, however, will not be able to provide the one-shot large dose of capital to
50 push economic growth beyond those levels where population increases eat up the incremental advances.

The final argument concerns the relationship between delayed development and the state.
55 Countries wishing to industrialize today have more competitors, and these competitors occupy a more differentiated industrial terrain than previously. This means that the available niches in the international system are more limited. For
60 today's industrializers, therefore, the process of industrialization cannot be a haphazard affair, nor can the pace, content, and direction be left solely to market forces. Part of the reason for a strong state presence, then, relates specifically
65 to the competitive international environment in which modern countries and firms must operate.

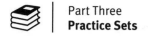
7. The passage suggests that all of the following are arguments for state economic intervention EXCEPT:

    O   The start-up costs of initial investments are beyond the capacities of many private investors.

    O   The state must mediate relations between the demand and supply sides of the economy

    O   The pace and processes of industrialization are too important to be left solely to market trends.

    O   The livelihoods and security of workers should not be subject to the variability of industrial trends.

    O   Public amenities are required to facilitate a favorable business environment.

8. Which of the following best states the central point of the passage?

    O   Without state intervention, many less developed countries will not be able to carry out the interrelated tasks necessary to achieve industrialization.

    O   Underdeveloped countries face a crisis of overpopulation and a lack of effective demand that cannot be overcome without outside assistance.

    O   State participation plays a secondary role as compared to private capital investment in the industrialization of underdeveloped countries.

    O   Less developed countries are trapped in an inescapable cycle of low production and demand.

    O   State economic planning can ensure the rapid development of nonindustrialized countries' natural resources.

9. The author suggests all of the following as appropriate roles for the state in economic development EXCEPT

    O   safeguarding against the domination of local markets by a single source of capital

    O   financing industries with large capital requirements

    O   helping to coordinate demand among different economic sectors

    O   providing capital inputs sufficient for growth to surpass increases in per capita consumption

    O   developing communication and transportation facilities to service industry

10. The author suggests which of the following about the "technical indivisibilities in social overhead capital" (lines 14–15) and the "low-level equilibrium trap" (lines 34–35)?

    O   The first leads to rapid technological progress; the second creates demand for technologically sophisticated products.

    O   Both enhance the developmental effects of private sector investment.

    O   Neither is relevant to formulating a strategy for economic growth.

    O   The first is a barrier to private investment; the second can attract it.

    O   The first can prevent development from occurring; the second can negate its effects.

11. Which of the following, if true, would cast doubt on the author's argument that state participation is important in launching large-scale industries?

  ○ Coordination of demand among different economic sectors requires a state planning agency.

  ○ Private investors might be willing to help pay for improvements to public utilities, transport, and communications facilities.

  ○ When surveyed, most citizens in underdeveloped countries say they strongly prefer that the government not play a large role in launching large-scale industries.

  ○ Associations of private sector investors can raise seemingly unlimited amounts of capital by pooling their resources.

  ○ State participation in launching large-scale industries often introduces new problems that wouldn't otherwise exist.

12. According to the passage, the "low-level equilibrium trap" in underdeveloped countries results from

  ○ the tendency for societies to produce more than they can use

  ○ intervention of the state in economic development

  ○ the inability of market forces to overcome the effects of population growth

  ○ the fragmented and disconnected nature of the demand side of the economy

  ○ one-shot, large doses of capital intended to spur economic growth

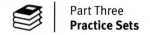

Answers and Explanations

1. B	4. A	7. D	10. E
2. C	5. C	8. A	11. D
3. D	6. E	9. A	12. C

PASSAGE 1—Ecology

Topic and Scope: A basic scientific principle: "Population size is partly a reflection of available food resources." Specifically, the author uses two experiments (one by Berger, one by Bryant) to illustrate how changes in food supply can dramatically affect the size of rodent populations.

Purpose and Main Idea: Author wants to demonstrate that the relationship between population and food supply "is more complex than formerly thought."

Paragraph Structure: In paragraph 1, the second sentence is key: "Recent experiments suggest that the relationship is more complex than formerly thought." *You can guess from these words that the passage will go on to discuss these experiments.* The next sentence identifies the nature of the complexity—rodent browsing affects plant chemicals, which in turn affect the rodents. Paragraph 2 details Berger's experiment, which studied how plant chemicals *trigger reproductive activity among voles.* Paragraph 3 details Bryant's experiment, which studied the effect of plant chemicals on *declining populations of snowshoe hares.* Paragraph 4 discusses possible future research involving lemmings, another rodent with fluctuating populations.

1.   B

With a question like this, you need to check each choice against the passage. A faster way to eliminate choices is to remember that the correct answer often fits with the main idea, here the food-population relationship. Thus, (A) is wrong because it ventures away from this. (B) looks excellent, because the author devotes several lines at the end of paragraph 2 to explaining the importance of timing for vole

reproduction. (C) is simply never covered. (D) is wrong because the author discusses the significance of 6-MBOA but not its biologic mechanism. As for (E), why the hares overpopulate is dismissed in the third paragraph with the words "for reasons that are unclear." The correct answer is (B).

2.   C

This question asks about a detail from paragraph 2. The cited sentence says that timing is crucial because voles are short-lived and the timing of plant growth is unpredictable. You can infer that the plant-rodent relationship increases the vole population at times when food is more plentiful. The best restatement of this inference is (C). (A) goes the wrong way; 6-MBOA triggers breeding—it doesn't discourage it. (B), (D), and (E) are never mentioned anywhere.

3.   D

The lemmings are mentioned in the last paragraph, which speculates that lemmings might, like voles, be affected by a plant trigger for breeding behavior. Some answer choices mention Berger and some mention Bryant. The lemmings are likened to voles, so Berger is the pertinent researcher here. This eliminates (A) and (B). (E) conflicts with the main idea. The author wants to prove something, not disprove it.

That leaves (C), supporting Berger's specific findings, and (D), indicating whether Berger's findings can be generalized. The paragraph doesn't talk about proving Berger's specific results with the voles; those are accepted as given. It does say that the lemmings, like voles, may be affected by a plant trigger. This implies (D), that Berger's findings may be applicable to other animals.

4. A

The answer to this Global question has to focus on something about the complex relationship between food and population size, including the rodent examples; it should also encompass the entire passage. Thus, the best answer is (A). (B) is a detail appearing only in the second paragraph, while (E) appears only in paragraph 3. (C) is too general, and (D) mentions a topic the author never covers.

5. C

When you read about the hares, notice that Bryant's conclusion is pure speculation. He sees that the hares don't eat resinous shoots and concludes that this "may play a role" in population decline. The assumption is that there's a connection between not eating the plants and a population reduction. Choice (C) is correct; the avoidance of plants would lead to starvation and population decline.

(A), if true, would *weaken*, not strengthen, Bryant's conclusion. (B) is irrelevant—the cause of the rise is unknown and doesn't concern Bryant; it's the decline that interests him. (D) mixes up the hares with the voles and their breeding behavior. The hare experiment has nothing to do with breeding and reproduction. Finally, (E) is never suggested. Bryant concluded that the population decline was caused by *avoiding* the shoots, not by *eating* them.

6. E

Because the question stem refers to both experiments, you need to find the statement that describes only one of the experiments. Choice (A) was part of both: Berger measured how voles changed breeding behavior, and Bryant measured how hares changed eating behavior. (B) also appears in both: Berger measured the rise and fall of vole populations, while Bryant measured hare populations. (C) and (D) apply to both experiments, since both scientists fed the animals chemically treated foods and noted consumption. (E) is correct: Only Berger's experiment dealt with the effect of food on breeding behavior. Bryant's hare experiment dealt with the effect of food on *eating* behavior.

PASSAGE 2—State Role in Development

Topic and Scope: The underdeveloped countries' economies; specifically, the four arguments for state participation in economic development.

Purpose and Main Idea: The author's purpose is to argue for state participation in economic development in underdeveloped countries.

Paragraph Structure: The first paragraph introduces the topic and mentions the first argument: size of obstacles. The second paragraph mentions the next argument: many sectors of industrialization. The third paragraph addresses the third argument: the low-level equilibrium trap and population. The fourth paragraph mentions the final argument: the relationship between delayed development and the state.

7. D

Here's a good example of why it's helpful to be done with the passage quickly. Some of the answers to this Detail question are pretty tricky. You're looking for a reason *not* given in the passage, which means that the four wrong answers are in there somewhere. "Start-up costs of initial investments" from (A) fits with "entrance requirements in terms of financial capital" in lines 6–7. (B) is trickier. "Demand" is pretty clearly mentioned at the top of paragraph 2, but what about "supply"? A quick look at paragraph 3 provides what you need: society will eat what they make at subsistence levels, and per capita income increases will only serve to increase population to match. The author feels that the private sector cannot break this cycle on its own. (C) mirrors the author's explicit opinion in lines 63–66. Spotting those Emphasis key words would make for quick elimination of this answer choice. (D) talks about "livelihoods and security of workers," two subjects mentioned nowhere in the passage. Could public "amenities" in (E) mean "public utilities, transport, and communications facilities" from lines 15–16? It's certainly plausible. So, (E) should be eliminated as well. Only (D), the correct answer, remains.

8. A

The passage, as a whole, presents reasons state intervention is necessary for the industrialization of many less developed countries. (B) focuses only on paragraph 2 and paragraph 3. It also introduces the new idea of outside assistance ("state presence" doesn't mean "foreign presence"). (D) also draws only on those two paragraphs and confuses them to boot. (C) is the opposite of the author's main point, and (E) overstates the case with the extreme words "rapid" and "ensure."

9. A

You need what's *not* in the passage. (B) and (E) are mentioned in paragraph 1, (C) in paragraph 2, and (D) in paragraph 3. "Safeguarding against the domination of local markets by a single source of capital" is not mentioned.

10. E

Context is critical for any question that references a specific part of the passage, and Inference questions are no exception. The sentence talking about "technical indivisibilities in social overhead capital" begins with the key phrase "[i]n addition," indicating that the "technical indivisibilities" are another example of what was discussed in the previous sentence. That sentence lists imposing obstacles, so the "technical indivisibilities" must be another obstacle. That eliminates all the choices except (D) and (E). Notice that you don't need to understand the dense jargon in this sentence to understand its role in the paragraph.

Now on to "low-level equilibrium trap." The context here isn't as clear, but at this point your job is simpler—you only need to figure out which of the two remaining answer choices is supported by the passage. There is no language in paragraph 3 that fits with attracting investment. But lines 40–44 say "additional income . . . [will] force society back to its former subsistence position." That fits (E) nicely.

11. D

Every now and again, you'll see a Weaken question in Reading Comprehension. Don't panic, as you can deal with it just as you would a Critical Reasoning question. The author makes four arguments here, and it wouldn't be efficient to try to analyze them all and create four different predictions. It'll be best to go choice by choice. (A) fits with the author's main point, so it's hardly reasonable to think that it would weaken any of his arguments. (B) is out of scope. The author doesn't argue that the problem is how to pay for improvements to these services, just that these services have to already exist before industrial development can even begin. As for (C), the author only deals with what is needed to get large-scale industries going, not what citizens want or don't want. (D) contradicts both paragraph 1 and paragraph 3, and is therefore the correct answer. In paragraph 1, the author argues that the required large capital investments will be barriers for private investors. If private investors can join together, as (D) says, this won't be as big a problem. Similarly, the end of paragraph 3 discusses private investors' inability to provide a large "dose of capital." Again, (D) provides a possible solution to this. (E) might be true, but it deals with the consequences of state participation in launching large-scale industries, whereas the author is concerned merely with what is needed to launch the industries in the first place. Thus (E) doesn't weaken the author's argument.

12. C

This question is technically a Detail question, but even so, it tests your big-picture knowledge of the passage, as will many seemingly detail-oriented questions. You know from your Passage Map that you need to look in paragraph 3 for the answer. Perhaps you read for context only the first two sentences of that paragraph. Even so, you could have eliminated (A), which is the exact opposite of the second sentence. It's not likely that state intervention is the problem, as you know from the author's purpose that he's arguing in favor of such intervention. (B), then, should be eliminated. (D) also is out on big-picture grounds, as it is drawn from the wrong paragraph. (E) seems to be in the paragraph, but read the whole sentence—the author doesn't mention "one-shot, large doses of capital" as a cause of the trap. Rather, it's the private sector's inability to provide those doses that's the culprit. (C), then, is correct.

Reading Comprehension Practice Set Two

Directions: The questions in this group are based on the content of a passage. After reading the passage, choose the best answer to each question. Base your answers only according to what is stated or implied in the text.

Questions 1–5 refer to the following passage.

In 1943, Baade obtained photographs of stars in the galaxy Andromeda. Using these photographs, Baade divided stars into two groups. The brightest members of Population I were hot,
5 blue stars with surface temperatures up to 30,000 kelvins. The brightest Population II stars (called "red giants") were large, cool, and red, and fainter than Population I stars. Later observations showed that most Population I
10 stars occur in the arms of spiral galaxies, while Population II stars are most common between the arms and in the centers of spiral galaxies, and in elliptical galaxies.

According to Baade, the two populations
15 compose distinct stellar age groups. Since the rate at which stars consume their fuel is directly proportional to their brightness, and brightness increases with mass, large, bright stars burn their fuel more quickly than dimmer stars. Baade
20 concluded that the brightest Population I stars were probably less than one million years old while Population II stars were older.

Baade found support for his views in the distribution of red giants. It is believed that most
25 of a star's hydrogen fuel is gradually converted to helium. When the helium core comprises about one-tenth of a star's mass, the star expands and its surface cools. This phase lasts until the red giant consumes all of its fuel and
30 disintegrates in either a single explosion or a series of outbursts. Most red giants occur in Population II.

The composition of red giants supports Baade's conception. It is thought that all elements
35 evolved from hydrogen as a result of nuclear reactions in stars. When a star explodes, it throws out heavy elements. Thus, the dust and gas from which new stars are produced gradually become richer in heavier elements.
40 Studies of red giants in both populations reveal that heavier elements are more abundant in Population I giants. Thus, Population II stars evolved from material poor in heavier elements and are older.

45 Analyses of stars in our galaxy have shown variations in concentrations of heavy elements, indicating that the stars must be of assorted ages. As a consequence, stars are now classified into five distinct populations.

1. The primary purpose of this passage is to

   O explain how to determine the age of a star

   O describe a system of star classification and some of the evidence supporting it

   O discuss Population II stars

   O compare and evaluate competing theories of stellar evolution

   O examine the importance of Baade's contributions to astronomy

2. According to the passage, Baade considered all of the following to be characteristics of Population I stars EXCEPT:

   O They are relatively young stars.

   O The brightest members are hot, blue stars.

   O They are found mainly between the arms of spiral galaxies.

   O They are brighter than Population II stars.

   O They have surface temperatures of up to 30,000 kelvins.

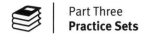
3. According to the passage, when the core in which hydrogen has been totally consumed amounts to approximately one-tenth of a star's mass, then

   O the star will expand and its outer layer will cool

   O its life as a normal star will end

   O the star may disintegrate in a single explosion

   O the star will throw out the heavy elements it has produced

   O its classification will change from Population I to Population II

4. The passage suggests which of the following about red giants?

   O They appear mostly in the arms of spiral galaxies.

   O Each red giant is cooler than it once was.

   O Population II giants evolved from Population I giants.

   O They have a low percentage of heavy elements.

   O Many have surface temperatures over 30,000 kelvins.

5. The passage provides support for all of the following statements EXCEPT:

   O The death of a star involves either one major or several minor explosions.

   O The chemical compositions of red giants support the classification of stars into different age groups.

   O Population II stars are older than Population I stars.

   O Elliptical galaxies have existed for a longer period of time than spiral galaxies.

   O The chemical composition of a star is indicative of its age.

Questions 6–9 refer to the following passage.

Desert plant populations have evolved sophisticated physiological behavioral traits that aid survival in arid conditions. Some send out long, unusually deep taproots; others utilize
5 shallow but widespread roots, which allow them to absorb large, intermittent flows of water. Certain plants protect their access to water. The creosote bush produces a potent root toxin which inhibits the growth of competing root
10 systems. Daytime closure of stomata exemplifies a further genetic adaptation; guard cells work to minimize daytime water loss, later allowing the stomata to open when conditions are more favorable to gas exchange with the environment.

15 Certain adaptations reflect the principle that a large surface area facilitates water and gas exchange. Most plants have small leaves, modified leaves (spines), or no leaves at all. The main food-producing organ is not the leaf but
20 the stem, which is often green and non-woody. Thick, waxy stems and cuticles, seen in succulents such as cacti and agaves, also help conserve water. Spines and thorns (modified branches) protect against predators and also
25 minimize water loss.

6. The passage suggests that which of the following weather-related conditions would most benefit plants with shallow root systems?

   O An unusually prolonged drought

   O A windstorm

   O A flash flood

   O A persistent fog

   O A winter snowfall

7. The adaptations of desert plants to their environment would tend to support the statement that

    O the rate of genetic evolution is greater in the desert than in more temperate surroundings

    O structures in a plant that usually perform one function may, under certain conditions, perform different functions

    O while the amount of leaf surface area is critical for a desert plant, it is much less so for plants in most other environments

    O desert plants do not have many physiological and behavioral traits in common with other plants

    O desert plants could probably adapt to life in a variety of harsh ecosystems

8. All of the following are mentioned as examples of adaptation by desert plants EXCEPT

    O deep roots

    O shallow roots

    O poisonous roots

    O food-producing leaves

    O spines and thorns

9. The passage suggests that the adaptations of desert plants function to do all of the following EXCEPT

    O protect the plants' access to water

    O prevent the loss of water during the day

    O maximize the water and gas exchange

    O shield the plants from daytime heat

    O guard against predators

Questions 10–12 refer to the following passage.

Shopping mall developers seek to attract large department stores that will act as "anchors"—high-traffic stores that will bring many customers into their complex. However, when a
5 department store chain seeks to site a new store, it must take into consideration that the high level of customer traffic generated by the new store may be exploited by nearby smaller retailers. It will decline to build if it is judged that
10 the large store's "positive externality" will serve primarily to increase sales at nearby small competitors. Mall developers can circumvent this problem and retain a mixture of large and small retailers by internalizing the department store's
15 externality—that is, by bringing some of the benefits associated with the department store back to the store itself.

The ability of malls to do so lies in the fact that their developers own the entire complex. They
20 can charge rents that reflect not only the contribution that each store makes to the mall's overall revenues, but also the business that a store brings to the mall's other tenants. Recent studies of malls in the American Midwest show
25 that in a mall with two or three department stores, a small shoe store or restaurant might pay rent per square foot that is five times the rate charged to department stores in the complex, while a jeweler in a mall with four or
30 five department stores could pay twenty times the rate paid by the mall's anchors.

The partiality shown department stores increases with mall size, even though the study shows that department stores in different-sized complexes
35 usually generate about the same sales per square foot. The disparity in the rents charged between department stores and small retailers cannot be explained simply by the fact that small stores make greater sales per square foot of floor space;
40 rather, the smaller stores are willing to subsidize the department stores for the sales that department stores generate for them, and the greater the traffic, the more they are willing to pay.

10. The author's primary purpose in writing this passage is to

O indicate the competitive advantages that malls have over traditional shopping districts

O introduce the concept of positive externality and explain its relevance to shopping malls located in the American Midwest

O argue that mall owners exploit small stores by manipulating their rents so that large store owners benefit

O explain how mall developers attempt to increase customer traffic for a mall by varying rental rates for different kinds of stores

O demonstrate how mall developers maximize the number of retailers in their malls by internalizing the benefits of positive externality

11. Which of the following can be inferred from the passage?

O Jewelers in small malls pay more rent per square foot than do shoe stores in large malls.

O Department store chains consider more than potential sales per square foot when determining where to locate stores.

O If mall developers were to charge the same rent per square foot for every store, malls would likely experience a surplus of department stores and a shortage of smaller retailers.

O Positive externality is a greater problem for small stores than for larger department stores.

O If not for the phenomenon of positive externality, malls would not be able to attract large department stores as tenants.

12. Which of the following statements about large malls and small malls can be logically inferred from the passage?

   O   Department stores in large malls generate more sales per square foot than do department stores in small malls.

   O   Small malls tend to attract more specialized stores than large malls, and therefore do not need as many anchor stores.

   O   The disparity in rent per square foot between small retailers and anchor stores is greater in larger malls than smaller malls.

   O   Small retailers in large malls often resent paying higher rent than anchor stores, and eventually move to smaller malls where the disparity is less pronounced.

   O   Because larger malls are normally assumed to attract an upscale clientele, they can charge small retailers more rent per square foot than smaller malls can.

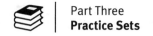

Answers and Explanations

1. B	4. B	7. B	10. D
2. C	5. D	8. D	11. B
3. A	6. C	9. D	12. C

PASSAGE 1—Baade

Topic and Scope: Baade's star observations; specifically, his system for classifying stars.

Purpose and Main Idea: The author's purpose is to describe Baade's star classification scheme and the evidence behind it. Since this is a descriptive passage, the author doesn't offer a specific main point of his own.

Paragraph Structure: The first paragraph introduces Baade's scheme by differentiating Population I and II stars. The second paragraph picks up on this contrast, distinguishing the two groups by age. The third and fourth paragraphs provide evidence in support of the notion that Population II stars are older: first, the more frequent occurrence of red giants in this population and, second, the composition of red giants themselves. The last paragraph indicates that, although Baade's basic insights are still considered valid, his two star categories have now been expanded to five.

1.   B

If you put the purpose of the passage into your own words, you should have come up with something like "describe Baade's star categories and show how evidence supports them." (B) contains these ideas, though in more general terms.

Remember that the correct response to a Global question must cover everything in the passage. (A) ignores the first and last paragraphs, which are not concerned with star ages. (C) focuses only on Population II stars, while the passage clearly differentiates between Population I and II stars. No theories of stellar evolution are presented, so (D) is wrong. (E) might have been tempting because it focuses on Baade, but it does so without mentioning his star categories, which are the main focus of the passage; (E) would be appropriate for a more general and biographical passage than this one.

2.   C

"According to the passage" indicates a Detail question, so the correct answer is to be found in the text itself. Population I stars are discussed in the first two paragraphs: they are bright (brighter than Population II stars), they are hot (up to 30,000 kelvins), the brightest among them are blue, they are young, and they occur *in* the arms of spiral galaxies. Since this is also an "all/EXCEPT" question, the correct answer cannot be one of these facts. This eliminates (A), (B), (D), and (E). That leaves (C), which is indeed correct, because it is Population II stars that are found *between* the arms of spiral galaxies.

3.   A

This development is discussed in the third paragraph. "When the helium core comprises about one-tenth of a star's mass, the star expands and its surface cools." (A) paraphrases this development. Notice that (B), (C), and (D) come from either too far along in the third paragraph or from the fourth paragraph. Choice (E), logical as it may appear, is never mentioned at all.

4.   B

According to the passage, red giants occur primarily among Population II stars and are older, cooler, dimmer, and redder than Population I stars. Their hydrogen has mostly changed to helium, and they are poorer in heavier elements than are other stars. (A) is not a valid inference because it's Population I stars that appear mostly in the arms of spiral galaxies, not Population II stars. (B) is correct because red giants have converted most of their hydrogen to helium, and as they do this their surface cools. As for (C), there is nothing in the passage to suggest any evolutionary relationship between Population I and Population II giants. (D) is not supported by the passage either. Paragraph 4 just says that heavy elements are "more abundant" in

Population I red giants than in Population II red giants, but you don't know anything about a "low percentage." (E) is contradicted by paragraph 1, which says that Population I stars have surface temperatures "up to" 30,000 kelvins and that Population II stars are cooler. There is no indication that many, or even any, of the stars in either group have surface temperatures *over* 30,000 kelvins, especially the cooler red giants.

5. D

Remember to look for the choice that is *not* supported by information in the passage. (A) appears nearly verbatim at the end of the third paragraph. (B) and (E), which get at the same point, constitute the principal focus of the fourth paragraph. (C)'s point is made several times in the passage. (D), however, looks different immediately. Elliptical galaxies are mentioned only once—at the end of the first paragraph—where it's stated that older Population II stars are found in them. But these stars are found in spiral galaxies as well, so it can't be concluded that elliptical galaxies are older than spiral galaxies. (D), therefore, is correct.

PASSAGE 2—Desert Plants

Topic and Scope: Desert plant adaptations and how they aid in these plants' survival.

Purpose and Main Idea: The author is trying to describe the physiological traits that desert plants have adapted in order to survive in arid conditions.

Paragraph Structure: The first paragraph describes some general adaptations. The second paragraph discusses adaptations based on the principle that a large surface area facilitates water and gas exchange.

6. C

The stem is looking for the weather-related condition that would especially benefit plants with shallow root systems. Shallow root systems are mentioned up in the second sentence, and the point is that these specially adapted roots allow desert plants to take advantage of heavy, irregular flows of water. One example would be a very heavy, torrential downpour. The only choice that comes close to this is a flash flood. Flash floods result from unexpected, torrential

rainfall. (A) and (B) are impossible; neither drought nor windstorms provide water. (D) won't work because a persistent fog doesn't deposit large, intermittent flows of water. (E), finally, is also unsuitable. First, this choice doesn't suggest a *heavy*, intermittent snowfall, and second, nothing is said in the passage to suggest snow would be of special benefit to shallow rooted plants.

7. B

The second paragraph contains several examples of structures that in desert plants perform different functions than those they normally perform in plants in other environments. Spines and thorns in desert plants are modified leaves and branches to reduce water loss. And, as a result of their lack of normal leaves, most desert plants produce their food in their green, fleshy stems. As for the wrong choices, three of them—(A), (D), and (E)—simply can't be answers. There's no information to support any of these statements. Finally, in choice (C), while the passage does indicate that a small leaf surface area is a critical factor for desert plants, nothing suggests that leaf surface area isn't critical for plants in most other environments. Since the general principle is that a large surface area facilitates gas and water exchange, one can infer that the larger leaf surface area of other plants helps in this process.

8. D

You are told in the second paragraph that most desert plants produce food in their stems, not their leaves. Therefore, (D) is the correct answer: it names something that's not mentioned in the passage. Choices (A), (B), and (C) are mentioned in the first paragraph, and (E) is mentioned in the second paragraph.

9. D

The passage mentions several different adaptations and the purpose of each. The creosote bush produces a toxin that prohibits competing root systems from intruding on its space, therefore protecting its access to water. Guard cells function to "minimize daytime water loss." The second paragraph starts by talking about adaptations that facilitate gas and water exchange. Spines and

thorns are adaptations that protect against predators. There is no mention of any adaptation shielding plants from the heat, so (D) must be the answer.

PASSAGE 3—Malls

Topic and Scope: The relationship between shopping mall owners and their tenants.

Purpose and Main Idea: To explain that mall owners need to attract large department stores that will bring in many customers to the mall by charging such stores lower rents.

Paragraph Structure: The first paragraph introduces the problem: large department stores bring many advantages to a mall that may end up being detrimental to the store itself, so mall owners must provide other benefits to the store in exchange. The second paragraph describes how small stores are often charged much higher rents than large department stores, and the third paragraph explains why: the small stores are subsidizing the larger stores due to the increased customer traffic that department stores bring to the mall.

10. D

The primary purpose is set up in the first paragraph: mall developers seek department stores because they bring a lot of customers to the malls; however, in order to get those department stores, they have to make it worthwhile for them. The next two paragraphs explain how developers solve this problem by varying rents to compensate the department stores. So, the primary purpose is concisely stated in choice (D), to explain how mall developers attempt to increase customer traffic by varying rental rates for different kinds of stores. Choices (A) and (E) state ideas that are not present in the passage: a comparison with other shopping districts is not made, and maximizing the number of retailers is not discussed. Choice (C) is way too strongly worded and contrary to the tone of the passage; it is never suggested that small stores are exploited, and in any event, hiking rents on small stores is not the main point of the passage. Choice (B) may be tempting, because the concept of positive externality

clearly is important to the passage, but it's too specific, referring only to the American Midwest. The studies of Midwestern malls are brought up only to support the author's argument.

11. B

The question provides no clues as to where to look in the passage for the answer, so work from the answer choices. Choice (B) is correct because the passage states that department store chains will decline to build in a mall if their presence will "primarily" benefit other stores. Therefore, it can't be just their own sales that concern them: they also consider the benefit they provide to other stores. (B) is also a fairly softly worded answer choice, which is usually true of the correct answer to an Inference question. (A) goes too far; while the passage gives examples of jewelers in malls with more department stores paying more rent than shoe stores in malls with fewer anchors, there is no way to infer a generalization for the opposite cases of jewelers in small malls and shoe stores in large malls. (C) states the opposite of what the passage implies. Department stores demand lower rents per square foot to compensate for their "positive externalities," so a developer offering the same rates to all stores would have a dearth of department stores. (D) likewise contradicts the passage; smaller stores are never said to have "positive externalities," only department stores. Even if smaller stores have that "problem," nothing in the passage implies that smaller stores suffer more from that problem than do larger ones. Finally, (E) gets it wrong because the passage never suggests that positive externality is what attracts department stores to malls. The developers want the department stores for their "positive externalities," not vice versa.

12. C

(A) is contradicted by the passage, which says that sales per square foot for department stores are about the same for large and small malls. (B) is nowhere suggested by the passage; differences between the mix of stores in large and small malls are never discussed. (C) is a winner. The passage states that "the partiality [in rent] shown department stores increases with mall size," which is equivalent to saying that the disparity in rent between anchor (department) stores and small stores is greater for larger malls than smaller malls. (D) is way off base. Resentment never comes up in the passage, nor do the feelings of developers or store owners. (E) makes a claim about "upscale clientele," which is not supported by the passage; the passage explains rental rates based on only customer traffic, not on how chic the store is. Remember to stick closely to the text on Inference questions.

Reading Comprehension Practice Set Three

Directions: The questions in this group are based on the content of a passage. After reading the passage, choose the best answer to each question. Base your answers only according to what is stated or implied in the text.

Questions 1–6 refer to the following passage.

Although it is well documented that women face difficulties in reaching senior positions in business, studies indicate that business proprietorship offers one way forward.

5 Stanworth and Curran suggest that members of ethnic and religious minorities have often started their own businesses as a means of advancement. One advantage of ownership is the absence of "organizational selectors"—

10 proprietors need not meet employment criteria based on age, gender, or experience. Recent data confirm that women perceive self-employment as a means for overcoming subordination. In 1985, 4 percent of employed women in Britain

15 were self-employed; more recent estimates are put at 6 percent. Between 1977 and 1980, the number of woman-owned enterprises in the United States increased by 33 percent.

Goffee and Scase classify self-employed women

20 into four types by considering commitments to both entrepreneurial and conventional female values. Innovative entrepreneurs question conventional assumptions about the social position of women. Innovators seek business

25 ownership because of their inability to fulfill ambitions within more common career structures. Work is a central interest and is much more important than conventional female roles. In a related category are radicals—

30 proprietors who are active in collective political and economic ventures which promote female issues. Unlike innovators, their businesses are not oriented mainly to profit making; rather, accumulated assets are used to further the

35 long-term interests of women. Goffee and Scase designate a number of women as conventionals. Committed to entrepreneurship, they also remain attached to conventional female roles.

Unlike many innovators, resentment about

40 limited career prospects is rarely a motive for a business start-up. According to Goffee and Scase, conventionals "are less likely to have been previously employed in large-scale organizations. Before starting their businesses, most were

45 'secondary' workers who moved in and out of the labor market depending upon employment prospects and according to domestic commitments." Goffee and Scase suggest that entrepreneurs in a fourth category, domestics,

50 have a limited commitment to entrepreneurial ideals and are strongly attached to a traditional female role. These women "regard their business as secondary to their roles as mothers and wives. Proprietorship offers opportunities for

55 self-fulfillment and autonomy within parameters delineated by their other obligations."

1. Which of the following correctly describes one of the four types of female entrepreneurs discussed in the passage?

   ○ A conventional has a strong attachment to conventional gender roles and a weak attachment to entrepreneurial ideals.

   ○ An innovator has a limited attachment to both conventional gender roles and entrepreneurial ideals.

   ○ A radical has a limited attachment to conventional gender roles and a strong attachment to entrepreneurial ideals.

   ○ An innovator has a strong attachment to both conventional gender roles and entrepreneurial ideals.

   ○ A domestic has a limited attachment to entrepreneurial ideals and a strong attachment to conventional gender roles.

2. Which of the following summarizes the main idea of the first paragraph?

   O   There are few fundamental distinctions among female entrepreneurs.

   O   Women entrepreneurs, in their motives and objectives, do not differ significantly from their male counterparts.

   O   Entrepreneurship is increasingly seen by women as providing access to formerly unavailable economic opportunities.

   O   The development of a single set of policy guidelines designed to facilitate female entrepreneurship is desirable.

   O   Numbers of female entrepreneurs continue to grow despite opposition within the predominantly male business world.

3. Which of the following addresses a distinction made in the passage between innovators and radicals?

   O   Innovators attempt to revise current definitions of women's social roles; radicals do not.

   O   Innovators are committed to organizing cooperative business ventures; radicals are not.

   O   Innovators view work primarily as a means of securing personal and financial success; radicals do not.

   O   Radicals are motivated by antagonism toward previous employers; innovators are not.

   O   Radicals direct themselves mainly toward profit-making goals; innovators do not.

4. According to the passage, which of the following is true of conventionals?

   O   A commitment to entrepreneurship affects their attachment to a traditional female role.

   O   Their entrepreneurial values are shaped by past job-related experiences.

   O   Their political values are similar to those of domestics.

   O   Their previous participation in the labor market was often irregular.

   O   An attachment to a conventional female role inhibits their business activities.

5. The information given in the passage about the work of Goffee and Scase supports each of the following generalizations about female proprietorship EXCEPT that it

   O   fosters links among minority groups

   O   offers opportunities for nonmonetary rewards

   O   provides a means for political advances

   O   allows access to previously unattainable economic goals

   O   curtails the importance of the conventional female role

6. Goffee and Scase's distinction between innovators and radicals would be most weakened if it were shown that relatively few women

   O   become self-employed because of anger toward former employers

   O   use business profits to combat male dominance in society

   O   start a business in order to avoid organizational selectors

   O   are able to enter and leave the labor force at will

   O   feel that sex discrimination plays a major role in their lives

Questions 7–12 refer to the following passage.

The great migration of European intellectuals to the United States in the second quarter of the twentieth century prompted a transformation in the character of Western social thought. The
5 influx of Continental thinkers fleeing fascist regimes had a great impact on American academic circles, leading to new developments in such diverse fields as linguistics and theology. But the greatest impact was on the emigrés
10 themselves. This "migration experience" led expatriates to reexamine the supposedly self-evident premises inherited from the Continental intellectual tradition. The result, according to H. Stuart Hughes in *The Sea-Change*, was an
15 increased sophistication and deprovincialization in social theory.

One problem facing newly arrived emigrés in the United States was the spirit of anti-intellectualism in much of the country. The empirical orientation
20 of American academic circles, moreover, led to the conscious tempering by many European thinkers of their own tendencies towards speculative idealism. In addition, reports of oppression in Europe shook many Old World
25 intellectuals from a stance of moral isolation. Many great European social theorists had regarded their work as separate from all moral considerations. The migration experience proved to many intellectuals of the following generations
30 that such notions of moral seclusion were unrealistic, even irresponsible.

This transformation of social thought is perhaps best exemplified in the career of the German theologian Paul Tillich. Migration confronted
35 Tillich with an ideological as well as a cultural dichotomy. Hughes points out that Tillich's thought was "suspended between philosophy and theology, Marxism and political conformity, theism and disbelief." Comparable to the fusion
40 by other expatriate intellectuals of their own idealist traditions with the Anglo-American empiricist tradition was Tillich's synthesis of German Romantic religiosity with the

existentialism born of the twentieth-century war
45 experience. Tillich's basic goal, according to Hughes, was to move secular individuals by making religious symbols more accessible to them. Forced to make his ethical orientation explicit in the context of American attitudes,
50 Tillich avoided the esoteric academic posture of many Old World scholars, and was able to find a wide and sympathetic audience for his sometimes difficult theology. In this way, his experience in America, in his own words,
55 "deprovincialized" his thought.

7. The author's main concern in the passage is to

O characterize the effects of migration on U.S. history

O show how Paul Tillich's career was representative of the migration experience

O discuss the effects of the great migration on modern social thought

O reveal the increased sophistication of post-migration thought

O contrast European social thought with that of the United States

8. The author probably mentions H. Stuart Hughes (lines 13–14) in order to

O give an example of a European intellectual who migrated to America

O cite an important source of information about the migration experience

O demonstrate how one American academic was influenced by European scholars

O pay tribute to Americans who provided European thinkers with a refuge from fascism

O name a leading disciple of Paul Tillich

9. According to the passage, Tillich achieved which of the following?

    O   He engendered sympathy for the esotericism of Old World scholarship without himself taking an esoteric posture.

    O   He found an audience for his difficult theology without having to reveal his own ethical orientation.

    O   He adjusted his ideas so that they were suspended between philosophy and theology.

    O   He simplified his difficult theology so that he could find a wider audience.

    O   He elucidated religious symbols in a secular context without sacrificing their impact.

10. According to the passage, "reports of oppression in Europe" (lines 23–24) affected social thinkers by forcing them to

    O   rethink their moral responsibilities

    O   reexamine the morality of European leaders

    O   analyze the effects of migration on morality

    O   reconsider their antisocial behavior

    O   justify the moral value of social thought

11. It can be inferred that postmigration social thought is distinguished from premigration thought by its

    O   less secular nature

    O   greater social consciousness

    O   more difficult theology

    O   diminished accessibility

    O   more theoretical nature

12. The passage suggests that the migration experience

    O   had little major effect on American academic circles

    O   led to the abandonment of the idealist philosophical tradition

    O   made American intellectuals sensitive to oppression in Europe

    O   caused emigré social thinkers to question certain beliefs they had held

    O   negated Tillich's influence on modern social thought

Answers and Explanations

1.	E	4.	D	7.	C	10.	A
2.	C	5.	A	8.	B	11.	B
3.	C	6.	B	9.	E	12.	D

PASSAGE 1—Self-Employed Women

Topic and Scope: Different motives and values that lead different women to start their own businesses.

Purpose and Main Idea: The author summarizes the four categories into which Goffee and Scase have divided female entrepreneurs.

Paragraph Structure: The first paragraph provides a general introduction to the topic. It says that a significant number of women have started their own businesses as a way of avoiding the discrimination to which they are often subject in male-owned businesses. The second paragraph sorts women who start their own businesses into four categories: *innovators*, who are motivated mainly by the desire for career success; *radicals*, whose motivation is primarily ideological; *conventionals*, who are committed both to their businesses and to traditional female roles; and *domestics*, for whom traditional female roles are the first priority.

1. E

This is a Detail question, so the answer's in the text itself. In fact, all this question requires is that you check the choices against the definitions in the second paragraph. (A), (B), (C), and (D) are "half-right, half-wrong" choices. Each combines a correct piece of information with an incorrect piece. Only (E) gets the definition completely right.

2. C

"Prephrasing" the answer to this Global question would have allowed you to move quickly and confidently through the answer choices. The first paragraph makes the point that comes up in (C).

(A) contradicts the passage; the second paragraph reveals that there are many fundamental distinctions among female entrepreneurs. (B) is outside the scope of the passage, since the text never even mentions male

entrepreneurs. (D) is wrong because the author describes "female entrepreneurship" without advocating any particular official actions to "facilitate" it. Finally, (E) distorts information in the first paragraph, which mentions that women have difficulty reaching senior positions in business. However, the author never claims that female entrepreneurship is opposed by the business world; certainly, this is not a main idea of the passage.

3. C

Paying close attention to terms can sometimes make it easy to relocate details. According to the second paragraph, innovators are very committed to their work and start their own businesses to fulfill their ambitions—sentiments that often clash with conventional gender roles. Radicals, though they also reject traditional female roles, start businesses not for profit but primarily to advance general female interests. The choice that gets at this distinction is (C): innovators work primarily for personal and financial success but radicals do not. (A) and (B) ascribe the motives of radicals to innovators, while (D) and (E) do the precise opposite, attributing innovator qualities to radicals.

4. D

This is yet another Detail question, so, again, the answer is right there in the text. Conventionals, according to the passage, are committed to both entrepreneurship and traditional female roles. They are not motivated by resentment about limited careers and tend to be people who have "moved in and out of the labor market." These facts contradict (A), (B), and (E), while political values, (C), are never even mentioned. However, (D), irregular participation in the labor market, is a nice paraphrase of "in and out of the labor market" and is the correct answer.

5.   A

The correct answer to this "all/EXCEPT" question either will not be mentioned at all in the passage or will refer to something in the wrong part of the passage. This question concerns Goffee and Scase, who are featured in the second paragraph. Since the only mention of minorities is in the first paragraph, (A) is correct: the work of Goffee and Scase pertains to women, not minorities. The remaining four choices are all supported by the research of Goffee and Scase: "non-monetary rewards," (B), for domestics; "political advances," (C), for radicals; "access . . . to goals," (D), for all; and "curtails the importance of the conventional female role," (E), for innovators.

6.   B

Look at the distinction at issue. Innovators want personal success while radicals want to further the interests of women in general. Thus, you're looking for an answer that denies this difference in motivation. You can eliminate (C), which plays on information in the first paragraph, and applies to many women in business. Choice (D) is also poor, because it applies to conventionals, not the two categories mentioned. (A) is mentioned in regard to innovators, but you can get rid of it because it does not address the difference between personal and political motivation. (B) and (E) address this distinction, but (B) is stronger because it directly states that few women are in business to advance a political agenda. This does deny the main difference between the two groups. (E) is fuzzier—even if most women don't feel discriminated against, they may still have distinctly different goals.

PASSAGE 2—Migration

Topic and Scope: The great migration; specifically, how the migration experience transformed the social thought of European intellectuals who came to America, especially Tillich.

Purpose and Main Idea: The author's purpose is to describe the changes in the social thought of European intellectuals who immigrated to America, using Tillich as an example. The main idea is simply that, as a consequence of the migration experience, European thinkers in America transformed their ideas to have more relevance to "real-world" issues.

Paragraph Structure: The first paragraph introduces the topic and scope of the passage. The second paragraph describes in general terms how the social thought of European intellectuals was transformed. And the third paragraph provides a specific example of this transformation by describing the case of Tillich.

7.   C

To answer this question, it's important to realize that the author's purpose is to discuss the transformation of social thought that resulted from the great migration. Tillich is merely an example of how this transformation manifested itself among European emigrés; he is not the primary focus of the passage. Therefore, (B), which places emphasis on Tillich, is out. (A) fails to mention "social thought." (D) mentions only "thought," not "social thought," and doesn't mention the migration. Finally, (E) gets in the idea of social thought but leaves out the migration experience. (C), which includes the important elements of the author's purpose—the effects of the great migration on social thought—is correct.

8.   B

Hughes is mentioned in the first paragraph as the author of a book that says something about European expatriates in the United States. He's also cited in the third paragraph in the course of analysis of Tillich's thought. In other words, Hughes is cited as a source of information, as (B) suggests.

Choices (A), (C), and (D) are incorrect because the passage doesn't tell you whether Hughes was a European or an American, or whether he had any direct contact with the emigrés. Choice (E) may have been a bit more tempting, since the author cites Hughes's interpretation of Tillich's ideas, but that doesn't mean that Hughes is a disciple—a follower—of Tillich. Choice (B) is the only answer that's really supported by the passage.

9. E

Before you check the choices, review the information about Tillich in the last paragraph. He combined religiosity with existentialism and made religious symbols more meaningful to secular people. This is echoed in (E). (A) is a distortion. While it's true that Tillich avoided the esoteric academic posture of many Old World scholars, he did nothing to gain sympathy for that posture. (B) is contradicted by paragraph 3, which says that Tillich was forced to state his ethical orientation. (C) is incorrect because it was Hughes who pointed out that Tillich's thought was "suspended between philosophy and theology . . ." It wasn't that Tillich adjusted his ideas to match this description. As for (D), Tillich did indeed find a wider audience for his theology, but it was not by simplifying that theology. It was actually despite its difficulty.

10. A

This is a Detail question, so the correct answer is there in the text—in this case, in the second paragraph, which says that oppression forced social thinkers to reject moral isolation. (A) gets at this notion. (B) brings in "leaders," but they aren't mentioned in the passage. (C) substitutes "morality" for "moral isolation." They are not the same, and the morality of the emigrés was never in question. (D) is entirely wrong; the passage doesn't accuse the emigrés of "antisocial behavior." While (E) may have been tempting, "rethink" in (A) is much more characteristic of the thrust of the passage than the word "justify" in (E). Don't answer Detail questions on a hunch. Go back to the text and find the answer.

11. B

The passage uses the word "deprovincialization" twice to characterize the transformation of social thought. Among the choices, the closest paraphrase is (B), greater social consciousness. Notice that two choices, (A) and (C), allude to Tillich, but the question asks about social thought in general, not about him. Besides, these choices distort Tillich's approach. (D) and (E) are contrary to the passage.

12. D

This Inference question doesn't ask about a specific part of the passage, so jump into the answers and look for a choice that is consistent with the author's purpose and the passage's main idea. (D) is consistent with the passage's thesis, and is correct.

Looking at the other choices, (A) is contradicted in the first paragraph. Also, it deals with a minor point that the author doesn't pursue in the remainder of the text. The word "abandonment" makes (B) too broad a choice. Be suspicious of choices that make sweeping generalizations. (C) focuses on American rather than European thinkers. Finally, (E) goes contrary to the passage. If anything, the migration experience enhanced Tillich's influence.

Reading Comprehension Practice Set Four

Directions: The questions in this group are based on the content of a passage. After reading the passage, choose the best answer to each question. Base your answers only according to what is stated or implied in the text.

Questions 1–3 refer to the following passage.

The relevance of formal economic models to real-world policy has been a topic of some dispute. The economists R. D. Norton and S. Y. Rhee achieved some success in applying
5 such a model retrospectively to the Korean economy over a fourteen-year period; the model's figures for output, prices, and other variables closely matched real statistics. The model's value in policy terms, however,
10 proved less clear-cut. Norton and Rhee performed simulations in which, keeping long-term factors constant, they tried to pinpoint the effect of short-term policy changes. Their model indicated that rising
15 prices for imported oil would increase inflation; reducing exports by five percent would lower Gross Domestic Product and increase inflation; and slowing the growth of the money supply would result in slightly
20 higher inflation.

These findings are somewhat startling. Many economists have argued that reducing exports will lessen, not increase, inflation. And while most view escalating oil costs as
25 inflationary, few would think the same of slower monetary growth. The Norton-Rhee model can perhaps be viewed as indicating the pitfalls of a formalist approach that stresses statistical "goodness of fit" at the
30 expense of genuine policy relevance.

1. The author is primarily concerned with

   O proposing a new type of economic analysis

   O describing the limitations of an overly formal economic model

   O advocating the use of statistical models in determining economic policy

   O suggesting an explanation for Korean inflation

   O determining the accuracy of Norton and Rhee's analysis

2. The author mentions "a fourteen-year period" (line 6) in order to

   O indicate how far into the future Norton and Rhee's model can make accurate predictions

   O acknowledge the accuracy of Norton and Rhee's model in accounting for past events

   O explain the effect of reducing exports on inflation

   O demonstrate the startling nature of Norton and Rhee's findings

   O expose the flaws in Norton and Rhee's model

3. The most significant criticism leveled against Norton and Rhee's model is that it

   O excludes key statistical variables

   O is too abstract to be useful in policy making

   O fails to adjust for Korea's high rate of inflation

   O underestimates the importance of economic growth

   O fails to consider the effect of short-term variations in the economy

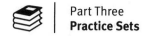

Questions 4–8 refer to the following passage.

Many aspects of coral reefs remain puzzling to scientists. One mystery concerns the relationship between Scleractinia, the coral type whose colonization produces reefs, and their symbiotic

5 partners, unicellular algae present in the coral's endodermic tissues. Both organisms play an integral part in the formation of a reef's foundation by working together to secrete and deposit calcium carbonate, which reacts with sea

10 salt to form a hard limestone underlayer. Scientists also know that, because of algal photosynthesis, the reef environment is oxygen-rich, while similarly high amounts of carbon dioxide are removed rapidly. All of this accounts

15 for the amazing renewability of coral reefs despite the erosion caused by waves. The precise manner in which one symbiotic organism stimulates the secretion of calcium carbonate by the other, however, remains unclear.

20 Scientists have proposed various theories to explain the transformation of "fringing reefs" (those connected above sea level to land masses) into "barrier reefs" (those separated from shorelines by lagoons) and finally into island

25 atolls. Although Darwin's view of the transformation is considered partially correct, some scientists feel that the creation of reef formations has more to do with the rise in sea level that occurred at the end of the last Ice Age

30 than with a gradual submergence of the volcanic islands to which fringing reefs were originally attached. However, recent drillings at one atoll have revealed a substantial underlayer of volcanic rock, which suggests that Darwin's

35 explanation may be largely correct.

The term "coral reef" is something of a misnomer. The *Scleractinia* themselves generally comprise only 10 percent of the total mass of life forms of an average reef community: Algae,

40 along with foraminifera, annelid worms, and assorted mollusks, can account for up to 90 percent of the reef mass. Moreover, the conditions under which reef growth occurs are determined by the needs of the algae, not those

45 of the coral. Reefs flourish only in shallow, highly saline waters above 70° F, because the algae require such an environment. Non-reef-building coral, meanwhile, occur worldwide.

4. The author suggests that coral reefs are able to survive the process of erosion

    O primarily through the activities of algae

    O despite the high oxygen content of the reef environment

    O as a result of the combined relations of coral and algae

    O only if they have an above-surface connection to the shoreline

    O because of the volcanic rock at their base

5. It can be inferred from the passage that Darwin

    O believed that reefs became atolls through the sinking of volcanic islands

    O should have expanded his studies of reefs to include those found at atolls

    O theorized that each reef formation was formed by an entirely different process

    O is less persuasive on the topic of reef formation in light of recent discoveries

    O was more interested in algae and coral than in other organisms living at reefs

6. The passage does NOT discuss the relationship between

    O algal photosynthesis and high oxygen content

    O Darwin's views and evidence supplied by recent research

    O volcanic rock and the life forms found at reefs

    O sea salt and calcium carbonate

    O wave action and the renewal of reefs

7. Which of the following questions is most completely answered by the passage?

    O   What percentage of coral worldwide is of the reef-building type?

    O   How do rises in sea level affect reef formation?

    O   What are the requisite environmental conditions for coral reef growth?

    O   How does coral stimulate the calcium carbonate secretions of symbiotic algae?

    O   What is the principal reason for the transformation of fringing reefs into atolls?

8. It can be inferred that the author would agree with all of the following statements EXCEPT:

    O   Coral cannot produce reefs without algae.

    O   The water around a coral reef contains high levels of oxygen.

    O   Darwin's theory about the causes of reef formation is at least partly accurate.

    O   The term "coral reef" should be abandoned by scientists.

    O   Some coral are more resistant to cold temperatures than the algae that live in their tissues.

Questions 9–12 refer to the following passage.

For many years, the observation that certain intensely bright young stars are concentrated along the spiral arms of disk-shaped galaxies remained unexplained. But recent research
5   suggests both a solution to the puzzle of these "O-stars," which are a million times brighter than the sun, and a mechanism that may partially explain the process of star formation in general.

10   Astronomers have long been aware that stars are made up of interstellar gas and dust, but until recently the specific sequence of events that signaled their birth was a mystery. Today, however, the stars in spiral arms of disk-shaped
15   galaxies are thought to result from density waves induced by gravitational fluctuations at the galactic center. These waves appear to function as the lines along which scattered clouds of interstellar gas and dust collect into
20   much larger clouds, which then coalesce into clumps of high concentration, out of which different types of stars, including O-stars, eventually emerge. Extensive mapping of these cloud complexes, or nebulas, has established a
25   correlation between these complexes and O-stars—a coincidence too striking, in view of the expanse of empty space within galaxies, to be the result of chance.

Since they produce a red fluorescence, O-stars
30   are usually found in glowing nebulas that astronomers have labeled H II regions. O-stars cannot migrate out of these regions because their lifespans are too short. Therefore, astronomers have studied H II regions to
35   determine how clouds and O-stars interact.

These observations suggest that the interaction between clouds and O-stars is a self-perpetuating cycle in which stars will be produced until the cloud material is used up.
40   O-stars consume their fuel rapidly and release huge amounts of energy. Moreover, O-star radiation contributes to driving a shock wave

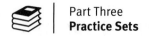
into these clouds, compressing gas and dust there. Out of this tremendous compression of gas and dust arises a second generation of young stars, among them new O-stars.

9. Which of the following best describes the organization of the passage?

   O   A puzzle is presented and then two possible scientific solutions are discussed.

   O   A new phenomenon is described and then the scientific methods used to study it are discussed.

   O   Recent scientific research is described and then applied to solve an existing problem.

   O   A previously known phenomenon is described and then explained by scientific observations.

   O   A number of scientific hypotheses are discussed and then observations concerning their validity are described.

10. The passage states all of the following about O-stars EXCEPT:

   O   They consume their fuel quickly.

   O   They are found in glowing nebulas.

   O   They are much bigger than the sun.

   O   They emit large amounts of radiation.

   O   They cannot migrate out of H II regions.

11. According to the passage, interstellar gas and dust coalesce into "clumps of high concentration" (line 21)

   O   only in H II regions of space

   O   because of gravitational fluctuations in galactic arms

   O   when O-stars migrate out of H II regions

   O   after releasing huge amounts of energy

   O   before new stars are formed

12. The author mentions "O-star radiation" (lines 41–42) in order to

   O   explain why O-stars have short lifespans

   O   indicate the role of O-stars in star formation

   O   emphasize the reddish glow of certain nebulas

   O   prove that O-stars interact with cloud complexes

   O   predict the rate at which nebulas use up their gas and dust

Answers and explanations follow on the next page. ▶ ▶ ▶

Answers and Explanations

1.	B	4.	C	7.	C	10.	C
2.	B	5.	A	8.	D	11.	E
3.	B	6.	C	9.	D	12.	B

PASSAGE 1—The Norton and Rhee Model

Topic and Scope: A discussion of the relevance of formal economic models to real-world policy. The author uses the model applied to Korea by Norton and Rhee to show shortcomings of such models.

Purpose and Main Idea: Author wants to reveal the shortcomings of formal economic models.

Paragraph Structure: Paragraph 1 describes the Norton and Rhee model. Paragraph 2 shows how the results of the application contradict the general trends of real-world economic policy.

1. B

The passage begins by posing the question of how useful formal models are and concludes by calling Norton and Rhee's model an example of the "pitfalls" of formalism. (B) captures this critical approach and is the correct answer. There's nothing that indicates that Norton and Rhee's method of analysis was "new," (A), nor is the author "proposing" it; on the other hand, she doesn't propose any *other* approach. (C) is what the author is very skeptical about; certainly she doesn't "advocate" using such models. (D) is incorrect. Norton and Rhee were examining how various economic factors would affect inflation (not explaining Korean inflation as a whole), and the author is not doing that at all, but rather is discussing Norton and Rhee's work. (E) is incidental to the broader purpose of criticizing "formalism."

2. B

The passage says that Norton and Rhee "achieved some success in applying such a model retrospectively to the Korean economy over a fourteen-year period." In other words, the model is fairly effective in analyzing past events, as (B) suggests.

Since the "fourteen-year period" refers to the past, not the future, (A) is clearly wrong; in fact, one of the

main points of the passage is that Norton and Rhee's model is not particularly useful for predicting the future. Choices (C), (D), and (E) refer to matters discussed later in the passage.

3. B

The whole passage is critical of Norton and Rhee, but the last sentence offers the only explicit criticism: their approach is "formalist" (or abstract) and lacks "policy relevance." (B) paraphrases this criticism. The only economic factors specifically excluded from the model, (A), are the long-term factors mentioned in the middle of paragraph 1; there is no suggestion that Norton and Rhee should be criticized for this procedure. (C) is something that the model does do, since it is aimed at finding the effect of various factors on inflation. The "importance" of economic growth, (D), is not discussed at all and certainly not underestimated. (E) is contradicted by paragraph 1: these are exactly the factors Norton and Rhee *did* consider.

PASSAGE 2—Coral Reefs

Topic and Scope: Coral reefs; specifically, the renewability, transformation, and composition and environment of coral reefs.

Purpose and Main Idea: The author's purpose is to discuss several aspects of coral reefs. Since this is a descriptive passage rather than an argumentative passage, the author makes no specific point.

Paragraph Structure: The first paragraph talks about the renewability of coral reefs. The second paragraph discusses their transformation, summarizing two theories on this issue. And the third paragraph describes the composition of coral reefs and the environment in which they can exist.

4.   C

The answer to this question appears in the first paragraph. The paragraph's next-to-last sentence states that "All of this accounts for . . . renewability . . . despite . . . erosion." Thus, the answer must appear in the previous sentences. These sentences discuss the symbiotic relationship between coral and algae, so the correct answer is (C). (A) might have been tempting because the sentence before "All of this accounts . . . " refers to algae, but the focus of the first paragraph is on symbiosis, so the correct answer must include both coral and algae. (B) distorts the logic of the passage— oxygen contributes to renewability; "despite" is not appropriate here. (D) and (E) come from the wrong part of the passage—from later paragraphs that don't deal with the issue of erosion.

5.   A

Darwin is discussed in the second paragraph of the passage. This paragraph mentions his theory of reef transformation: the theory of gradual submergence of volcanic islands. That makes (A) correct. (B), (C), and (D) contradict the passage. (E) is not discussed in the passage; the text does not address the question of what parts of the reef most interested Darwin.

6.   C

The relationships in (D), (A), and (E) are discussed in the third, fourth, and fifth sentences of the first paragraph, respectively. (B) is mentioned in the second paragraph. (C), however, connects items that are not associated with each other in the passage. Volcanic rock is discussed in the second paragraph, while life at reefs is brought up in the third.

7.   C

(A) is tricky because it tries to get you to look at the third paragraph and see "10 percent." This percentage, however, refers to a particular type of reef life form; no percentage is given for reef-building coral worldwide. (B) appears promising since sea level and reefs appear in the second paragraph, but the mechanism by which sea level contributes to reef-building is never explained. (C), though, looks good; the second-to-last

sentence provides considerable detail about where reefs can form. Checking the last two choices, (D) can be eliminated because the author specifies in the last sentence of the first paragraph that the answer to this question is unknown. Likewise, (E), the transformation of reefs, is never resolved. Two theories are presented and the author leans toward one of them, but never gives a definitive answer.

8.   D

While it's true the author says "the term 'coral reef' is something of a misnomer" in lines 36–37, there is no indication that the author is adamant that people should stop using that phrase. Be wary of extreme language in Reading Comp answer choices. Typically they indicate a wrong answer, but in this EXCEPT question the extreme "should" in (D) is a giveaway that the author would not necessarily agree.

For the record, (A) and (B) can be found in paragraph 1, (C) in paragraph 2, and (E) can be confirmed in paragraph 3.

PASSAGE 3—Bright Young Stars

Topic and Scope: The passage is about O-stars, a type of particularly bright young star.

Purpose and Main Idea: This is an explanatory passage; the author has written it to answer the question of how O-stars are formed and their interactions with their environment.

Paragraph Structure: The first paragraph describes a previously unanswered question: how are O-stars formed? It then introduces the idea that recent research may have answered that question. The second paragraph describes the mechanism by which these stars are thought to be created in certain kinds of nebulas. The third paragraph introduces the idea that O-stars can only exist in these nebulas and that scientists are studying the interactions between star and nebula. The final paragraph describes the cycle of dying O-stars contributing to the creation of new O-stars.

9. D

The good news about "hard" science passages is that you don't actually have to understand the science to get the correct answer. This Global question asks about the organization of the passage, so after quickly reading through the passage, attack the answer choices aggressively. Paragraph 1 mentions a previously known phenomenon: the location of O-stars in the spiral arms of disk-shaped galaxies. The rest of the passage explains the why and the what of this phenomenon: why O-stars form there and what function they serve there. Choice (D) accurately reflects this organization and is the correct answer.

The first part of (A) is okay: a "puzzle" is presented; but this choice hops the tracks when it mentions two solutions. This is one of those "half-right, half-wrong" choices that you should watch out for. No new phenomenon is described, nor are scientific methods ever discussed; (B) is therefore incorrect. This choice violates the scope of the passage. (C) has things backwards: in the passage, the problem comes before the research. Like (B), (E) violates the scope: the author doesn't discuss a "number of scientific hypotheses."

10. C

The only comparison made between O-stars and the sun appears in lines 6–7, which say that O-stars are brighter than the sun, not that they're bigger. Choice (C) is correct. Lines 40–41 say that O-stars "consume their fuel rapidly" (A) and "release huge amounts of energy" (D); lines 30–32 indicate that they're "usually found in glowing nebulas" (B) and "cannot migrate out of" H II regions (E). Note that in EXCEPT questions, you're looking for the choice that is not true. Use process of elimination to throw out true choices.

11. E

Since the question stem sends you back to line 21, the answer is to be found in the middle of the second paragraph. The third sentence of this paragraph explicitly states that gas and dust are concentrated into dense clumps prior to the birth of stars, which is what (E) says. (A) and (C) refer to the wrong part of the passage: the third paragraph; moreover, (C) flatly contradicts information in that paragraph. (D) also refers to the wrong part of the passage, the fourth paragraph, and besides, it pertains to O-stars, not interstellar gas and dust. Finally, (B) gets the paragraph right, but like (C), flatly contradicts the passage.

12. B

Line 42 says that O-star radiation "contributes to driving a shock wave" that compresses gas and dust in clouds. The following lines go on to say that new stars emerge out of this compressed gas and dust.

The short lifespans of O-stars (A) and the reddish glow of "certain nebulas" (C) are brought up in paragraph 3, but aren't linked to O-star radiation. (D) misrepresents the author's purpose: he's not out to "prove that O-stars interact with cloud complexes," he's out to explain how the two interact. (E) also misrepresents the author's purpose: he doesn't "predict" anything. Note that most questions to "hard" science passages tend to be very specific Detail questions, in which either a line reference will be provided or the wording in the question will help you to locate the relevant information in the passage. Even if you don't fully understand the passage, you can often get these questions right.

CHAPTER 7

Critical Reasoning Practice

Critical Reasoning Practice Set One

Directions: For each question in this practice set, you will be presented with a short argument, a set of statements, or a plan of action. Select the best answer from the choices provided.

1. Because competition for viewers has become increasingly fierce, many so-called news programs are reporting less "hard" news in favor of the more entertaining celebrity stories that have been dubbed "info-tainment." In fact, the more popular a news show is, the more likely it will cover important national and international issues fleetingly, if at all. As a result, viewers who routinely watch the most popular television news shows tend to be poorly informed on matters of national and international issues.

   Which of the following is an assumption on which the argument relies?

   O News programs should not be forced to compete for viewers the way entertainment programs do.

   O Celebrities are never involved in "hard" news stories.

   O Network news shows have an advantage over cable outlets, since cable shows are available to fewer households.

   O Viewers who routinely watch popular news shows typically do not consume news from other media sources.

   O News shows that don't feature celebrity stories are more popular with most viewers.

2. Executive: Even though Country X is currently in the middle of a destructive civil war, opening a new manufacturing plant in Country X is not inadvisable, despite what critics of the plan may say. Ten years ago, we opened our plant in Country Y in the middle of a revolution; that plant has been generating substantial profits ever since.

   Which of the following provides the strongest support for the executive's argument?

   O Some businesses are more profitable during periods of conflict than during periods of peace.

   O Country X is a more politically stable nation than is Country Y.

   O Critics of the proposed plant in Country X are likely to be biased.

   O Despite the effects of the civil war in Country X, the new manufacturing plant will still generate profits.

   O The proposed plant in Country X will be more successful than the plant in Country Y.

3. An ecology magazine regularly publishes articles on tree diseases. This year, the number of articles on *Ophiostoma ulmi,* the fungus that causes Dutch elm disease, is significantly smaller than the number of such articles that appeared last year. Clearly, fewer researchers studied *Ophiostoma ulmi* this year than did so last year.

    Which of the following, if true, weakens the above conclusion?

    ○   Many researchers publishing articles are currently studying *Stegophora ulmea,* a fungus that causes elm leaf spot.

    ○   Since its introduction, Dutch elm disease has killed half of the elm trees in North America.

    ○   Research on Dutch elm disease that focuses on prevention receives more funding than research that focuses on finding a cure.

    ○   A new strain of the fungus *Rhytisma acerinum* infested maple trees at an unprecedented rate this year.

    ○   All articles go through at least a one-year review process before publication.

4. Air travel is becoming increasingly dangerous. In the last year, there have been seven major collisions resulting in over 700 deaths, more deaths than in any previous year.

    Which of the following, if true, would most weaken the argument above?

    ○   The volume of air traffic last year was higher than in any previous year.

    ○   Training programs for pilots no longer adequately instruct pilots on how to fly planes with the most recent technology.

    ○   Mortality per passenger mile is lower for air travel than for any kind of surface transportation.

    ○   The increase in deaths due to collision in air travel has proceeded at a rate identical to that for deaths in all other major forms of transportation.

    ○   Last year, the average number of passengers per flown plane was significantly lower than that of previous years.

5. According to a recent study, attending a single-sex high school aids an adolescent's physical growth. Cited as evidence is the finding that during the first two years of high school, the average boy in an all-boys school grew five inches, and the average girl in an all-girls school grew four inches.

   The answer to which of the following questions is needed in order to evaluate the reasoning presented in the study?

   O   Why was it that the first two years of high school were chosen as the focus of the study?

   O   Did some of the boys in the study grow less than five inches while they were in high school?

   O   How much do the average male student and the average female student in a coeducational school grow during their first two years of high school?

   O   Did the girls in the study have as nutritious a diet as the boys during the time the study was being conducted?

   O   What was the average height of the boys and the average height of the girls upon entering high school?

6. Which of the following best completes the passage below?

   In a survey of freshmen at University X, two-thirds claimed never to have plagiarized while in high school. However, the survey may overstate the proportion of freshmen at University X who did not plagiarize in high school because _____.

   O   some people who do not attend University X probably plagiarized in high school

   O   some people who plagiarized in high school may not do so in college

   O   some people who claimed to have plagiarized once may have done so many times

   O   at University Z, one-half of the freshmen admitted to having plagiarized in high school

   O   some freshmen who did plagiarize in high school might have claimed on the survey that they did not do so

7. Archaeologists have discovered various paintings on the walls and ceiling of a Chinese cave whose entrance was blocked by a volcanic eruption in the 25th century B.C. and only recently cleared by an earthquake. Since the paintings depict warriors using Type C bronze weapons, these archaeologists have concluded that Type C bronze weapons were already widely used in this area by 2500 B.C., far earlier than was previously believed.

    Which of the following pieces of additional evidence would most seriously weaken the archaeologists' conclusion?

    O   Another entrance to the cave remained clear until a second volcanic eruption 1,000 years after the first.

    O   Archaeologists have evidence that Type C bronze weapons were in wide use in areas of present-day India as early as 2500 B.C.

    O   Alternative methods of dating place the time of the volcanic eruption somewhat earlier, at around 3000 B.C.

    O   Most experts believe that Type C bronze weapons were not in use anywhere in present-day China until 2000 B.C.

    O   The paintings were very faded when the archaeologists found them, making identification of the depicted weapons difficult.

8. Considering the current economy, the introduction of a new brand of cereal is unlikely to expand total sales of cereal, but rather will just cause some existing buyers of cereal to switch brands. So, it makes no sense for the Coolidge Corporation to introduce another brand of cereal, since they will only hurt sales of the brands of cereal they already produce.

    Which of the following, if true, would most seriously weaken the argument above?

    O   In focus group research, consumers rated the new brand very favorably.

    O   Many new brands of cereal sell extremely well for the first year of their existence.

    O   Coolidge Corporation currently produces fewer brands of cereal than its competitors do.

    O   Some cereal buyers regularly switch from brand to brand, even when no new brands have been introduced.

    O   Research indicates that the new brand will attract more buyers of competitors' cereals than buyers of other Coolidge brands.

9. A public health official reported that 60 percent of the children at summer school have never had the measles or chicken pox, and that, of this 60 percent, not one child has ever been observed to eat the cheese served in the school lunches. From this he concluded that children who abstain from cheese products protect themselves from most childhood disease.

    Each of the following, if true, would strengthen the official's argument EXCEPT:

    O   Medically speaking, whatever serves to inhibit measles and chicken pox will generally inhibit the entire spectrum of childhood diseases.

    O   The observations the official carried out were extremely accurate, and all those observed to abstain from cheese at school did, in fact, abstain.

    O   The children's eating habits are the same at school as anywhere else, and those who abstain from cheese products at school do so in general.

    O   Recent research has indicated that a diet deficient in cheese products is one of the major causes of measles and chicken pox infections.

    O   Most cheeses and cheese products harbor microorganisms that are known to be causative agents for many childhood diseases, such as measles and chicken pox.

10. Director: Our engineers are considering two different sites—one on the Abaco River and one on the Bornos River—for a hydroelectric plant. Although we have the technical expertise to build roughly the same plant in either place, producing roughly the same amount of electricity per hour, building the plant on the Abaco site will cost over twice as much money. With our budget currently in deficit, we should build the dam at the Bornos site.

    Which of the following, if true, best explains the difference in building costs for the two proposed dam sites?

    O   Many farms along the lower Bornos River valley would benefit from the controlled flow of water a dam would make possible.

    O   The Abaco site is in an inaccessible area, requiring the building of new roads and the importation of laborers.

    O   The Bornos site is near a large city whose residents could use the resulting lake for inexpensive recreation.

    O   The Abaco site is in an area that contains many endangered species that would be threatened by the new dam.

    O   The Abaco River has a relatively low volume of flow, making it impossible to expand an Abaco plant to meet future electricity needs.

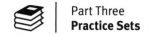

Answers and Explanations

1. D	4. A	7. A	9. D
2. D	5. C	8. E	10. B
3. E	6. E		

1. D

The Conclusion: Viewers who watch the most popular television news shows tend not to know a lot about national and international issues.

The Evidence: The more popular a news show is, the less it covers national and international issues.

The word "assumption" in the question stem is a clear indicator of an Assumption question. An argument's central assumption is something that must be true for the conclusion to follow from the evidence. This argument's conclusion can be true only if viewers do not get information about hard news stories from sources other than television news. (D) matches this prediction precisely.

There's no indication that the author believes (A) to be true. The author is stating the consequences of competition among news programs; you have no idea of his or her opinion about the existence of competition in the first place. (B) is too extreme. This argument still works even if celebrities are occasionally involved in a news story of national or international significance. (C) makes an irrelevant comparison between network news and cable news. It doesn't matter what kind of TV channel delivers the news. (E) goes in the opposite direction from the argument by telling you that infotainment is actually not that popular with viewers. The author would certainly never assume this.

2. D

The Conclusion: It's not a bad idea to open a new manufacturing plant in Country X, even though that country is in the middle of a civil war.

The Evidence: A plant opened in Country Y during a revolution 10 years ago has always generated substantial profits.

The author draws an analogy between the two plants. Since the one in Country Y has made money, so too, she implies, will the one in Country X. The reasoning here only makes sense if the revolution in Country Y and the civil war in Country X are comparable; if, for example, the civil war is going to be much more destructive to the infrastructure of Country X than the revolution was to the infrastructure of Country Y, then the argument doesn't hold together. Choice (D) strengthens the argument by affirming that yes, the plant will indeed make profits in Country X.

As for the other choices, choice (A) is too vague and weakly stated. Just because some businesses might be profitable during times of war doesn't mean that *this* business will be profitable in *this* war. The author presents the two countries as similar, so she's not arguing that (B), one is more stable than the other. The author is attacking her opponents' argument, but not (C), their motives. She makes no judgment, (E), as to which plant will be more successful. Remember, comparing and contrasting things that are considered equivalent in the stimulus is a common wrong answer type for Inference questions.

3. E

The Conclusion: Fewer researchers studied *O. ulmi* this year than did so last year.

The Evidence: The number of articles on *O. ulmi* appearing in a particular ecology magazine this year is much smaller than the number that appeared last year.

As with all Weaken questions, you want to understand the argument and look for its assumption. The argument basically says that because the number of articles on a particular topic dropped this year, you can safely conclude that fewer researchers are working on that topic this year. The argument shifts scope from the number of articles appearing in a given year to the number of researchers studying that topic in that year, so it must assume that a correlation exists between those two numbers in any one year. To weaken the argument, you need to find the answer that explains how fewer articles doesn't necessarily mean fewer researchers. (E) does this—if it takes more than a year to clear an article for publication, then the number of articles in one year can't be representative of anything else in that same year.

4.   A

The Conclusion: Air travel is becoming more dangerous.

The Evidence: In the last year, there have been seven collisions and over 700 deaths, the highest number of deaths ever.

You want something that suggests that the increase in fatalities doesn't prove an increase in danger. If, as (A) says, the volume of air traffic has increased, then an increase in the number of deaths doesn't prove that air travel is becoming more dangerous. The question of how dangerous air travel is can't be answered unless you know the proportion, not the number, of passengers who get killed.

Stating that pilots are no longer being trained correctly, (B), provides support for the argument. Pointing out more dangerous methods of transportation, (C), doesn't deny that the danger of air travel is increasing. Likewise, the fact that other forms of transportation are also getting more dangerous, (D), doesn't dent the author's claim. Fewer passengers per plane, (E), means more collisions, but you already know how many collisions there were.

5.   C

The Conclusion: Attending a single-sex high school promotes growth.

The Evidence: During the first two years, the average student in an all-boys school grew five inches and the average girl in an all-girls school grew four inches.

The question stem tells you that something has been left out of the argument. The conclusion compares single-sex schools to coed schools, but the evidence only cites data from single-sex schools. Until you know how much the

average student grows in co-educational schools, you have no evidence that attending a single-sex school promotes growth. (C) provides just that information.

Even if you knew the answer to (A), you'd still have no evidence from the coed schools. (B) is irrelevant; the scenario deals with average growth, so you'd expect some boys to grow more than the average and some less. The reasons for the growth difference between boys and girls, (D), isn't relevant to the growth differences between coed and single-sex schools. Since the study is only interested in how much students grow during the first two years of high school, it's irrelevant how tall they are to start with, (E).

6.   E

The Conclusion: The survey may overstate the proportion of students who did not plagiarize in high school.

The Evidence: The key word "because" indicates that the blank should be completed with evidence that best supports the conclusion.

(A) is incorrect because you're only concerned with students at University X who answered the survey. (B) is irrelevant to the argument; the survey is concerned only with how many students plagiarized in high school, not how many may plagiarize in college. (C) doesn't work because the survey asks only whether a student ever plagiarized, not how often. (D) tells you that the proportion of those who did not plagiarize is lower at another school, but like (A), this has no bearing on the proportion at University X as reported by the survey. (E) is correct: it tells you that some plagiarizers might have denied doing so on the survey. If that's true, then the survey results are inaccurate, and the actual proportion who did not plagiarize is lower than two-thirds.

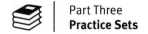
7. A

The Conclusion: People must already have been using Type C weapons in this area by 2500 B.C.

The Evidence: Depictions of the weapons exist on the walls of a cave that was sealed off in 2500 B.C.

To weaken this argument, find a choice that suggests that either the paintings don't depict weapons that were in use during that time, or that the paintings were made after 2500 B.C. The archaeologists are assuming that there was only one entrance to the cave. If there's another entrance to the cave that was only sealed much later, then people could have entered the cave and made the paintings long after the first entrance was sealed. (A) brings up exactly this point.

If anything, the existence of the weapons in India, (B), might be considered to strengthen the argument, since it shows Type C weapons were in existence as early as 2500 B.C. Pushing the date of the eruption back, (C), also strengthens the argument by making it likely that the paintings were done even earlier than claimed. Without some evidence to back it up, the opinion of the experts, (D), isn't worth much. That identification was difficult, (E), is not the same as its being uncertain or controversial.

8. E

The Conclusion: Introducing a new cereal will only hurt the brands Coolidge already produces, so Coolidge shouldn't introduce another brand of cereal.

The Evidence: The introduction of a new brand of cereal doesn't increase the total number of cereal buyers, but only encourages those who already buy cereal to switch brands.

The assumption here is that the new brand will only attract those who currently buy other brands of Coolidge's cereal. If the new brand steals buyers from competitors' cereals, then it will help Coolidge by adding to its total sales.

Even if people like the new cereal, (A), a new brand might still hurt the sales of Coolidge's established cereals. The new cereal may sell well, (B), but if that just means it's stealing lots of buyers from other Coolidge cereals, what good is it? The fact that Coolidge has only a few brands, (C), doesn't make it likely that a new cereal brand would steal buyers from competitors' brands rather than from other Coolidge brands. Neither does the fact that some brand switching is usual even when a new brand isn't introduced, (D).

9. D

The Conclusion: Not eating cheese protects children from childhood diseases.

The Evidence: All the children at summer school who have never had measles or chicken pox have also never eaten the cheese served in the school lunches.

The author deduces a causal relationship: not eating cheese leads to protection from childhood diseases. I hope you saw that this has numerous holes. Four of the choices help to fill those holes; the fifth does not. That fifth choice is (D). If research shows that abstaining from cheese products is a major cause of some childhood diseases, then the health official's claim that children can protect themselves from disease by not eating cheese is flat-out wrong.

It's important that the author be able (A) to connect measles and chicken pox (in the evidence) to other childhood diseases. Also necessary is that the observations be accurate, (B), and the students' behavior at home mirror their behavior at school, (C). Each of those speaks to the legitimacy of the correlation. Most important, though, is that there really be a causal connection, (E), rather than just a correlation, between cheese eating and childhood illness.

10. B

The Director's Conclusion: We should build the dam at the Bornos site.

Her Evidence: Although the same plant can produce the same amount of electricity at either site, building at Abaco will cost twice as much money.

Looking at the question stem first here really helps you narrow your focus when reading the stimulus. The only thing you're interested in is why the Abaco site will cost more than twice as much as the Bornos site. The stimulus doesn't give you any hint as to how the sites are different, so you'll have to rely on the correct answer to provide a complete explanation by itself. If the Abaco site is in the middle of nowhere and requires constructing new roads and importing laborers, then, of course, it's going to be more expensive to build there.

The benefits of the Bornos plant to farms, (A), don't explain its lower cost of construction. Neither do the benefits to nearby city residents, (C). Possible environmental damage caused by a plant built at Abaco, (D), is another reason for building at Bornos, but it's a different reason. The issue of expansion, (E), like the environment, might merit consideration, but it's not a factor in determining the cost of building.

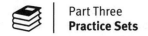

Critical Reasoning Practice Set Two

Directions: For each question in this practice set, you will be presented with a short argument, a set of statements, or a plan of action. Select the best answer from the choices provided.

1. Although excessive air pollution causing illness was previously thought to exist almost exclusively in our nation's cities, the recent dramatic increase in the number of persons suffering from illnesses attributed to excessive air pollution leaves us no choice but to conclude that pollution in nonurban areas is on the rise.

   Which of the following, if true, would most seriously weaken the conclusion of the argument above?

   O The nation's cities have seen a marked decrease in levels of air pollution.

   O The nation has experienced a sharp decrease in the number of people moving out of its cities.

   O Illnesses due to air pollution are among the least common causes of death to urban dwellers.

   O Many illnesses that were until very recently thought to be unrelated to air pollution are now considered to be caused by it.

   O As a result of the problems in urban areas, nonurban areas have passed strict pollution control measures.

2. Statistics show that although consumption of low-calorie alternative sweeteners has gone up in each of the past five years, so has the percentage of the population that is obese. According to sugar manufacturers, this shows that the low-calorie alternative sweeteners are not effective weight loss aids.

   Which of the following assertions, if true, would most weaken the sugar manufacturers' conclusion?

   O Many people who use low-calorie alternative sweeteners eat some foods that are not low-calorie.

   O Some low-calorie alternative sweeteners can increase the appetite, making a person eat more than he or she normally would.

   O Many people use low-calorie alternative sweeteners to accompany a well-balanced, low-calorie diet.

   O Obesity has declined among people who have consistently used low-calorie alternative sweeteners.

   O The rise in the consumption of low-calorie alternative sweeteners is primarily due to an increase in the number of users rather than an increase in the amount each user consumes.

3. It has long been commonplace in medical literature that the ingestion of Drug L, in combination with the application of Lotion M, causes the appearance of adverse reaction O. Recently, however, a doctor has put forth the claim that Lotion M plays no role in the appearance of adverse reaction O.

   Which one of the following research findings would, if true, most support the doctor's claim?

   O the appearance of adverse reaction O following the ingestion of Drug L and the application of Lotion M

   O the absence of adverse reaction O following the ingestion of Drug L

   O the ingestion of Drug L and the appearance of adverse reaction O in the absence of Lotion M

   O the appearance of adverse reaction O following the application of Lotion M

   O the disappearance of adverse reaction O following the ingestion of Drug L and the application of Lotion M

4. The candy manufacturer's claim that employee theft costs the company thousands of dollars a year in potential sales is greatly overstated. Most of the candy eaten on the job and not paid for is eaten one piece at a time by workers who would not be willing to buy an entire box of it anyway.

   Which of the following, if true, most weakens the argument above?

   O The workers eat only defective candies that could not be sold.

   O Candy eaten by employees represents lost potential sales to nonemployees.

   O A few workers account for most of the candy that is eaten but not paid for.

   O Most of the candies eaten by employees are consumed during the holiday season, when production outputs are at their highest.

   O The amount of candy eaten by employees is only a small fraction of the candy sold by the company.

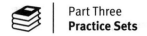

5. Children who attend private high schools may initially feel that they can succeed without doing the work required, but as they grow older, they realize the necessity of serious study. This is obvious from the fact that each year, the overwhelming majority of students disciplined for plagiarism and cheating on their exams are first-year students.

The argument above would be most weakened if which of the following were true?

O   As they move up in grade, students learn how to cheat without being caught.

O   First-time offenders for plagiarism and cheating on exams are not disciplined.

O   The ratio of proctors to students is the same during the exams of first-year students as it is during the exams of other students.

O   Acts of vandalism are most often committed by members of the sophomore class.

O   Public school students are no less likely than private school students to believe that they can succeed in life without working hard.

6. To improve the physical fitness of its students, School District 4 instituted a policy whereby students would be given extra credit in physical education for participating in extracurricular athletic activities. School officials call the program a success, since participation in after-school sports has doubled since the program was instituted.

Which of the following, if true, most seriously weakens the claim of the school officials?

O   Most students who joined after-school sports did so only to get extra credit.

O   Most children who are in poor physical condition cannot be persuaded to join after-school sports by such an incentive program.

O   Few students who joined after-school sports during the extra credit program will continue to play the sport after the school year ends.

O   Most of the new athletes are students who had never before participated in after-school sports.

O   A majority of students who participate in after-school sports programs for extra credit assume non-athletic roles such as statisticians and equipment managers.

7. It takes four weeks for a team of five professional window washers working regular full-time hours to properly clean every window of a large downtown office building. The building's owner demands that all the windows always be clean. Yet even if the five washers work consistently throughout their regular work week, they will not be able to finish cleaning all the windows before some windows will again need cleaning.

   If the statements above are true, which of the following must also be true?

   ○ If a window in the downtown office building is to be kept clean, it must be cleaned by a professional window cleaner.

   ○ The owner's demand for proper cleaning of all the windows will never be fulfilled.

   ○ If a team of five window washers cleans all of the windows in the downtown office building in less than four weeks, some of the windows will not be properly cleaned.

   ○ In order to ensure that all of the windows in the downtown office building are clean, the owner must have his window washers work overtime.

   ○ Some of the windows in the downtown office building must be cleaned more frequently than once every four weeks if they are to be kept clean.

8. Cultural anthropologists who have been observing and interviewing customers in retail stores have announced a definitive theory to explain the effect that in-store product displays have on consumer purchasing behavior.

   Each of the following, if true, would support a claim that this theory will be beneficial to retailers EXCEPT:

   ○ The new theory will allow retailers to determine which product displays fail to increase sales.

   ○ The new theory will allow retailers to gain insight into how consumers determine whether or not to buy a particular product.

   ○ The new theory will make consumers aware of how product displays influence their purchasing decisions.

   ○ The new theory will determine what types of retail display gimmicks produce a negative reaction in consumers.

   ○ The new theory will explain why consumers often purchase at different stores goods that could be bought at just one store.

9. Archaeologists have recently found, in various grave sites in the Mexican state of Veracruz, small ceramic animals with attached wheels. At first, this find might seem to discredit the belief that the wheel and its uses were unknown in pre-Columbian culture. On reflection, however, it would seem that the discovery actually bears out this belief. To be familiar with these toys and yet not to apply the principle of the wheel to daily tasks such as carting, transportation, and pottery making must indicate a lack of understanding of the wheel and its potential benefits.

Which of the following best expresses the argument made in the passage above?

- ○ If the pre-Columbian people of Veracruz had understood the principle of the wheel, they would not have attached wheels to ceramic animals.

- ○ If the pre-Columbian people of Veracruz had understood the principle of the wheel, they would have adapted it to everyday use.

- ○ If the pre-Columbian people of Veracruz had uses for the wheel in their everyday lives, they would have adapted the idea of the wheel from the wheeled ceramic figures.

- ○ The pre-Columbian people of Veracruz must have known of the wheel and its uses because they attached wheels to ceramic animals.

- ○ Since the pre-Columbian people of Veracruz did not know of the wheel or its uses, the ceramic animals found in the grave sites must be the remains of later cultures.

10. Doubling the cost of public transportation to compensate for money lost by declining ridership would be disastrous. The greater expense would only further discourage commuters who are already dissatisfied with the poor condition of buses and trains. If the fares are increased, many commuters will choose to drive their cars instead, causing pollution and traffic congestion. As a result, the city will lose money and become even more noisy and smog-filled than it is now.

Which of the following is an assumption made in the argument above?

- ○ Commuters who decide to drive instead of using public transportation will not share rides with one another.

- ○ Commuters will not park their cars in garages and thereby spend more money than they would by using buses or trains.

- ○ The condition of public transportation will not improve as a result of the fare increase.

- ○ Commuters who use their own cars currently outnumber those who use buses and trains.

- ○ Many people who now use public transportation have cars or can easily obtain them.

Answers and explanations follow on the next page. ▶ ▶ ▶

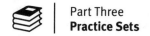

Part Three
Practice Sets

Answers and Explanations

1. D
2. D
3. C

4. B
5. A
6. E

7. E
8. C

9. B
10. E

1.　D

The Conclusion: Pollution in nonurban areas is now on the rise.

The Evidence: An increase in the number of persons suffering from illnesses attributable to air pollution.

The argument draws a link between an increase in the number of people suffering from illnesses attributed to air pollution and a rise in air pollution. But if there's anything else that would explain the rise in illnesses besides an increase in air pollution, then the argument would be weakened. That's what (D) does: it brings up the possibility that air pollution has always been a problem, and it's only a change in our understanding of how air pollution causes illnesses that accounts for the rise of illnesses *attributed* to pollution. The GMAT test makers are fond of this trick.

(A), "decreased air pollution in the cities," doesn't weaken an argument that says it's rising outside cities. (B) says fewer people are moving out of cities, and this has no clear effect. The new sufferers from air pollution would be nonurban, so the idea that not many urban dwellers die from air pollution, (C), won't weaken the argument. Antipollution measures, (E), are irrelevant. There could still be lots of pollution in nonurban areas, pollution that floated out from urban areas, for example.

2.　D

The Sugar Manufacturers' Conclusion: Low-calorie sweeteners aren't effective in helping people lose weight.

The Sugar Manufacturers' Evidence: Statistics show that although the consumption of these sweeteners has gone up, so has the percentage of obese people.

The manufacturers assume that the sweeteners are in some way responsible for the public's failure to lose weight. But if the consumers of the sweeteners aren't becoming more obese, then, despite the increase in the percentage of the public that is overweight, those using alternative sweeteners actually lost weight. (D) weakens the argument by showing that those who use the sweeteners have actually lost weight.

(A) is incorrect because there's no indication of whether this diet had any effect on weight loss or gain. (B) strengthens the manufacturers' claim, saying that some low-calorie sweeteners actually increase appetite. (C) tells you nothing about how effective low-calorie sweeteners may or may not be. And the sugar manufacturers' claim doesn't depend on an increase in the amount each user consumes, (E), rather than an increase in the number of users.

3.　C

The Conclusion: Adverse reaction O is caused solely by Drug L, not Lotion M.

The Evidence: This is what you're looking for: What would support this claim?

In (C), Lotion M is absent, yet O has taken place with Drug L. O in the absence of M suggests that M is superfluous and provides the support you need.

(A) has Drug L plus Lotion M resulting in adverse reaction O, just as was always thought. (B) doesn't test Lotion M and so is not useful, while (D) provides evidence to the contrary of the doctor's claim. In (E), adverse reaction O disappears, but the reversal of the reaction is not within the scope of this argument, which focused on the appearance of adverse reaction O only.

148 K

4. B

The Conclusion: Candy manufacturers don't really lose thousands every year in potential sales through workers eating candy.

The Evidence: Workers eat the candy one piece at a time and wouldn't buy a whole box anyway.

The argument as stated assumes that the candy would, if not eaten, only be sold to the people who are eating it—the workers. We can undermine this assumption by pointing out that the candy could easily be sold to other people.

If the workers eat only candy that couldn't be sold, (A), then the manufacturers probably aren't losing potential sales. It doesn't matter how many workers are eating the candy, (C); what's important is how much is disappearing and whether it could be sold if it weren't being eaten. The issue of when the candy is eaten, (D), is irrelevant to whether the company is losing potential sales. Even if the eaten candy is a small fraction of the candy sold, (E), it could still represent a substantial loss of potential sales money.

5. A

The Conclusion: Private high school kids start out willing to let academics "slide," but they learn the value of serious study as the years go by.

The Evidence: Most kids caught and punished for cheating are first year students.

The assumption is that older students don't cheat as much, but if they learn how to cheat without getting caught, the link between evidence and conclusion is severed.

A policy of going easy on first offenders, (B), has no impact on the logic—the statistics remain the same. (C) removes the alternative possibility that proctors are more lenient for older students; if anything this choice strengthens the argument. Vandalism (D) has nothing to do with the matter at hand. Equally irrelevant is (E)'s distinction between private and public school students' attitudes toward life.

6. E

The School Officials' Conclusion: A program intended to increase the physical fitness of students has been a great success.

The Evidence: Participation in after-school sports has doubled since the program began.

It's assumed that participation in after-school programs necessarily leads to better physical fitness. Denying this weakens the argument. Maybe the after-school sports are pool and bowling, which provide little physical conditioning. (E) brings up this point, but does so using a different example. Students could be involved in the program in non-athletic roles that might not be improving their physical fitness.

The students' motivation, (A), is irrelevant; the end result of the program is what's important here. The school officials' claim concerns students in general, not just ones in poor condition, (B), so the program could still be a success even if the truly sickly don't join. How long students take part in after-school sports, (C), doesn't really matter. And (D)'s claim strengthens the argument by making it reasonable that the policy has encouraged the new athletes.

7. E

The Conclusion: Even if the five washers work consistently throughout the regular week, they won't finish cleaning before some windows need to be cleaned again.

The Evidence: It takes four weeks for the team of five washers to clean every window.

What can be concluded? If any given window can be revisited four weeks later, yet some of them already need another cleaning, then some windows won't stay clean if attended to only once every four weeks. They get dirty more quickly than this, which is what the correct answer (E) states.

(B), (C), and (D) are wrong because they ignore the possibility of two teams working, or of washers working overtime. There's no reason why the

owner's demand couldn't be fulfilled by having two teams of five washers or by having one team work overtime, (B). And it's possible that one team working overtime could properly clean all the windows in less than four weeks, (C). Contrary to (D), it may be that three teams of washers working part-time can accomplish the task. As for (A), no distinction between professional and amateur washers has been or can be made.

8. C

The Conclusion: A group of anthropologists claim to have formulated a "definitive" theory of consumer purchasing behavior, and it will be beneficial to retailers.

The Evidence: There isn't any provided.

Find a choice that would be *least* likely to represent a benefit of the theory to retailers. Clearly, if the theory makes consumers aware of how displays influence them, as (C) states, they will be less at the mercy of crafty retailers. This is a benefit to consumers, not retailers.

Another effective way to approach this question is to identify and eliminate wrong answers. In this question, any choice that helps retailers understand consumer behavior will be incorrect. (A) and (D) point out that retailers will be able to use the new theory to display products to maximum advantage by cutting costs and pleasing customers. (B) names the overall benefit of the new theory: it will tell retailers why shoppers buy a particular product. And (E), if true, would help a retailer maximize the amount of shopping that customers do in her particular store.

9. B

The Conclusion: The pre-Columbian people of Veracruz must not have understood the principle and uses of the wheel.

The Evidence: Ceramic animals with attached wheels were found in Veracruz grave sites. Yet this culture did not use the wheel for tasks like carting, transportation, and pottery making.

The author argues that these people didn't understand the wheel because they didn't employ it in their everyday activities. Thus, if these people had understood the uses of the wheel, they would have used it in their daily lives.

The author never hints that if they understood the wheel they wouldn't have used it on the animals, (A). Nor does the author argue that they didn't have uses for the wheel, (C); it's that they didn't understand the wheel enough to make use of it in their daily lives. As for (D), the author states the opposite, that they must not have known of the wheel's uses despite the wheels on the animals. (E) is way off topic—the author doesn't even hint that the animals came from a later culture.

10. E

The Conclusion: If the cost of public transportation is doubled, the city will lose money and become even more noisy and smog-filled.

The Evidence: The added expense will deter commuters from using trains and buses—they will drive instead, resulting in pollution and congestion.

To state that the fare increase would have a major impact on the level of pollution and congestion by increasing the use of private cars, the author must assume that enough people have ready access to cars to make this impact.

People could, contrary to (A), share rides and still have a great negative impact on pollution and congestion, so long as the number of cars increases significantly. The amount of money commuters spend, (B), isn't the issue—the effect on the city is. Even if public transportation conditions did improve, (C), people would have already abandoned the commuter system. Nor does the author have to assume that drivers outnumber those in buses and trains, (D). The actual numbers aren't a part of this argument.

Critical Reasoning Practice Set Three

Directions: For each question in this practice set, you will be presented with a short argument, a set of statements, or a plan of action. Select the best answer from the choices provided.

1. A tariff against computers made in Country Z is needed to protect domestic computer manufacturers. With such a tariff, domestic computer manufacturers would see increased sales of their own products, and increased sales frequently lead to reduced prices.

   If the above statements are true, which of the following conclusions can most properly be drawn from them?

   ○ A tariff is a less drastic means of applying international economic pressure than an embargo.

   ○ A drop in computer prices is likely to create more jobs in the computer industry.

   ○ Domestic manufacturers will decrease computer production if a protective tariff is not established.

   ○ The lack of a protective tariff has hampered computer production in this country.

   ○ A tariff would probably lead to a drop in prices for buyers of domestically produced computers.

2. According to a recent study, a diet that is free of meat and dairy products greatly reduces the risk of suffering a heart attack. The study cites the fact that only 10 percent of those who consume such a diet suffer a heart attack at some point in their lives.

   Which of the following would most seriously weaken the argument above?

   ○ Diets free of meat and dairy are low in calcium, which can lead to decreased bone density.

   ○ Those who consume only dairy but not meat are twice as likely to suffer a heart attack as those who consume neither meat nor dairy.

   ○ Some people who consume neither dairy nor meat suffer two or more heart attacks over the course of a lifetime.

   ○ Meat and dairy products are high in low-density cholesterol, which is known to harden arteries and cause other heart problems.

   ○ Of those who consume dairy and meat, 7 percent regularly suffer heart attacks over the course of their lifetime.

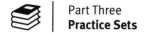

3. At Food World Supermarket, built in 1975, the number of successful thefts has risen dramatically in the past few months. Food World has a reliable electronic security system at all customer exit doors, and this system is always in operation. Therefore, the thefts must have been committed by people who used exits other than the regular customer exit doors.

    Which of the following is an assumption that would make the conclusion above logically correct?

    O   If a surveillance system is installed in a supermarket, it is always equipped at every possible exit.

    O   If an employee so wishes, he is allowed to leave through an exit that is not monitored by surveillance equipment.

    O   If a store has a reliable security system, it is impossible to pass unpurchased goods through the system undetected.

    O   If a supermarket was built before 1980, it often has exits that cannot be equipped with electronic surveillance.

    O   If a store has a reliable electronic security system but is still experiencing a rise in theft, it must be the case that the employees are stealing.

4. The sanitation chief, hailing the success of her voluntary conservation program, reported that the amount of garbage produced per capita in the city decreased dramatically last year. But that statistic is deceptive. Last year, the city incorporated three villages from the surrounding suburban area, increasing its population by almost 30 percent. It is this increase, rather than the conservation program, that explains the statistical drop.

    Which of the following, if true, would seriously weaken the objection to the sanitation chief's claim?

    O   Because of differences between urban and suburban life, most suburban areas produce less garbage per capita than do urban areas.

    O   The voluntary conservation program was not implemented in the three incorporated villages until very late last year.

    O   The year before last, the three villages produced as many pounds of garbage per capita as did the city.

    O   The statistics cited by the sanitation chief do not include commercial waste or garbage collected by private carters.

    O   Due to a three-week strike, some of the garbage produced by the city during the year before last year was not counted in the statistics.

5. A spokesperson for the Reader's Book Club (RBC) recently hailed the club's free gift program as a big boost for sales. A year ago, RBC began offering a free gift to any member ordering five or more books in a single month. Since then, the number of members ordering five or more books at a time from RBC has risen by nearly 35 percent.

    Which of the following, if true, would most seriously weaken the spokesperson's assessment of the program's effect on sales?

    O The number of members ordering fewer than five books in a single month did not rise in the last year.

    O Most members ordered the same number of books over the year but concentrated their orders in specific months.

    O The cost of providing free gifts nearly offset the increased revenue from higher sales.

    O Most other book clubs, many of which also sponsored free gift programs, saw a drop in sales last year.

    O The membership of the Reader's Book Club rose by more than 20 percent over the last year.

6. The United States will soon begin spot-checking all shipments of imported coffee for tainting by sandfly larvae. Any coffee found to be so tainted will be destroyed. Officials predict that the spot checks will result in the destruction of approximately 10 percent of all coffee imported into this country. Even so, the checks will miss about half of the tainted coffee sent here, since it is estimated that 20 percent of all coffee worldwide is tainted by sandfly larvae.

    The author of the passage above is necessarily assuming which one of the following?

    O Spot inspections will not succeed in preventing unacceptable amounts of tainted coffee from entering the country.

    O Inspectors can detect sandfly larvae in only half of the tainted shipments they inspect.

    O The proportion of imported coffee tainted by sandfly larvae is representative of the proportion of coffee so tainted worldwide.

    O Spot-checking will mean that only 10 percent of all imported coffee will be inspected for tainting by sandfly larvae.

    O The 80 percent of imported coffee shipments that are not tainted by sandfly larvae should not be inspected.

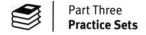

7. The Burbington dockyard is one of the largest employers in the Burbington area, but antiquated facilities are prompting so many customers to go elsewhere that the dockyard may be forced to close unless major renovation is completed. However, to modernize the facility so that it would be competitive again would require an investment beyond the reach of the dockyard owners. Therefore, they have appealed to the city council of Burbington to offer them tax breaks and an interest-free loan to allow them to modernize. Hoping to avoid a significant increase in local unemployment, the city council is giving the request serious consideration.

    Which of the following would be the most important question for the city council of Burbington to answer before deciding whether to grant the dockyard owners' request?

    O   Will the owners of the dockyard be able to relocate operations to another state for less than the cost of renovation?

    O   Will the renovation include improved environmental protections?

    O   To be competitive, would the Burbington dockyard need to automate several labor-intensive functions, thereby allowing it to achieve significant reductions in its workforce?

    O   Will the dockyard be able to build more ships annually after the renovations?

    O   Do the fiscal costs of tax breaks typically outweigh the benefits of increased economic activity?

8. Time and time again, it has been shown that students who attend colleges with a low student-to-faculty ratio get the most well-rounded education. As a result, when my children are ready for college, I'll be sure they attend a school with a very small student population.

    Which of the following, if true, identifies the greatest flaw in the reasoning above?

    O   A low student-to-faculty ratio is the effect of a well-rounded education, not its source.

    O   Intelligence should be considered the result of childhood environment, not advanced education.

    O   A very small student population does not, by itself, ensure a low student-to-faculty ratio.

    O   Parental desires and preferences rarely determine a child's choice of a college or university.

    O   Students must take advantage of the low student-to-faculty ratio by intentionally choosing small classes.

9. Sam: Statistics show that hospital patients who have no health insurance generally get fewer diagnostic procedures and leave the hospital sooner than do patients who are insured. People without insurance are obviously not being cared for properly.

    Dan: On the contrary, what your statistics show is that people insist on undergoing all sorts of unnecessary procedures when they know that someone else is footing the bill.

    Which of the following best describes Dan's response to Sam?

    O   He denies the truth of Sam's statistical evidence.

    O   He shows that Sam's argument is based on a logical fallacy.

    O   He provides counterevidence contradicting that cited by Sam.

    O   He shows that Sam's argument is biased because of an unfair preconception.

    O   He provides an alternative explanation for the facts cited by Sam.

10. Though the number of nurses employed in the United States has risen over the past 10 years, 15 percent of nursing positions in hospitals are vacant today. The situation will worsen unless hospitals improve working conditions and nursing schools attract students who have not traditionally been drawn to the profession. More scholarships and loans may make nursing education more affordable, and alternative routes to nursing may prompt adults interested in nursing to go back to studying in an undergraduate program.

    Which of the following can be logically inferred from the paragraph above?

    O   Nursing school recruitments are now at their lowest level in a decade.

    O   In the past 10 years, the number of practicing hospital nurses has fallen.

    O   Financial considerations are the principal reason for the current nursing shortage.

    O   The supply of nurses has been rising, but not as fast as the demand for them.

    O   Working conditions in hospitals have become significantly worse in the past decade.

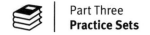
Answers and Explanations

1.	E	4.	C	7.	C	9.	E
2.	E	5.	B	8.	C	10.	D
3.	C	6.	C				

1.   E

The Conclusion: A tariff should be imposed on Country Z's computers.

The Evidence: A tariff will increase sales of domestic computers. Increased sales often result in lower prices.

Basically, it's putting one and one together. If the tariff will increase sales and if increased sales often lower prices, then there's a good chance that the tariff will lower domestic computer prices.

Embargoes, (A), are outside the scope of the argument, which concerns the effects of a tariff, not alternatives to it. (B) refers to a possible effect of the tariff—reduced prices; unfortunately, though, there's no mention in the stimulus of this resulting in increased jobs. A tariff, you're told, will lead to increased production; that doesn't mean, though, that *no* tariff will force *reduced* production, (C). (D) is an overstatement. The tariff will increase sales and probably production; that doesn't mean, however, that lack of a tariff has hampered production.

2.   E

The Conclusion: A meat-free, dairy-free diet greatly reduces the risk of a heart attack.

The Evidence: Only 10 percent of those consuming such a diet ever suffer a heart attack.

The word "weaken" in the question stem indicates that this is a Weaken question. The argument says that "only" 10 percent of those on a meat-free, dairy-free diet have a heart attack. To draw the conclusion that this diet *causes* fewer heart attacks, the argument must assume that more than 10 percent of people who do eat meat and dairy have heart attacks. An answer choice that makes this assumption less likely weakens the argument. Our prediction should be something like "fewer than 10 percent of

people who eat meat and dairy get heart attacks." This is exactly what (E) says.

(A) provides a good reason for eating meat and dairy but not a reason that weakens *this* argument, which is that such diets would increase risk of heart attack. (B) comes closer to strengthening the argument than weakening it, and it is also out of scope, since the passage doesn't mention people who eat dairy but not meat. (C) states that some of the people who eat neither meat nor dairy have more than one heart attack. Because there is no parallel statistic about how many dairy- and meat-eating heart attack sufferers experience more than one heart attack, this information does not affect the argument in either direction. (D) strengthens the argument because it explains in more detail exactly how meat and dairy consumption is responsible for heart problems.

3.   C

The Conclusion: The thefts *must* (note that key word) have been committed by people who used exits other than the regular customer exit doors.

The Evidence: The number of successful thefts has risen even though Food World has a reliable electronic security system at all customer exit doors.

In order to conclude that the thefts aren't taking place out the customer doors, the author must assume that the security system works. However, "reliable" doesn't necessarily mean infallible.

(A) plainly can't be assumed, since the author is concluding that the thefts took place at unequipped doors. (B) and (E) both play off the same red herring: employee theft. The issue is where the thefts are occurring, not who is committing them. The author seems to think that noncustomer exit doors are the problem, but there's no need to assume that these can't be equipped with a surveillance system, (D).

4. C

The Conclusion: The drop in per capita garbage is not due to the chief's conservation program.

The Evidence: The city incorporated three villages, whose extra residents accounted for the per capita drop.

Well, the author believes (assumes) that the suburban villagers are deflating the per capita garbage figure, so he assumes that suburbanites produce less garbage. If, though, they produce every bit as much garbage, then the drop can't be due to their incorporation into the city and the statistics.

He assumes (A), so it strengthens rather than weakens his argument. (B) makes it less likely that the conservation program is responsible for the drop, which also strengthens his argument. As long as the same type of garbage is eliminated from both years' statistics, (D), the effect of this on the different arguments is anyone's guess—a clear sign of a wrong answer. More garbage the year before last year, (E), just increases the drop; it does not, however, affect the author's attempt to explain this drop.

5. B

The Conclusion: The free gift program increased sales.

The Evidence: The number of orders of five or more books has increased by 35 percent.

The representative argues from evidence of sales of five books or more to a conclusion about total sales. If the large sales have increased at the expense of other sales, then it's not necessarily the case that total sales have risen. People may be taking advantage of the offer without buying any more books.

If smaller orders did not rise, (A), then the argument is strengthened, since that means that the only increase in sales was in the larger orders that were targeted by the free gift promotion. The argument concerns sales, not revenue, so (C) is off the point. If the argument concerned the competitiveness of RBC, then (D) might be relevant. As it stands, though, other clubs and their promotions have no effect on the representative's claims. And membership, (E), like revenues, is off the point. The representative hails the program as a success based on supposedly increased sales.

6. C

The Conclusion: The spot checks will miss half of the imported coffee tainted by sandfly larvae.

The Evidence: Only 10 percent of imported coffee will fail the spot checks, whereas 20 percent of coffee worldwide is tainted.

The evidence contains a figure for coffee worldwide; the conclusion, for coffee imported to the United States. Here you have a twist on a common GMAT theme. The argument isn't *based* on a sample; it *concludes* something about a sample (imported coffee) based on evidence about the whole (all coffee). The same key issue is at work, though: the sample must be representative. In order for the math to work, 20 percent of imported coffee (the same figure as for all coffee) must be tainted.

The author assumes that spot checks will detect some tainted coffee; there's no evidence, though, that this amount (10 percent) is unacceptable, (A). (B) is incorrect because it's not clear that they will miss half of the tainted coffee they inspect. These are spot checks; they may miss half the tainted coffee because they don't check that coffee. (D) misreads the numbers: it's not that 10 percent will be inspected, but that spot inspections will destroy 10 percent of the imported coffee. (E) is nonsensical. If inspectors knew which 80 percent was untainted, there would be no need for inspections.

7. C

The Council's Conclusion: Helping the Burbington dockyard modernize will help the city avoid increased unemployment.

Its Evidence: Customers are going elsewhere due to antiquated facilities.

You are asked to find an important question that the city council should address before granting a request. This is a variation on the Strengthen/Weaken question type, since the answer to the "most important question" will presumably make the council's decision to grant the request more or less likely. As you read, pay particular attention to what the request is and what information the council lacks. The owner's request is for financial assistance to modernize the dockyard, a major employer in the city. You're told that the dockyard's outdated facilities are to blame for its potential demise. So, you can see what's in this for the dockyard owners—they'd get someone to help bail out their declining business. But the question stem tells you to concentrate on what's in this for the city. The answer is in the final sentence. The council hopes to avoid "a significant increase in local unemployment." The question the council members need to ask is whether modernizing the dockyard will keep the jobs at home. You can safely predict that the right answer will raise a question whose answer would illuminate something about saving jobs.

That's what (C) does. If the dockyard reduces its workforce after modernization, then granting the request would potentially fail to accomplish the council's goal. On the other hand, if the dockyard could be modernized in such a way that jobs aren't lost, then granting the request would meet the council's aim. (A) might be an important question for the dockyard owners to consider, but not one that the city council need address. (B) might be an important question generally, but it is not related to the city council's expressed goals. (D), concerning how productive the dockyard will be, is not directly relevant to the council's concern—saving jobs. After all, if the yard can build more ships while cutting its workforce, then the council will not have achieved its goal. (E) is too general: balancing the costs of this plan against its benefits is surely a good idea, but how they "typically" balance doesn't tell you how they balance in this specific case.

8.　C

The Conclusion: My child will get a well-rounded education at a school with a small student population.

The Evidence: Well-rounded education comes from schools with low student-to-faculty ratios.

To find a flaw, determine the error in reasoning that exists in the argument. Typically this means finding the specific disconnect between evidence and conclusion. You might paraphrase the argument like this: the most well-rounded education comes from schools with low student-to-faculty ratios, so I will send my kids to

colleges with low student populations. The author assumes that a low student population is the same thing as a low student-to-faculty ratio. That's an error—a school with a large student population could have a low student-to-faculty ratio by hiring lots of faculty. Similarly, a school with few students could have proportionally even fewer faculty, resulting in a high ratio. So, our prediction would be something like this: having a low student population doesn't mean a school must have a low student-to-faculty ratio. That's exactly what (C) says, which is why it's the correct answer.

(A) claims that the author confuses cause and effect, but that isn't a big flaw here; even if (A) is right, the stimulus points out that the two are highly correlated, so the author's strategy would still likely work. (B) is out of scope, as "intelligence" and "well-rounded education" don't mean the same thing. (D) touches on the issue of whether the plan is practical, which is outside the scope of the argument. Nothing in the argument indicates whether this parent has influence. (E) is also outside of the scope because it addresses not college choice but what happens after admission.

9.　E

Sam's Conclusion: The uninsured get poor hospital care.

Dan's Conclusion: The insured insist on unnecessary tests.

The Evidence (for both): Hospital patients who have no health insurance generally get fewer diagnostic procedures and leave the hospital sooner than do patients who are insured.

As the breakdown points out, the two agree on the facts, they just disagree on what the facts mean. Each has a different explanation for the discrepancy in hospital procedures. Dan, then, accepts the evidence but provides as a conclusion an alternative explanation for it.

Choices (A), (B), and (C) all have Dan disputing the evidence, or basis for Sam's argument. It's the interpretation that he disputes. He doesn't show a bias or preconception, (D).

10. D

The Conclusion: Unless steps are taken, the nursing shortage will worsen.

The Evidence: The number of employed nurses has risen over the past decade, but there's still a 15 percent vacancy rate that looks likely to get worse.

More than a straightforward argument, the stimulus is an exploration of the nursing shortage and approaches to handling it. Prephrasing here might give you the idea that working conditions aren't ideal or that there aren't enough students enrolling in nursing programs. As it turns out, though, it's simpler than that. If there are more nurses than ever, yet the shortage is worsening, then demand is rising faster than the supply.

There's no evidence that enrollments are actually down, (A), and you know that the number of nurses hasn't fallen, (B). Financial considerations, (C), seem to hurt nursing school enrollments, but that's a far cry from being "the principal reason for the nursing shortage." The same reasoning eliminates (E): working conditions have something to do with the shortage, and they need improving, but you can't infer that they have worsened significantly.

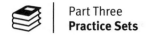
Critical Reasoning Practice Set Four

Directions: For each question in this practice set, you will be presented with a short argument, a set of statements, or a plan of action. Select the best answer from the choices provided.

1. Recent experiments in the Southern Ocean offer the promise of controlling the threat of global warming by creating organic "sponges" for carbon dioxide, which is widely considered the main culprit for rising global temperatures. Scientists were able to grow a lush strip of phytoplankton 150 kilometers long by fertilizing a patch of the ocean with hundreds of kilograms of an iron compound. Phytoplankton presently accounts for over half of the photosynthesis on Earth, the process by which carbon dioxide is absorbed and converted into oxygen. A major limiting factor in the production of phytoplankton is lack of iron, but by fertilizing oceans with iron compounds, scientists hope to be able to reduce carbon dioxide levels and reverse the greenhouse effect.

   Which of the following, if true, casts the most serious doubt upon the advisability of using the fertilization method described above to control carbon dioxide levels?

   O In some oceans, the growth of phytoplankton is also limited by how much nitrogen, phosphorus, and silicon are available.

   O The cost of fertilizing the oceans with sufficient quantities of iron to reverse the greenhouse effect is likely to be very high.

   O Iron naturally reaches the seas in the form of wind-blown mineral dust, which becomes more or less abundant as conditions on land change.

   O Fertilization efforts will do nothing to curb the production of more carbon dioxide emissions.

   O Some studies have indicated that higher levels of iron may inhibit the photosynthetic ability of other organisms.

2. University systems that use graduation rates to determine which campuses are allotted additional funds are acting counter to their stated goals. The universities say they are trying to raise academic standards, yet they are actually encouraging campuses to graduate students regardless of achievement.

   Which of the following statements, if true, would help to validate the approach taken by the university systems mentioned above?

   O Graduation rates for university systems with this policy are among the highest in the nation, but the graduates from these systems score poorly on tests of basic skills.

   O The campuses that need the additional funds the most are the ones that have the lowest graduation rates.

   O The new funds will be used toward facility upgrades, not new faculty positions or staff pay increases.

   O Graduation examinations currently exist that require every graduate at each university to demonstrate a minimum level of achievement.

   O An opposing plan focuses on providing extra funding based not on graduation rates, but on the percent of students that pass basic skills tests.

3. In 1998, 50 people with emotional disturbances underwent hypnosis to be cured of their mood swings. A follow-up survey in 2003 revealed that five had fairly stable emotional conditions at the time of the survey. These five subjects can therefore serve as models of the types of people for whom hypnosis is likely to be successful.

    Which of the following, if true, casts the most doubt on the suitability of the five subjects as models in the sense described?

    O   The five subjects have very different personalities and backgrounds.

    O   Since 1998, the five subjects have experienced dramatic mood swings interspersed with periods of relative stability.

    O   Those people who were still suffering from unstable emotional conditions at the time of the 2003 survey had shown no improvement since 1998.

    O   Many psychologists are less concerned about a patient's mood swings than about the patient's willingness to express his or her problems and fears.

    O   The emotional condition of most of the 45 subjects who were still unstable at the time of the 2003 survey had actually worsened since 1998.

4. The cause of the peculiar columnar growth pattern displayed by junipers growing near burning underground veins of lignite coal has never been convincingly explained. Until recently, the accepted theory posited that the abundance of carbon monoxide in the local atmosphere caused the columnar growth. However, a new theory holds that the cause is the persistent heat present near these underground fires that, while not intense enough to inflame the trees, can nonetheless change their normal growth pattern.

    The existence of which of the following would provide the strongest support for the new theory?

    O   a columnar juniper growing in an atmosphere of intense heat and an absence of carbon monoxide

    O   a normal juniper growing in an atmosphere of intense heat and an absence of carbon monoxide

    O   a columnar juniper growing in an atmosphere of normal heat and a high concentration of carbon monoxide

    O   a normal juniper growing in an atmosphere of intense heat and a high concentration of carbon monoxide

    O   a columnar juniper growing in an atmosphere of intense heat and a high concentration of carbon monoxide

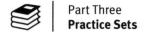
5. The cost of transatlantic airfare has nearly doubled over the past five years, yet airlines are doing a booming business. Clearly, people today have more money to spend on vacations than they did five years ago.

    Each of the following, if true, would weaken the argument above EXCEPT:

    ○   Most people buying transatlantic tickets today use them for business trips, so airfare is refunded by their companies.

    ○   There are far fewer airlines offering transatlantic service today than there were five years ago.

    ○   People are taking shorter vacations and staying in cheaper hotels than they used to.

    ○   The past five years have seen a drastic overall decline in the number of vacation travelers on domestic flights.

    ○   Domestic airline flights have also seen a steady increase in passengers in the last five years.

6. Truck driver: The gasoline tax is too high and it must be lowered. It has been raised every year for the past five years, while other sales taxes have not. If the government persists in unfairly penalizing truck drivers, our increased operating costs will either hurt consumers or put us out of business.

    State official: But your gasoline tax dollars maintain and improve the very roads you depend on. Without those additional revenues, road conditions would deteriorate, costing you and consumers much more in maintenance and repairs.

    The state official's response to the truck driver

    ○   points out that the truck driver's proposal will actually worsen the problem it is intended to solve

    ○   is circular, assuming the truth of its conclusion in order to justify its conclusion

    ○   points out that the truck driver is selfish because more people are aided by the gasoline tax than are penalized

    ○   is merely an attempt to excuse the government's policies without providing any justification for those policies

    ○   points to an inherent contradiction between the cause the truck driver cites and the effects the truck driver thinks will follow from the cause

7. Archaeologists recently unearthed a prehistoric statuette, portraying the figure of a woman, that had been carved from a mastodon bone. A team of researchers carefully studied the statuette, which they named the Venus of Orleans. Since it was similar in shape and design to another bone carving, the so-called Venus of Grenoble, they concluded that in all likelihood it was carved at the same time, about 70,000 years ago. Skeptics point out, however, that carbon-14 testing indicates that the recently discovered statuette is only about 50,000 years old.

    Which of the following, if true, would most weaken the skeptics' objection?

    O   Carbon-14 dating places the age of the Venus of Grenoble at 70,000 years.

    O   No other similar statuettes have been found at the site where the Venus of Orleans was unearthed.

    O   The carbon-14 dating process is unreliable for objects dating from before 60,000 B.C.

    O   The carbon-14 dating process has provided unreliable dates for many objects older than 100,000 years.

    O   Some speculation persists that the Venus of Orleans was carved out of the femur or thigh bone of a prehistoric ox.

8. Cowonga lion cubs in the wild often engage in aggressive and even violent play with their siblings. This activity is apparently instigated by the parent lions. Cowonga lion cubs born in captivity, however, rarely engage in aggressive play. Zoologists have concluded that this form of play teaches the young lions the aggressive skills necessary for successful hunting in the wild and that such play is not instigated in captivity because the development of hunting skills is unnecessary there.

    The zoologists' conclusion would be most strengthened by demonstrating that

    O   Cowonga lions raised in captivity are unable to hunt successfully in the wild

    O   the skills developed from aggressive play are similar to those used for hunting in the wild

    O   the young of other types of predatory animals also engage in aggressive play

    O   parent lions that were raised in captivity do not instigate this play in their young

    O   none of the Cowonga lions raised in the wild are incapable of hunting successfully

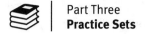
9. Which of the following best completes the passage below?

    The question of whether a child's personality is the result of genetic material inherited from the parents or the nurturing and environment provided by the parents is a perennial subject of debate. While no one would deny that environment and upbringing play some limited, superficial role, the genetic traits the child inherits provide the basic blueprint for who, and what, the child becomes. After all, if one plants tomatoes, _____.

    ○ one must tend them carefully in order to gather good vegetables

    ○ one had better choose the variety and location with equal care

    ○ one will eventually get tomatoes, but not necessarily good tomatoes

    ○ one must expect tomatoes to grow, not cucumbers or daffodils

    ○ one must be sure to tend them well, regardless of the quality of the seeds used

10. Zoologists have determined that the size of the litters produced by mating pairs of Beringer sloths is largely determined by the parent animals' diet. Sloths that feed primarily on catalpa trees tend to produce smaller numbers of offspring than do those that feed primarily on tulip trees. A new theory posits that the parent sloths vary their diet to achieve optimal population size for a given year, producing fewer offspring in dry years when food scarcity would threaten a large population.

    Which of the following, if true, would provide the strongest support for the theory that Beringer sloths vary their diets to suit the conditions of a given year?

    ○ In a forest dominated by catalpa trees, parent sloths ate far more tulip leaves than catalpa leaves in dry years.

    ○ In a forest dominated by tulip trees, parent sloths ate somewhat more tulip leaves than catalpa leaves in wet years.

    ○ The population of sloths in a particular area varied widely over several years during which precipitation remained relatively constant.

    ○ In a forest with roughly equal numbers of catalpa and tulip trees, parent sloths ate far more catalpa leaves than tulip leaves in dry years.

    ○ In a forest with roughly equal numbers of catalpa and tulip trees, parent sloths ate far more tulip leaves than catalpa leaves in dry years.

Answers and explanations follow on the next page. ▶ ▶ ▶

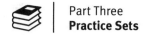
Answers and Explanations

1. E	4. A	7. C	9. D
2. D	5. E	8. A	10. D
3. B	6. A		

1. E

The Conclusion: A plan to fertilize the oceans with iron compounds will be able to reverse the greenhouse effect.

The Evidence: By fertilizing the oceans with iron compounds, phytoplankton will grow, creating organic "sponges" to soak up carbon dioxide, widely believed to be responsible for global warming.

Look for the answer that does the best job at weakening the argument. This is a causal argument, which concludes that a plan to fertilize the oceans with iron compounds will be able to reverse the greenhouse effect. The chain of reasoning goes like this: by fertilizing the oceans with iron compounds, phytoplankton will grow, creating organic "sponges" to soak up carbon dioxide, widely believed to be responsible for global warming. Look for an answer that weakens this chain of causality. (E) indicates that fertilizing the ocean with iron may have the unintended side effect of reducing the photosynthesis rates of other plants. If this is true, the plan might not reduce carbon dioxide levels after all.

Of the wrong answers, (A), which discusses *some* oceans, is too weak to affect the argument. There's nothing in the argument to suggest that *all* the oceans need to be fertilized. (B), which mentions the high cost of the plan, is beyond the scope of the argument. The argument does not suggest the cost is a factor; after all, we're discussing a plan to save the planet! (C) is completely irrelevant to the issue at hand. Who cares about how iron naturally reaches the sea? And finally, (D) does nothing to invalidate the plan. Sure, emission-reduction plans may also be in order, but that doesn't mean we shouldn't try to reduce present carbon dioxide levels.

2. D

The Conclusion: Using graduate rates to determine which universities get additional funds is a bad idea.

The Evidence: It will encourage universities to graduate everyone, rather than just rewarding schools with good academic performance.

The trickiest part of this question is understanding whose position you're trying to validate and whose you're trying to attack (it gets confusing when the argument involves opposing positions, as it does here). Here, you're trying to validate the approach taken by the university systems, which the author argues is flawed; in other words, you're trying to weaken the author's critique. So, what is the approach taken by the university systems? And what is the author's critique? The systems use graduation rates to determine which universities are awarded extra funds. This, the author argues, encourages campuses to graduate everyone, *regardless of achievement.* (D), which notes that exams exist that require every graduate to prove a minimum level of achievement, attacks the author's contention that the approach will lead to people graduating regardless of achievement.

Of the wrong answers, (A) strengthens the author's argument, as it agrees with his contention that achievement standards are being disregarded. (B) points out a downside to the university system's plan: that the money isn't going to schools that need it. (C) makes a completely irrelevant point. What's at issue is not how the money is *spent* by schools, but how it is *allotted* to them. And (E) doesn't validate the approach taken by the university systems but in fact hints that there may be a fairer approach out there.

3.   B

The Conclusion: These five people can serve as models for the type of person who can be helped by hypnosis.

The Evidence: A study showed that these five previously disturbed hypnosis subjects had stable emotional conditions.

The survey only found that at the time of the study, the five seemed to be doing okay. Remember, these people were originally suffering from mood swings; maybe the study just caught them on a good day. If that's the case—if, since 1998, these people have been experiencing dramatic mood swings and occasional periods of health—then hypnosis hasn't really helped them and they're not good models.

The author presented the people as models of different types of people who can be helped, not as a single model of a single personality type, so they needn't be similar, (A). It doesn't matter that the other 45 people who underwent hypnosis didn't get better, (C); the argument is based on and concerns only the 5 who were stable. (E) fails to weaken the argument for the same reason. The concern of many psychologists, (D), is well outside the scope. You need a statement that speaks about hypnosis and these 5 subjects.

4.   A

The New Theory's Conclusion: Heat (from the burning coal) causes columnar growth in junipers near burning underground coal veins.

The New Theory's Evidence: None really, except the correlation of columnar growth with these areas with underground fires.

The Old Theory's Conclusion: The abundance of carbon monoxide causes columnar growth.

The Old Theory's Evidence: None really, except the correlation of columnar growth with these areas with high carbon monoxide.

When you scan the choices, you see that each presents a case of the cause with or without the effect or the effect with or without the cause. Since the two theories are in opposition, weakening the old theory is a way of strengthening the new one. (A) describes a scenario in which the growth trigger stated in the new theory (heat) is present, while the growth trigger stated in the old theory (carbon monoxide) is not present. This would support the new theory and cast doubt on the old theory.

(B), where you get the new theory's alleged cause (intense heat), without the alleged effect (columnar junipers), is of no help at all. A columnar juniper in an atmosphere with high carbon monoxide but no extra heat, (C), strengthens the old theory. A case with both alleged causes without the expected effect, (D), weakens both theories. Likewise, columnar growth in the presence of both causes, (E), does nothing to promote one theory over the other.

5.   E

The Conclusion: People have more money to spend on their vacations.

The Evidence: Airlines are doing fine even though they're charging high fares to cross the Atlantic.

Since this is a Weaken/EXCEPT question, all four incorrect answer choices will weaken the argument by severing the assumed connection between the booming transatlantic airline business and an increase in people's vacation budgets. The correct answer will either strengthen this connection or be out of scope. Only (E) fails to weaken the argument, as domestic business is outside the scope of this argument. If anything, this answer choice might strengthen the argument that vacation travelers have more money, as both domestic and transatlantic business is booming.

The fact that most of the flights presented as evidence aren't bought by vacationers, (A), breaks the connection between booming business and vacation money. Airlines can do a booming transatlantic business even if business as a whole is down, as long as there are fewer airlines offering transatlantic service, (B). If people are skimping elsewhere, (C), then even if they're paying a lot for airfare, they needn't have more vacation money. And if (D) is true, it may be the case that people's vacation budgets are down overall; however, what vacations they are taking involve transatlantic flights.

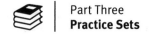

6.   A

The Truck Driver's Conclusion: The gas tax must be lowered.

The Truck Driver's Evidence: Increased costs will either put the truckers out of business or will hurt consumers.

The Official's Conclusion: The tax must remain.

The Official's Evidence: Highways will fall into disrepair without tax revenues, costing truckers and consumers even more.

The official wants the trucker to realize that cutting gas taxes won't help, but will likely raise costs for both industry and consumers. So, she's arguing that the trucker's proposal, if carried out, will actually make matters worse.

(B)'s circular argument would be more or less a restatement of the conclusion—that's not what's happening here. The official doesn't accuse the trucker of selfishness, (C); moreover, the trucker also warns of the harm done to consumers by the gas tax. The official does provide justification of the tax policy, (D); the revenue pays for road upkeep. There's no inherent contradiction between high taxes and the destruction of the trucking industry, (E), nor does the official claim there is.

7.   C

The Skeptics' Conclusion: The Venus of Orleans isn't 70,000 years old.

The Skeptics' Evidence: Carbon-14 testing indicates that the statue is only about 50,000 years old.

The skeptics contend that the 70,000-year dating is false. As evidence, they present carbon-14 dating results that show the statuette to be only 50,000 years old. This argument is weakened if results from carbon-14 dating are unreliable when the object predates 60,000 B.C. Basically, if the archaeologists are right, the skeptics' tests are worthless. So, the issue is still open and the skeptics' evidence is greatly weakened.

(D) works along similar lines, but no one believes the statuette to be over 100,000 years old. (A) deals with the other statuette and, rather than casting doubt on its date, affirms it. The skeptics' argument doesn't rely on other statuettes having been found, (B), or on the material of which the statuette is composed, (E).

8.   A

The Zoologists' Conclusion: The play teaches the young lions the aggressive skills necessary for successful hunting in the wild.

Their Evidence: Cubs in the wild often engage in aggressive play with their siblings, play that is instigated by their parents. Cubs born in captivity, however, rarely engage in aggressive play.

There's cause and effect here. The zoologists believe that the play teaches hunting skills. Where there is need of the effect (hunting skills), there is the cause (play); where there is no need of the effect, the cause is lacking. That's a correlation, but the key issue remains: Does the play cause the hunting skills? The fact that lions raised in captivity, without the play, can't hunt tells you that without the alleged cause, there is no effect. This greatly strengthens the connection between the two.

The fact that the play and hunting are similar, (B), does little to show that the former leads to the latter; both could be effects of something more basic and instinctive. The behavior of other animals, (C), is beyond the scope of the zoologists' argument. Presumably, the parents raised in captivity, (D), are raising their young in captivity, so this adds nothing new. And the fact that wild lions learn to hunt, (E), has no effect on the hypothesis; the question is how they learned to hunt.

9. D

The Conclusion: Children's personalities are primarily the result of genetics.

The Evidence: Genetics provide the basic blueprint for who a child becomes.

There's not much evidence given (it's a restatement of the conclusion). The sentence with the blank is intended to provide more: an example or illustration, in which tomatoes are compared to children. Since the author believes in the primacy of genetics, the completion should be an illustration of this same belief for tomatoes. If one plants tomatoes, then one will get tomatoes (it's genetic), not some other plant.

Careful tending, (A) and (E), parallels nurture or upbringing, which the author doesn't consider very important. Equal care devoted to variety and location, (B), would illustrate that both nature and nurture are equally important. (C), getting tomatoes but not necessarily good tomatoes, is close but no cigar. (D) does a better job of illustrating that certain outcomes are genetically impossible. Moreover, the issue of quality comes from nowhere, making this an incorrect GMAT argument completion.

10. D

The New Theory's Conclusion: Parent sloths vary their diet to achieve optimal population size for a given year by producing fewer offspring in dry years when food is scarce.

The Evidence: The size of the litters is largely determined by the parent animals' diet. Sloths that feed primarily on catalpa trees tend to produce smaller numbers of offspring than do those that feed primarily on tulip trees. With stimuli like this, it's often a good idea to jot down some shorthand describing what the theory says:

dry → scarce → catalpa

wet → not scarce → tulip

You want support. Nothing leaps to mind, so look to the choices. Each describes a scenario; you need the one that "fits" the new theory. Sloths deliberately going for tulips over catalpa in dry years, (A), is contrary to the theory. (B) is in line with the theory—tulip leaves in wet years—yet because this forest was dominated by tulip trees, it could just be that the sloths ate most what they found most. (C) tells you nothing about diet and it's not obvious what it means, so it's out. (D), however, gives what you want. Catalpa leaves in dry years is in line with the theory, and the trees are equally available. This makes it more likely that the sloths sought out the catalpa. Tulip leaves in dry years, (E), is directly counter to the theory.

CHAPTER 8

GMAT Verbal Practice

Practice GMAT Verbal Section

The following practice set contains a typical mix of medium-to-hard GMAT Verbal questions. If you can answer most of these questions correctly under timed conditions, you can expect to do well on the real GMAT.

One thing, however, that we could not simulate in this book is the computer-adaptive nature of an actual GMAT. If you want that experience (and we recommend it strongly), we have two suggestions.

First, you can get your hands on some of Kaplan's GMAT prep materials. One option is to pick up the latest edition of *Kaplan GMAT Prep Plus.* It comes with a suite of online resources that includes full-length, computer-adaptive practice tests, along with targeted practice quizzes.

You can also use Kaplan's Adaptive Qbank. You get more than 2,500 questions that you can access 24/7 from any internet browser or Kaplan's mobile app, each with comprehensive explanations. You can even customize your quizzes based on question type, and as you get more questions right, the Adaptive Qbank gives you harder questions, just like on the real GMAT. Best of all, you also get charts that show your progress. Visit **kaptest.com/GMAT** for details on the Adaptive Qbank and for more information on other practice and course options.

Your other option is to download the *GMAT® Official Starter Kit* software from the test maker's website, **mba.com**. It's free and contains two full-length CATs (explanations of answers are not included) and a short practice section for each question type, with answers and explanations.

How to Take This Practice Set

Before taking this practice section, find a quiet place where you can work uninterrupted for 65 minutes. Make sure you have a comfortable desk, a timer, a couple of pencils, and several sheets of scratch paper.

Answer the questions in order. As you know, there's no skipping around on the actual GMAT.

You'll find the answer key and explanations following this section.

Good luck!

Practice Section Answer Sheet

1. Ⓐ Ⓑ Ⓒ Ⓓ Ⓔ   13. Ⓐ Ⓑ Ⓒ Ⓓ Ⓔ   25. Ⓐ Ⓑ Ⓒ Ⓓ Ⓔ
2. Ⓐ Ⓑ Ⓒ Ⓓ Ⓔ   14. Ⓐ Ⓑ Ⓒ Ⓓ Ⓔ   26. Ⓐ Ⓑ Ⓒ Ⓓ Ⓔ
3. Ⓐ Ⓑ Ⓒ Ⓓ Ⓔ   15. Ⓐ Ⓑ Ⓒ Ⓓ Ⓔ   27. Ⓐ Ⓑ Ⓒ Ⓓ Ⓔ
4. Ⓐ Ⓑ Ⓒ Ⓓ Ⓔ   16. Ⓐ Ⓑ Ⓒ Ⓓ Ⓔ   28. Ⓐ Ⓑ Ⓒ Ⓓ Ⓔ
5. Ⓐ Ⓑ Ⓒ Ⓓ Ⓔ   17. Ⓐ Ⓑ Ⓒ Ⓓ Ⓔ   29. Ⓐ Ⓑ Ⓒ Ⓓ Ⓔ
6. Ⓐ Ⓑ Ⓒ Ⓓ Ⓔ   18. Ⓐ Ⓑ Ⓒ Ⓓ Ⓔ   30. Ⓐ Ⓑ Ⓒ Ⓓ Ⓔ
7. Ⓐ Ⓑ Ⓒ Ⓓ Ⓔ   19. Ⓐ Ⓑ Ⓒ Ⓓ Ⓔ   31. Ⓐ Ⓑ Ⓒ Ⓓ Ⓔ
8. Ⓐ Ⓑ Ⓒ Ⓓ Ⓔ   20. Ⓐ Ⓑ Ⓒ Ⓓ Ⓔ   32. Ⓐ Ⓑ Ⓒ Ⓓ Ⓔ
9. Ⓐ Ⓑ Ⓒ Ⓓ Ⓔ   21. Ⓐ Ⓑ Ⓒ Ⓓ Ⓔ   33. Ⓐ Ⓑ Ⓒ Ⓓ Ⓔ
10. Ⓐ Ⓑ Ⓒ Ⓓ Ⓔ   22. Ⓐ Ⓑ Ⓒ Ⓓ Ⓔ   34. Ⓐ Ⓑ Ⓒ Ⓓ Ⓔ
11. Ⓐ Ⓑ Ⓒ Ⓓ Ⓔ   23. Ⓐ Ⓑ Ⓒ Ⓓ Ⓔ   35. Ⓐ Ⓑ Ⓒ Ⓓ Ⓔ
12. Ⓐ Ⓑ Ⓒ Ⓓ Ⓔ   24. Ⓐ Ⓑ Ⓒ Ⓓ Ⓔ   36. Ⓐ Ⓑ Ⓒ Ⓓ Ⓔ

Verbal Section

36 Questions
Time—65 Minutes

There are three types of questions in the Verbal section: Critical Reasoning, Reading Comprehension, and Sentence Correction.

Directions: For each question, select the best answer of the choices given.

Each of the **Critical Reasoning** questions is based on a short argument, a set of statements, or a plan of action.

Each of the **Reading Comprehension** questions is based on the content of a passage. After reading the passage, answer all questions pertaining to it on the basis of what is **stated** or **implied** in the passage.

Each of the **Sentence Correction** questions presents a sentence, part or all of which is underlined. Beneath the sentence you will find five ways of phrasing the underlined part. The first of these repeats the original; the other four are different. Follow the requirements of standard written English to choose your answer, paying attention to grammar, word choice, and sentence construction. Select the answer that produces the most effective sentence; your answer should make the sentence clear, exact, and free of grammatical error. It should also minimize awkwardness, ambiguity, and redundancy.

You may review these directions at any time during the Verbal section.

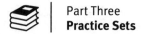
1. Fossils found recently in Pakistan provide evidence <u>supporting the theory of land mammals returning to the water that later</u> evolved into modern whales.

    O   supporting the theory of land mammals returning to the water that later

    O   supporting the theory that land mammals, after returning to the water,

    O   that supports the theory of land mammals that returned to the water and that later

    O   in support of the theory that land mammals returned to the water and that they later

    O   of support for the theory of land mammals that returned to the water and after

2. Although modern roller coasters have loops in which the cars turn upside-down, <u>old-fashioned roller coasters have more and longer straight drops</u>.

    O   old-fashioned roller coasters have more and longer straight drops

    O   the old-fashioned roller coaster has more and longer straight drops

    O   whereas old-fashioned roller coasters have more and longer straight drops

    O   old-fashioned roller coasters having more and longer straight drops

    O   old-fashioned roller coasters drop longer and straighter

3. The governor's recent direct mail survey on the environment showed that 80 percent of those who responded, and thus allegedly the vast majority of the state's residents, support increased state spending for the environmentally safe disposal of solid waste. But we should expect that most of the people who respond to an environmental survey are in favor of spending money to protect the environment.

    Which of the following best expresses the author's point?

    O   The survey was mailed only to those citizens who are environmentalists.

    O   Most citizens are poor judges of how the state's revenues should be spent.

    O   The survey failed because it neglected to ask citizens where the money for the increased spending would come from.

    O   Those who responded to the survey are not truly representative of the state's residents.

    O   The state does not need to spend more money to dispose of solid waste.

4. The dollar amount of federal tax revenues gained from personal income tax has increased markedly in recent years. Clearly, people are being more honest in declaring their annual earnings than they used to be.

    The argument above would be weakened by each of the following EXCEPT:

    O   Fewer income tax deductions are allowed now than in the past.

    O   The nation's population has increased.

    O   Tax revenue from the corporate sector has decreased.

    O   The average yearly income of the nation's residents has increased.

    O   The rate of personal income taxation has increased.

GO ON TO THE NEXT PAGE

Questions 5–7 refer to the following passage.

Having rejected Catholicism, English society after the Protestant Reformation felt compelled to impose new order on an uncertain universe. Claiming knowledge of a divine plan that linked
5 the celestial and natural worlds into one "great chain of being," some English thinkers depicted humans as the highest link on the portion of the chain representing the natural world. Furthermore, they conceived of human society
10 as a vertical series of political strata. One metaphor, occurring in Shakespeare's *Coriolanus*, among other places, likened society to the human body. Queen Elizabeth I chided a recalcitrant Parliament by asserting that "the
15 feet do not rule the head." Edward Forset echoed this assertion in 1606, when he elaborated a hierarchy in which the body was topped, literally and morally, by the head and the soul. In Forset's scheme, both soul and
20 monarchy possessed "unity" or "indivisibility"; the soul united and reigned over the physical body, and the sovereign united and reigned over the body politic. Popular acceptance of the idea of stability as God's will gave Elizabeth and her
25 immediate successors a potent, though short-lived, ideological restraint on rebellious thought and activity.

5. The passage suggests that many English people saw the idea of a new social order as

   O   necessary in order to fill a vacuum created by the decline of the monarchy

   O   an idiosyncratic viewpoint advocated by a few eccentric thinkers

   O   an amusing but not terribly urgent social issue

   O   a disguised attempt by the Catholic Church to restore its lost influence in English affairs

   O   unavoidable because an older order that had provided them with structure and security no longer existed

6. The passage suggests that, in the years following the Protestant Reformation, English monarchs were able to maintain their political influence primarily because

   O   popular opinion was tightly controlled by a small group of thinkers

   O   English society accepted that a hierarchical society was consistent with divine will

   O   monarchs accepted a social position basically equal to that of most other people

   O   Parliament was politically passive and offered no significant resistance

   O   English society traditionally supported a strong monarchical authority

7. Which of the following sentences would most logically follow the last sentence of this passage?

   O   Subsequently, popular acceptance of a divinely ordered social structure continued to shape English politics for an unusually lengthy period.

   O   However, because Forset's ideas were judged to be too radical, they initially failed to make a substantial impact on the balance of power in English government.

   O   Forset's arguments for a strict, hierarchically ordered society found especially enthusiastic support among many members of the English Parliament.

   O   This acceptance undoubtedly helped check growing assertiveness of those social classes that spoke through Parliament.

   O   Thus, freed of her problems with Parliament, Elizabeth was able to focus on the threat to social stability posed by Forset.

GO ON TO THE NEXT PAGE

8. When a movie that is panned by most film critics is a popular success, it is often taken as evidence of the poor taste of general audiences. But film critics belong to a fairly homogeneous class, and their preferences are often rooted in the prejudices of that class. Their opinions are no more likely to be an unerring guide to quality than are those of the average moviegoer.

The passage above best supports which of the following conclusions?

   O   Judgments of film quality by professional film critics are usually incorrect.

   O   Judgments of quality applied to movies are meaningless.

   O   Film critics usually consider popular movies to be of poor quality.

   O   Professional critics generally agree on the quality of any given movie.

   O   When film critics and general audiences disagree about a movie's quality, the critics' opinion is not necessarily more accurate.

9. John F. Kennedy increased the participation of the United States in the war in Vietnam, <u>which Lyndon B. Johnson did</u> when he succeeded Kennedy.

   O   which Lyndon B. Johnson did

   O   which Lyndon B. Johnson was to be doing

   O   as Lyndon B. Johnson

   O   as did Lyndon B. Johnson

   O   as Lyndon B. Johnson did do

10. <u>The reason why Scipio Africanus wept after his defeat of Hannibal is because he knew</u> that, having attained this stunning victory, his fortunes could only turn for the worse.

   O   The reason why Scipio Africanus wept after his defeat of Hannibal is because he knew

   O   Scipio Africanus's weeping after his defeat of Hannibal was because he knew

   O   Scipio Africanus wept after his defeat of Hannibal because he knew

   O   The reason Scipio Africanus wept after his defeat of Hannibal is because he knew

   O   Scipio Africanus wept after his defeat of Hannibal, the reason being that he knew

11. The Federal No Child Left Behind Act of 2001 <u>requires that students be present for at least 91 percent</u> of all scheduled school hours.

   O   requires that students be present for at least 91 percent

   O   requires that students to be present for at least 91 percent

   O   requires that students will be present for at least 91 percent

   O   has a requirement of students, being present for at least 91 percent

   O   has a requirement to have students be present for at least 91 percent

GO ON TO THE NEXT PAGE

Questions 12–15 refer to the following passage.

Corporate managers often work in groups because of the complexity of strategic problems. A consensus-seeking group's effectiveness may be impaired, however, if the group values
5 harmony over open evaluation of ideas. Consequently, some theorists advocate building decisional conflict into the group process. Doing so, they argue, should yield better decisions. While conflict potentially offers benefits, a
10 group's effectiveness also depends on members' reactions to group experiences. Ideally, the group process wins the commitment of its members. The process, though, may generate so much divisiveness that implementation and
15 future cooperation are undermined. Management groups thus face an apparent dilemma: decisional conflict may yield better decisions at the risk of weakening managerial effectiveness. Conversely, the harmony that
20 facilitates cooperation and implementation may come at the cost of inferior decisions.

Efforts to build conflict into group decision making have focused on two approaches, dialectical inquiry and devil's advocacy. Both
25 work by dividing the group into two competing subgroups, relying on formal debate to prevent uncritical acceptance of the seemingly obvious, and continuing until participants agree on a decision. The approaches differ in the roles
30 played by the subgroups. In dialectical inquiry, the subgroups present opposed sets of assumptions and recommendations, and debate until they reach agreement. In devil's advocacy, the second subgroup critiques the assumptions
35 and recommendations of the first, but offers no alternative. The first subgroup revises its ideas and presents them for a second critique. The process continues until the subgroups agree.

The varying roles of the subgroups have led to
40 disagreement among theorists over the effectiveness of the approaches. Mason and Mitroff claim that devil's advocacy does not identify suitable alternatives, whereas dialectical inquiry's juxtaposition of opposed sets of ideas
45 does so. Cosier, however, argues that dialectical inquiry adds potentially confusing steps to the process that would require extensive training, and may run counter to managers' accustomed ways of thinking; he also feels that this approach
50 may lead to excessive compromise.

12. The author's primary purpose in the passage is to

O emphasize the benefits of group decision making and reconcile two differing approaches

O describe the benefits and risks of decisional conflict and alternative means of its use

O defend an innovative method of group management against its critics

O argue that group decision making is superior to any other decision-making approach

O advocate one method of group decision making over another

13. It can be inferred from the passage that advocates of both the dialectical inquiry and devil's advocacy processes would agree with which of the following statements?

O Superior decisions often reflect compromises made between opposing views.

O Superior decisions stem from a consideration of opposing sets of proposals.

O Managers should avoid changing their customary ways of thinking.

O Formal debate can lead to a more thorough understanding of a problem.

O Effective group management requires extensive training.

GO ON TO THE NEXT PAGE

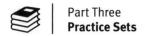
14. Which one of the following, if true, would counter Cosier's criticism of dialectical inquiry?

   O   Frequent compromises among managers may lead to ill-advised actions.

   O   Demanding that managers agree often weakens implementation of decisions.

   O   Encouraging conflict among managers improves the quality of decisions.

   O   Some managerial decisions must be made and implemented rapidly to be effective.

   O   Managers willing to alter their accustomed modes of thinking often make better decisions.

15. Which of the following exemplifies the functioning of management groups, as those groups are described in the passage?

   O   A citizens' group gathers to monitor the results of a closely contested election.

   O   A special prosecutor's office organizes to investigate alleged misconduct on the part of government officials.

   O   A committee of administrators forms to address the major problems of running a hospital.

   O   A panel of experts assembles to study an issue of growing public concern.

   O   A faculty committee forms to observe the search for a college president.

16. Manager: The success ratio for new businesses is lower than ever, with only 12 percent surviving the first two years. Furthermore, many businesses already operating are doing so at a loss, or with their lowest profit margin in decades. The blame must fall on the excessive demands of the workers. Profits drop in order to pay for new paint, radios, and artwork. We have lost sight of the fact that work is intended to be productive, not enjoyable.

Which of the following, if true, would most weaken the manager's argument?

   O   Workers, whether they are performing productively or not, often have very difficult and highly taxing duties.

   O   In most cases, improvements in the work environment increase productivity by increasing worker satisfaction.

   O   The failure of many businesses in the past was due to exorbitant taxation rather than excessive demands of the workers.

   O   The failure of a new business is not necessarily the same thing as the failure of an already existing business.

   O   The failure of a new business is not necessarily the same thing as operating an already existing business without a profit.

GO ON TO THE NEXT PAGE

17. Setting a distance record, in 1984 Joe Kittinger piloted his balloon from Maine to Italy, and he became the first balloonist to cross the Atlantic solo.

    O   Setting a distance record, in 1984 Joe Kittinger piloted his balloon from Maine to Italy, and he became the first balloonist to cross the Atlantic solo.

    O   In 1984, Joe Kittinger, setting a distance record, piloted his balloon from Maine to Italy, and he became the first balloonist to cross the Atlantic solo.

    O   In 1984, Joe Kittinger piloted his balloon from Maine to Italy, setting a distance record and becoming the first balloonist to cross the Atlantic solo.

    O   Having been first to cross the Atlantic solo, and with a voyage from Maine to Italy, Joe Kittinger set a balloon distance record in 1984.

    O   Joe Kittinger, in 1984, piloted his balloon from Maine to Italy, setting a new distance record, becoming the first balloonist to cross the Atlantic solo.

18. Crises in international diplomacy do not always result from malice; nations, like individuals, can find themselves locked into difficult positions, unable to back down.

    O   do not always result from malice; nations, like individuals, can find

    O   does not always result from malice; nations, just as individuals, finding

    O   do not always result of malice; nations, such as individuals, can find

    O   are not always the results of malice; nations in the same way that individuals can find

    O   are not resulting always from malice; just like nations and individuals who can find

19. Young ballet dancers and gymnasts sometimes fail to maintain good eating habits caused by the desire to be as thin as possible.

    O   Young ballet dancers and gymnasts sometimes fail to maintain good eating habits caused by the desire to be as thin as possible.

    O   Good eating habits sometimes fail to be maintained by young ballet dancers and gymnasts caused by desiring to be as thin as possible.

    O   Because they desire to be as thin as possible, good eating habits are sometimes not maintained by young ballet dancers and gymnasts.

    O   Good eating habits sometimes fail to be maintained by young ballet dancers and gymnasts because they desire to be as thin as possible.

    O   Young dancers and gymnasts sometimes fail to maintain good eating habits because they desire to be as thin as possible.

20. A talent agent analyzed her company's records in an attempt to determine why they were placing so few actors in roles. She attributed the company's poor performance to the fact that in a majority of the cases she reviewed, the actor sent to an audition did not conform to the description of the character in the casting notes. They were completely inappropriate for the role.

    Which of the following, if true, most supports the talent agent's thinking?

    O   An actor that does not conform to the description of a character in the casting notes will not get hired for the part.

    O   The actors her company represents are not very good.

    O   It is difficult to predict how appropriate an actor will be for a role.

    O   Her company does not send enough actors to audition for major roles.

    O   Directors often cast actors who are inappropriate for the role.

21. Patient: Doctor, you decreased my Olanon from seven milligrams to two but you eliminated the Doril-T entirely. You said you prescribed the Doril-T in order to prevent possible side effects of the Olanon. Since I am still taking the Olanon, shouldn't I also be taking the Doril-T?

Doctor: Since you did not experience any side effects from the seven milligrams of Olanon, there is no reason to fear side effects from two milligrams of Olanon.

Which of the following identifies a problem in the doctor's reasoning?

O   Medications cause side effects in proportion to the amount prescribed.

O   Without Doril-T, a mere two milligrams of Olanon may prove insufficient.

O   The Doril-T may have prevented side effects caused by the Olanon.

O   Since no side effects were experienced from seven milligrams of Olanon, the new prescription should have called for a greater, not lesser, amount.

O   The question as to why no Doril-T was prescribed is not addressed.

22. Analyst: This corporation is currently putting all its efforts into maximizing short-term profits. Whatever happened to our traditional philosophy of slow, steady growth and emphasis on long-term profitability? One aspect of the problem is seen in simple mathematics. Of our 57 district managers, only 7 have been with the corporation for five years or more. In addition, only 5 of our 16 vice presidents and only 2 of the 9 members of the board of directors have been with the corporation for five years.

Which of the following conclusions does the author of this passage most probably want the reader to draw?

O   The corporation needs to seek leadership from outside sources if it is to remain profitable in the long run.

O   One of the reasons that the corporation's traditional financial goals have been ignored is that very few of its high-ranking employees have much experience with the corporation.

O   The only reason that the corporation's traditional financial goals have been ignored is that very few of its high-ranking employees have much experience with the corporation.

O   The corporation's traditional financial goals are outmoded.

O   Even though the corporation's traditional financial goals are being ignored, company management has made great strides by bringing in leadership from outside sources.

GO ON TO THE NEXT PAGE ⟹

23. Hubert Humphrey's attempt in his campaign to dissociate <u>himself from Johnson's foreign policies was built around an emphasis on Humphrey's Senate career</u>.

    O himself from Johnson's foreign policies was built around an emphasis on Humphrey's Senate career

    O him from Johnson's foreign policies were built around an emphasis on Humphrey's Senate career

    O him from Johnson's foreign policies was built around an emphasis on Humphrey's Senate career

    O himself from Johnson's foreign policies were built around an emphasis on Humphrey's Senate career

    O him from Johnson's foreign policies was built around emphasizing the Senate career of the candidate

24. Since conscious patients often died of shock on the operating table, <u>the invention of anesthesia was essential to the development of surgery as the invention of the propeller was to the development of</u> powered flight.

    O the invention of anesthesia was essential to the development of surgery as the invention of the propeller was to the development of

    O inventing anesthesia was as essential for the development of surgery as the invention of the propeller was for the development of

    O the invention of anesthesia was as essential in the development of surgery much as the invention of the propeller had been for the development of

    O the invention of anesthesia was as essential to the development of surgery as the invention of the propeller was to the development of

    O the invention of anesthesia was essential to the development of surgery, so was the invention of the propeller essential to the development of

25. New evidence suggests that women may react differently than men to high blood pressure, or hypertension. Women with hypertension are less likely to suffer from ensuing complications, such as heart attacks or strokes, and are less likely to die as a result. Women's higher estrogen levels may be related to this phenomenon: after menopause, when estrogen levels lower, women gradually become more and more susceptible to cardiovascular disease.

Which of the following positions would be best supported by the statements in the passage above?

    O Very elderly women with high blood pressure are no less susceptible to complications than their male counterparts are.

    O When treating their female patients for hypertension, doctors should take into account whether or not the patient has gone through menopause.

    O Men with hypertension should receive immediate treatment, while women with high blood pressure may wait until their condition becomes severe.

    O Since women withstand high blood pressure more readily than men do, the benefits they receive from lowering it are relatively insignificant.

    O Women with very high blood pressure are as likely to suffer complications from their condition as are men with only slightly elevated blood pressure.

GO ON TO THE NEXT PAGE

26. Unlike football, which is played on a standardized field, <u>baseball fields vary considerably in both size and shape</u>.

    ○ baseball fields vary considerably in both size and shape

    ○ baseball fields vary considerably, in size as well as in shape

    ○ baseball is played on a field that varies considerably in both size and shape

    ○ baseball is played on fields that vary considerably in both size and shape

    ○ baseball is played on a field that varies considerably in size as well as in shape

27. <u>An important reason to be vaccinated would be that vaccination</u> prevents the spread of infectious diseases, such as cholera, typhoid, and typhus, that are prevalent in areas of the world that lack proper sanitation.

    ○ An important reason to be vaccinated would be that vaccination

    ○ Vaccination is important because it

    ○ An important reason to be vaccinated is because it

    ○ You should be vaccinated and this

    ○ An important reason to be vaccinated is that vaccination

Questions 28–31 refer to the following passage.

A pioneering figure in modern sociology, French social theorist Emile Durkheim examined the role of societal cohesion on emotional well-being. Believing that scientific methods should be applied to the
5   study of society, Durkheim studied the level of integration of various social formations and the impact that such cohesion has on individuals within the group. He postulated that social groups with high levels of integration serve to buffer their
10   members from frustrations and tragedies that could otherwise lead to desperation and self-destruction. Integration, in Durkheim's view, generally arises through shared activities and values.

Durkheim distinguished between *mechanical*
15   *solidarity* and *organic solidarity* in classifying integrated groups. *Mechanical solidarity* dominates in groups in which individual differences are minimized and group devotion to a common aim is high. Durkheim identified *mechanical solidarity*
20   among groups with little division of labor and high rates of cultural similarity, such as among more traditional and geographically isolated groups. *Organic solidarity*, in contrast, prevails in groups with high levels of individual differences, such as
25   those with a highly specialized division of labor. In such groups, individual differences are a powerful source of connection, rather than of division. Because people engage in highly differentiated ways of life, they are by necessity interdependent.
30   In such societies, there is greater freedom from some external controls, but such freedom occurs in concert with the interdependence of individuals, not in conflict with it.

Durkheim realized that societies may take many
35   forms and consequently that group allegiance can manifest itself in a variety of ways. In both types of societies outlined above, however, Durkheim stressed that adherence to a common set of assumptions about the world was a
40   necessary prerequisite for maintaining group integrity and avoiding social decay.

GO ON TO THE NEXT PAGE ⇒

28. The author is primarily concerned with illustrating how Durkheim

    O   supported a specific approach to the study of the integration of social groups

    O   compared different ways that group dynamics maintain allegiance among group members

    O   described how a highly specialized division of labor can protect individuals from depression

    O   helped people determine what type of society will best suit their emotional needs

    O   contrasted a traditional view of a social phenomenon with a more recent one

29. The passage contrasts *mechanical solidarity* and *organic solidarity* along which of the following parameters?

    O   the degree to which each relies on objective measures of group coherence

    O   the manner and degree to which members are linked to the central group

    O   the means by which each allows members to rebel against the group norm

    O   the length of time that each has been used to describe the structure of societies

    O   the effectiveness of each in serving the interests of its members

30. It can be inferred from the passage that

    O   as societies develop, they progress from *organic solidarity* to *mechanical solidarity*

    O   group integration enables societies to mask internal differences to the external world

    O   Durkheim preferred *organic solidarity* to *mechanical solidarity*

    O   individuals from societies with high degrees of *organic solidarity* would be unable to communicate effectively with individuals from societies that rest on *mechanical solidarity*

    O   the presence of some type of group integration is more important for group perpetuation than the specific form in which it is manifested

31. The passage states that *organic solidarity* predominates in societies with relatively high levels of intragroup dissimilarity because

    O   it enables individual differences to be minimized

    O   it causes societies to become more highly specialized, thus aiding industrialization

    O   individuals who engage in highly specialized activities must rely on others to ensure that their basic needs are met

    O   these societies are at greater risk of being affected by social stressors

    O   these societies are more likely to engage in shared activities and values

GO ON TO THE NEXT PAGE

32. The impact of the 1930s crisis on the different regions of Country X varied depending on the relationship of each region's economy to the international marketplace, with Region A most drastically affected. Interestingly, demand in foreign markets for Region A's tropical crops was only slightly affected by the drop in income levels after 1929; the same was true of foreign demand for the temperate-zone basic foodstuffs produced by Region B. However, Region B was better able to survive the crisis, largely avoiding the economic damage suffered by Region A's economy.

    Which one of the following provides the most reasonable explanation for the fact that Region A's economy was more drastically affected by the slight decrease in demand than was Region B's?

    O   Tropical crops like those produced by Region A usually command higher prices on the world market than do basic foodstuffs like those produced by Region B.

    O   Region B's economy was dependent on annual crops, the supply of which is easily adjusted because the plants are renewed each year, in contrast to the perennial crops grown in Region A.

    O   Because tropical goods are generally bought by more affluent consumers, demand for these products rarely declines even when overall income levels drop.

    O   The temperate-zone basic foodstuffs produced in Region B directly competed with similar crops produced by the countries that imported Region B's goods.

    O   Because Region B's economy was dependent on the export of basic foodstuffs, there was only a slight decline in demand for its goods even after income levels dropped.

33. Through their selective funding of research projects, pharmaceutical companies exert too much influence upon medical research in universities. Only research proposals promising lucrative results are given serious consideration, and funding is usually awarded to scientists at large institutions who already have vast research experience. As a result, only larger universities will be able to continue developing adequate research facilities, and graduate students will learn that their future research must conform to the expectations of the corporation. Research will continue to be conducted at the expense of human welfare.

    The reasoning of the argument above depends upon which of the following assumptions?

    O   As universities become primarily research institutions, teaching will be neglected.

    O   Graduate students are not motivated by humane interests.

    O   Smaller universities would be better suited to serve as product development laboratories for pharmaceutical companies.

    O   Medical research should be funded by government-regulated foundations.

    O   The interests of pharmaceutical companies and human welfare are usually incompatible in research.

GO ON TO THE NEXT PAGE

34. <u>Prosecutors use a reliable forensic method, graphology, in forgery cases, which</u> may also be used by employers to uncover clues to prospective employees' characters.

    O   Prosecutors use a reliable forensic method, graphology, in forgery cases, which

    O   Prosecutors in forgery cases that have used graphology as a reliable forensic method and

    O   Graphology, a reliable forensic method used by prosecutors in forgery cases

    O   As a reliable forensic method, prosecutors use graphology in forgery cases, which

    O   Prosecutors which use graphology in forgery cases, a reliable forensic method

35. Until recently, parents whose teenaged child had signed a purchase contract <u>without their written agreement were not</u> liable for the child's debt.

    O   without their written agreement were not

    O   that they do not agree in writing have not been

    O   and they had not agreed in writing had not been

    O   without them agreeing in writing had not been

    O   without their written agreement are not

36. The Laysan rail, an insectivorous bird once present on several of the Hawaiian Islands, can no longer be found and is thought to be extinct. Scientists originally thought that a decrease in the amount of ground vegetation available for nesting was responsible for the decline of the bird. However, they now believe that increased competition for food was ultimately responsible for the Laysan rail's inability to survive.

    Which of the following would best help to account for the change in the accepted explanation for the Laysan rail's extinction?

    O   The vegetation on the Laysan rail's home island was decimated when rabbits were introduced to the island in the 1910s.

    O   When attempts were made to relocate the Laysan rail to other islands, the birds lost the geographical cues on which they relied to find mating sites.

    O   The Laysan rail builds nests under dense ground cover to protect its eggs.

    O   A recent study found that an increase in the use of pesticides resulted in a decrease in the numbers of insects present in the Laysan rail's territory.

    O   Many species nested in the same types of vegetation as the Laysan rail.

Answers and Explanations

1.	B	10.	C	19.	E	28.	B
2.	A	11.	A	20.	A	29.	B
3.	D	12.	B	21.	C	30.	E
4.	C	13.	D	22.	B	31.	C
5.	E	14.	E	23.	A	32.	B
6.	B	15.	C	24.	D	33.	E
7.	D	16.	B	25.	B	34.	C
8.	E	17.	C	26.	D	35.	A
9.	D	18.	A	27.	B	36.	D

1. B

(A) contains a modification error: "the water that later evolved" is illogical, since the mammals, not the water, evolved into whales. Scanning the beginnings of the choices lets you eliminate (E), because "evidence of support" changes the meaning of the sentence. Also, "theory of land mammals that returned" is unidiomatic; the correct phrasing would be "theory that land mammals returned." (C) also uses this incorrect phrasing. By repeating "that," (D) is wordy. (B) expresses the intended idea clearly and correctly.

2. A

The author is contrasting new and old roller coasters. Roller coasters are correctly compared to other roller coasters, and the adjectives "more" and "longer" are correct for comparing two things. There is no error in this sentence. In (B), it doesn't make sense to refer to a singular old-fashioned roller coaster. The "whereas" in (C) is redundant and makes the sentence ungrammatical, given the "although" at the beginning. (D) lacks a main verb, turning the sentence into a fragment. (E) is unparallel; the first part of the comparison talks about features modern roller coasters "have," so the second part needs to say older rides "have" different features. Also, the original sentence doesn't say the drops are "straighter"; adding this comparison changes the meaning of the sentence.

3. D

The Conclusion: The governor's survey on solid waste disposal must have had skewed results.

The Evidence: Eighty percent of respondents support a rise in spending for environmentally safe disposal of solid waste.

The author assumes that most people who respond to this kind of survey will favor environmental safety—she's arguing that the respondents weren't representative of the population as a whole.

The author doesn't think that only environmentalists received the survey, (A), but that a disproportionate number of respondents are environmentalists. She isn't criticizing the judgment of "most citizens," (B). It's not that there's a problem with the survey itself, (C), but with the interpretation of the survey. And you don't know anything about the author's opinion on solid waste issues, (E).

4. C

The Conclusion: People aren't cheating on their taxes as much as they used to.

The Evidence: The amount, in dollars, of taxes collected from personal income tax has gone up appreciably in recent years.

The stimulus is only concerned with revenue from the personal income tax, so any information about the corporate taxes is outside the realm of interest.

All the wrong choices provide alternative explanations—explanations as to how more tax dollars can be collected without people being more honest in reporting their incomes. Fewer deductions, (A), would probably cause people to pay more money in taxes. A population increase, (B), would produce more tax payers. If average income went up, (D), then average tax paid would go up as well. And if the tax rate rose, (E), the government would very likely collect more money.

PASSAGE 1—Forset

Topic and Scope: A worldview prevalent in post-Reformation England.

Purpose and Main Idea: The author says that many English people after the Reformation conceived of the world as a system of hierarchies, in which the king's or queen's position as ruler is part of the natural order of things and reflects God's plan.

Paragraph Structure: In a single paragraph, the author explains why early English Protestants hungered for order, and how the concept of order that some thinkers came up with coincided with the will of the British monarchs.

5.   E

(E) is a fairly direct paraphrase of the idea stated in the passage's opening sentence, with the added inference that the Catholic Church formerly provided structure and stability to English society. There is nothing to suggest (A), that the monarchy was declining. Quite the contrary, according to the rest of the passage: Elizabeth and other monarchs managed quite well to maintain their grip on power, at least temporarily. The passage also implies something contrary to (B); rather than being seen as eccentric or peculiar, the "divinely inspired" hierarchical view of Forset and other thinkers won wide acceptance. Contrary to (C), the need for order was felt to be "compelling," as it's put in the first sentence. As for (D), there's no evidence for this idea. The passage mentions the Catholic Church simply as having been rejected, nothing more.

6.   B

This choice puts together the idea of hierarchy, as found in Forset and other thinkers, with the statement in the last sentence that people accepted stability as God's will. The implication is that Elizabeth and her successors maintained their influence and power because English society accepted the idea of a divinely prescribed social structure in which the monarch occupied the top of the social heap. Choice (A) exaggerates the role of the thinkers. Yes, they apparently had the ear of the public, but to say they were a small group that had tight, almost conspiratorial control is too extreme. It's inconsistent with the passage's tone. (C) puts things backwards; as the sentence about Elizabeth and Parliament make clear, the monarchs claimed a position far above that of most people. That same sentence also makes clear that Parliament, while apparently not mounting effective resistance to Elizabeth, was nonetheless "recalcitrant," not passive. Finally, (E) could be true, but there is nothing to suggest it in the passage; what the passage does do is tie Elizabeth's success to the idea of divine sanction for social hierarchy, and this should lead you back to correct choice (B).

7.   D

This choice is supported by two references in the passage. The first is the reference to a "recalcitrant Parliament"; the second is the veiled suggestion in the last sentence that there were restive elements in English society that had to be held down or kept in check by the monarchy, and that the English public's interim acceptance of a divine hierarchical scheme aided the monarchy in this situation. This choice completes the thought by adding the plausible idea that Parliament represented these rebellious interests. The other choices all fail, in one way or another, to follow the logic of the passage's ideas. Choice (A) contradicts the last sentence's suggestion that the monarchs' grip on power was short-lived. (B) contradicts the widespread acceptance and immediate influence of Forset's notions. (C) is inconsistent with the apparent opposition of Parliament to a political hierarchy in which the monarch was the unquestioned authority. (E), lastly, illogically pits Elizabeth against her staunch advocate, Forset.

8. E

The Conclusion: Critics' opinions aren't any more reliable than those of the average person.

The Evidence: Critics tend to have similar points of view that are rooted in the prejudices of their class.

The author seems to believe that critics' opinions aren't necessarily more significant than those of the average Joe, so (E), a restatement of the main idea, is a logical conclusion. Their opinions are no more likely to be a guide to quality, so when they disagree with the public, they're no more likely to be right.

Though the author says that critics' opinions aren't more correct than those of average moviegoers, he doesn't imply that they're usually incorrect, (A). It's not that there are no right or wrong judgments about films, (B), but that critics don't always make the right judgments. You don't know how frequently critics dislike popular movies, (C), just that it's often assumed that they have valid reasons for doing so. And (D), that critics agree about any given movie, is too strong, since the author only says that their opinions tend to reflect certain class prejudices.

9. D

The pronoun "which" needs to refer to a noun. The author means it to refer to "increasing U.S. participation in the war," but "increasing" is not in this sentence, and "which" cannot refer to the verb "increased." Eliminate (A). The correct connector is "as," and the verb "did" needs to be included to complete the comparison between Kennedy's action and Johnson's action. This makes (D) correct. (B) has the same pronoun problem as (A) and is wordy. (C) omits the verb that gives Johnson an action. (E) is redundant with "did do."

10. C

The wording "the reason . . . is because" is redundant, since the meaning of "because" is included in "reason." The correct phrasing is "the reason . . . is *that*." This phrasing does not appear in the choices, so the correct answer must solve the problem a different way. (D) commits the same error as (A). (B) has a pronoun error, because a possessive such as "Scipio Africanus's"

cannot be the antecedent of "he." In (E), "the reason being" is too informal and wordy. (C) states the author's idea clearly and correctly.

11. A

What follows the verb "requires" should be the word "that" and the infinitive form of the verb without the word "to" before it. Since the underlined portion already follows this guideline, this sentence is correct as written, and (A) is the correct answer. (B) incorrectly replaces the subjunctive "be present" with the infinitive "to be present." (C) changes the correct subjunctive verb phrase to the future "will be present." (D) and (E) use the wordy "has a requirement." In addition, "requirement of students' being" and "has a requirement to have" are unidiomatic.

PASSAGE 2—Group Management

Topic and Scope: The value of group management; specifically, the benefits and risks of using decisional conflict in group management.

Purpose and Main Idea: Author agrees that building conflict into group management is good (it leads to better managerial decisions), but stresses that there are potential risks. Experts are divided over what form of decisional conflict is best (and least risky).

Paragraph Structure: Paragraph 1 acknowledges the value of group decision making and the use of decisional conflict, and identifies the risks, the "dilemma," involved in using decisional conflict: "Decisional conflict may yield better decisions at the risk of weakening managerial effectiveness. Conversely, the harmony that facilitates cooperation and implementation may come at the cost of inferior decisions." Paragraph 2 identifies two methods of building conflict into group decisions (dialectical inquiry and devil's advocacy) and explains the similarities and differences. Paragraph 3 explains how experts disagree about which approach is better.

12. B

Choice (B) covers all the paragraphs. Paragraph 1 discusses the benefits and risks of decisional conflict, and paragraphs 2 and 3 focus on the two alternative approaches.

(A) ignores the discussion of the *risks* of decisional conflict. And the author never tries to "reconcile" the two approaches. The verb "defend" makes choice (C) suspect; the author never defends anything against critics. (D) doesn't work because the author never implies that group decision making is better than any other approach. As for (E), the author never indicates a preference for dialectical inquiry or devil's advocacy.

13. D

Paragraph 2 details similarities as well as differences between the two approaches. One similarity is that both rely on "formal debate," which clearly implies choice (D).

(A) is an irrelevant detail; the only mention of "compromise" is at the end of the passage where Cosier charges that dialectical inquiry could lead to compromises and inferior decisions. The problem with (B) is that only dialectical inquiry involves "opposing sets of proposals." (C) and (E), like (A), refer to irrelevant details in the last paragraph.

Note: Even without a line reference, the stem must steer you to paragraph 2. After a fast, *strategic* skimming of the passage, you should be equipped to recognize where the answer will be found.

14. E

You need the choice that's *inconsistent* with one of Cosier's criticisms, one of which is that dialectical inquiry "may run counter to managers' accustomed ways of thinking." (E) would cast doubt on this criticism: "Managers willing to alter their usual modes of thinking often make better decisions."

(A) doesn't work because it paraphrases—and therefore would support—one of Cosier's criticisms. With (B), Cosier implies nothing about "demanding that managers agree" about a decision. Choice (C) is a point that Cosier and everyone else connected with this passage would agree with. (D), like (B), is an irrelevant point;

Cosier says nothing about the need for some decisions to be made rapidly.

15. C

Application questions like this one ask you to recognize a choice that's consistent with information in the passage. (C) parallels the passage's *basic idea* about management groups: the opening sentence states that "corporate managers often work in groups because of the complexity of strategic problems." In a similar way, in (C), "a committee of administrators forms to address the major problems of running a hospital." The hospital is a type of corporation, and its administrators work as a group to solve its problems.

None of the other choices supplies a parallel situation: monitoring election results, (A), investigating governmental misconduct, (B), studying an issue of public concern, (D), and observing a college presidential search, (E), are all different from running a corporation.

16. B

The Conclusion: Money spent to make the workplace more pleasant is the cause of stumbling and failing businesses.

The Evidence: New businesses almost always fail, and many established businesses show little or no profit. Workers want expensive perks like paint and radios.

The assumption here is that providing these niceties works only to the detriment or disadvantage of the businesses—that it's as simple as spending money and getting no return. You weaken the argument by denying this assumption and showing that the perks increase productivity. In this case, the new paint, radios, and artwork might well be a wise investment.

Even if the workers work very hard, (A), it doesn't mean that they don't make excessive demands on their employers. It could be possible that in the past, businesses went under for other reasons, (C), and yet still be true that they are now going under because of the perks. The author hasn't claimed that different types of businesses are the same thing, as in (D) and (E), but rather, that they're in trouble for the same reason.

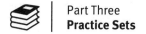
17. C

One way to start with this sentence is to try to figure out what's most important. Joe Kittinger seems to have done two equally important things: he set a distance record and he became the first balloonist to cross the Atlantic solo. Choice (C) puts these two achievements on an equal footing by expressing them both in participial phrases ("setting" and "becoming"). So does (E), but it omits the "and," which is necessary. Choices (A), (B), and (D) fail to make it clear that it was by piloting his balloon from Maine to Italy that Kittinger accomplished these two things.

18. A

First, "crises" is the plural form of "crisis," so (B), with the singular verb "does," is wrong. Next, "do not always result of malice" in (C) is unidiomatic, and "aren't resulting always from malice" in (E) is awkward. Whereas the original sentence logically compares "nations" to "individuals," (D) muddles this relationship, seeming to compare "the way" that nations do something to the way individuals do something. To make this comparison work, "that" would need to be "as." The sentence is correct as written, so choose (A).

19. E

The problem here has to do with the placement of the modifier. What is caused by the desire to be as thin as possible? Not good eating habits, though that's the impression you could get from (A), and not the ballet dancers and gymnasts, though that's the impression you could get from (B). Eliminate both these choices. And who or what desires to be as thin as possible? Again, not good eating habits, though you could get that impression from (C) or (D), both of which use the passive voice unnecessarily and confusingly. The correct answer is (E), in which pronoun reference and the placement of modifiers are perfectly clear.

20. A

The Conclusion: The reason why the talent agency is failing is because they are the wrong actors to audition for roles.

The Evidence: Few actors from the agency are being placed in roles, and the actors being sent to auditions do not fit the descriptions listed in the casting notes.

The talent agent must believe that sending actors who don't match the description of characters is a bad idea, and that's why her actors aren't getting hired. But what if it were true that casting directors enjoyed seeing different types of actors audition for roles, even those that didn't match the description in the casting notes? (A) removes this possible alternative, and in turn strengthens the talent agent's argument.

The actors' talent, (B), isn't questioned by the agent; she focuses on the types of roles. That it's hard to predict an actor's appropriateness, (C), needn't be assumed—it has no effect on the argument. She could, on the contrary, think it easy to judge a role's appropriateness, and just believe that her company employs incompetents. Major roles, (D), are outside the scope, since the agent doesn't mention them. And if it were true that directors often cast the wrong actors, (E), then the argument would be weakened, not strengthened.

21. C

The Doctor's Conclusion: The patient doesn't need to take Doril-T, the side-effect preventing drug.

The Doctor's Evidence: Since the patient didn't have side effects on 7 mg of Olanon, he won't have side effects on 2 mg.

What's the doctor missing here? The idea that the patient probably didn't have side effects on 7 mg because he was taking the Doril-T, the drug intended to prevent side effects. The doctor basically assumes that this drug had no effect yet presents no evidence.

The doctor seems to believe, (A), that the smaller the amount taken, the less likelihood of side effects—so this isn't a flaw. There is nothing to indicate that the two drugs work together, (B), to produce the desired effect. Why would the doctor prescribe more Olanon, (D)? Nothing is stated about the positive or negative effects of increasing the dose, so this is not a flaw in the doctor's reasoning. And (E) is just plain false, since the doctor does describe why no Doril-T was prescribed—because the patient hasn't had side effects.

22. B

The Analyst's Conclusion: The company is moving away from its long-term growth commitment and putting all its eggs into the short-term profits basket.

Her Evidence: Few of the company's top managers have been with the company for more than five years.

What does the author want you to think about all of this? That these "newcomers" have caused the shift in emphasis, and thus, traditional values have been ignored. Otherwise, why argue for the shift in policy by pointing to the relatively short tenure of many of the top managers?

The author wouldn't advocate bringing in more newcomers, (A), since she thinks that they've caused all the trouble. It is too extreme to conclude that the newcomers are the only reason for the trouble, (C), especially since she refers to them as "one aspect of the problem." The author yearns for traditional values, so she wouldn't want to argue that they are outmoded, (D). And strong support for the company's hiring of newcomers, (E), is counter to the apparent feelings of the author.

23. A

This sentence talks about what Humphrey attempted to do to Humphrey, so it requires the reflexive pronoun "himself," not "him." You can rule out (B), (C), and (E). Now, "attempt," the noun, is singular, so it has to govern a singular verb: "was," not "were," so (D) is out.

24. D

This sentence makes a comparison, so the correct answer will use the "as . . . as" construction. The first "as" is missing in (A). Choice (C) turns the second "as" into "much as," which spoils the construction. Choice (E) omits the "as . . . as" formula altogether and creates a run-on sentence. The things being compared must be in parallel form, and this is not the case in (B) with "inventing . . . the invention of."

25. B

The Conclusion: That's what you're looking for.

The Evidence: Women with high blood pressure are less likely to have heart attacks or strokes than are men with the same condition. This may be related to estrogen levels—after menopause, when estrogen is lowered, women are more likely to get cardiovascular disease.

What's a logical conclusion? That doctors would be wise to take into account whether their female patients are pre- or post-menopausal, since estrogen levels will probably have an effect on their treatment needs. Perfectly reasonable.

There's no information that would allow you to conclude (A), that old women are as susceptible as old men, or that (E), women with very high blood pressure face the same risks as men with only slightly high blood pressure. In addition, you can't go so far as to claim that women can wait for treatment, (C). (D) is another distortion. Even though women are less likely to suffer complications from high blood pressure, you can't infer that they receive almost no benefit from lowering their high blood pressure.

26. D

"Unlike" signals a comparison. Start by making sure that it's logical. Football can be compared with baseball, but not with baseball fields. This eliminates (A) and (B). And of course, a single field cannot vary in size and shape; it is different fields that vary. Since (D) uses the plural "fields," it is correct.

27. B

Would be? No, it is; eliminate (A). "The reason . . . is because," in (C), is redundant. In (D), there is no clear antecedent for "this." This leaves (B) and (E). Choice (E) unnecessarily repeats "vaccinated" and "vaccination."

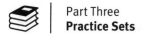
PASSAGE 3—Durkheim

Topic and Scope: Emile Durkheim's study of social cohesion in society.

Purpose and Main Idea: To describe Durkheim's beliefs regarding two different ways that societies can maintain social integration among their members.

Paragraph Structure: The first paragraph introduces Durkheim and his study of social groups. The second paragraph discusses two ways societies can maintain social integration. The third paragraph offers a broader context for interpreting the evidence in the second paragraph.

28. B

The final paragraph gives you the key to answering this Global question. The author describes how Durkheim's work illustrates the different ways that societies can function without choosing a side or advocating a specific position. You can rule out choice (A) immediately for its strong stand. Choice (C) distorts a detail beyond its acceptable scope. While the passage does discuss how social cohesion can function in societies with high degrees of labor specialization, this is not the author's main interest in Durkheim's work. Choice (D) takes a prescriptive stance, and neither the author nor Durkheim seek to directly help people here. Finally, choice (E) makes a comparison that is not there. Both of the mechanisms for maintaining social solidarity were developed by Durkheim at the same time and are part of the same worldview, namely, his. The comparison between a traditional and a recent view is inapplicable here.

29. B

What is the crucial difference between *mechanical solidarity* and *organic solidarity*? The level of homogeneity in the group in which each functions. Neither one relies on any measure, objective or otherwise, of group coherence. Rather, they describe the way societies function naturally, ruling out choice (A). Choice (C) introduces the notion of rebellion, a concept that is not mentioned in the passage and, hence, cannot be correct. Choice (D) is wrong because the two types of solidarity were developed at the same time by Durkheim; nothing in the passage indicates a traditional view and a more recent view of the same phenomenon, but rather two different ways that societies can function within the same worldview. Choice (E) brings into question the effectiveness of each, but the last paragraph makes it clear that either one can serve its members' needs equally well.

30. E

In this Inference question, you will need to think about the author's opinion as you approach the answer choices. Choice (A) is wrong because the author never discusses the two forms of *solidarity* as being related to each other, nor does he discuss the transformation of societies over time. Choice (B) is outside the scope, as the relationship of individual societies to the world at large is not an issue that concerns the author. Choice (C) makes a subjective statement about Durkheim that is never suggested by the passage. Choice (D) makes a comparison between the two types of social groups that is not supported by the passage. Choice (E), however, is closely matched by information in the final paragraph of the passage. The particular type of integration that exists within a given society is less important than that it is present in some form.

31. C

Look to the second paragraph, where *organic solidarity* is discussed, and you will see Durkheim's reasoning for why it exists in societies with high levels of heterogeneity. *Organic solidarity* prevails in societies with fewer similarities among members, because when a society is highly specialized, its members rely on each other out of necessity, as a way to ensure that everyone's needs are met. Reading through the answers, choice (C) should jump out at you as conveying this idea.

Choice (A) runs counter to the passage. In societies in which *organic solidarity* dominates, individual differences are relatively high. Choice (B) implies a causal relationship between *organic solidarity* and the way a society is organized, but *organic solidarity* is simply a term to describe the way a society *is* functioning; it is not an active agent of anything. Choice (D) uses information that was never mentioned in the passage—namely, that some societies are more likely to be affected by social stressors. Finally, choice (E) misappropriates information from the section on societies in which *mechanical solidarity* dominates. Societies that operate by *organic solidarity*, by contrast, tend not to comprise members who lead highly similar lives.

32. B

The Evidence: In an economic crisis, the demand for crops produced in both Regions A and B dropped only slightly, but Region B suffered less economic damage than Region A did.

Because the question stem says you are looking for an "explanation," this is an Explain question.

The two facts presented in the stimulus are (1) demand for the crops produced by Region A and for those produced by Region B dropped only slightly, and (2) Region B was better able to survive the crisis, while Region A's economy was devastated.

(A) might seem to explain Region A's difficulty in an economic crisis. But the stimulus says that demand fell only slightly for Region A's foodstuffs and that the demand for Region B's dropped by the same amount. So (A) is irrelevant.

(B) states that Region B can adjust the supply of its crops and Region A cannot. Even if you don't know what "perennial" means, the answer choice explicitly says that such crops cannot be easily adjusted. (B) is, therefore, the correct answer.

(C) explains why one might expect Region A to do well in an economic downturn, so it hardly constitutes an explanation for why it didn't. (D), if anything, would explain why Region B did poorly, not well. (E) is consistent with only part of the facts. It shows why Region B's demand didn't fall much, but you know that Region A's demand was affected similarly. So, this answer doesn't explain the differing fortunes of the two region's economies.

33. E

The Conclusion: Research at universities will be conducted at the expense of human welfare.

The Evidence: Research is funded by pharmaceutical companies, so research must be conducted in order to meet the expectations of the corporation.

You need an assumption, and if you compare evidence and conclusion (including the author's dire prediction), you find an element for which there's no evidence: the idea of "human welfare." The author must be assuming that the interests of these companies and human welfare are usually at odds in order to conclude that research conducted in the interests of the companies won't be compatible with human welfare.

The quality of university teaching, (A), has nothing to do with this argument. The author doesn't argue that grad students aren't interested in humane pursuits, (B), but rather that they must conform to the companies' expectations. That smaller universities are better for

research from the companies' perspective, (C), is way off—the companies, you're told, are only funding the larger universities. And government-regulated foundations, (D), are irrelevant. The author may well believe that some other type of funding is needed, but this particular remedy is not required by the argument.

34. C

By putting the pronoun "which" next to "forgery cases," (A) and (D) make it seem as if it's forgery cases that employers may use to learn about job applicants. But the employers are really using graphology to do this. (C) expresses this thought clearly. (B) is incomplete and nonsensical. (E) makes it sound as if forgery cases are a forensic method.

35. A

The nonunderlined verb "had signed" lets you know the author is talking about the past. So (E) is definitely out. The child didn't sign a "contract that they do not agree," so (B) can't be right. In (C) and (D), the phrases "and they had not agreed in writing" and "without them agreeing in writing" are unclear. They make it sound as if the parents need to agree with each other. In (A), "without their agreement" makes it clear that the parents need to agree to the contract to make it valid.

36. D

The Conclusion: Scientists now believe that the extinction of the Laysan rail was caused by a loss of food rather than a loss of ground vegetation.

The Evidence: There is none; this is what you'll need to find in the correct answer.

The question is very specific about what to look for: evidence that would explain why scientists changed their theory about why the Laysan rail is now extinct. Look closely in the stimulus to find the new theory. Scientists first attributed the extinction to a loss of ground vegetation, which the birds used for nesting, but now they believe the cause was a loss of food. Since the birds are insectivores, this means a loss of insects. What evidence would support this new conclusion? A reasonable prediction would be "data showing a decrease in the availability of insects." Sure enough, that's what (D) says.

Perhaps you missed the word "insectivorous" in the stimulus, so your prediction was the more general "less food available." In that case, both (A) and (D) might have seemed tempting. When this happens, check the stimulus again to get a clearer sense of the scope. Asking yourself, "So do these birds eat plants, per (A), or do they eat flies and moths, per (D)?" would lead you to the word "insectivorous."

PART FOUR

Analytical Writing Assessment

CHAPTER 9

Analytical Writing Assessment

> **LEARNING OBJECTIVES**
>
> After studying this chapter, you will be able to:
>
> - List important attributes of the Analytical Writing Assessment (AWA) section, including question format, timing, and scoring
> - Explain how the principles of language control, clarity, and logical organization will help you manage the AWA
> - Write an Analysis of an Argument essay that earns a satisfactory score on the AWA

At the beginning of the GMAT, you have the option to decide when to take the Analytical Writing Assessment (AWA). You can choose to take it as the first or the last section on your GMAT. Regardless of whether you choose to tackle it before or after the other sections, the AWA is always 30 minutes in length.

For the essay, you will analyze a given topic and then type your essay into a simple word processing program. It allows you to do only the following basic functions:

- Insert text
- Delete text
- Cut and paste
- Undo the previous action
- Scroll up and down on the screen

Spell-check and grammar-check functions are not available in the program, so you will have to check those things carefully yourself. One or two spelling errors or a few minor grammatical errors will not lower your score. But many spelling errors can hurt your score, as can errors that are serious enough to obscure your intended meaning.

Thirty minutes is not enough time to produce the same kind of essay you've written for college classes. Nor is it enough time to do a lot of trial and error as you type. It is, however, enough time to write a "strong first draft" if you plan carefully, and that's what the essay graders are looking for.

Essay Format and Structure

At the start of the AWA, you'll be given a brief tutorial on how to use the word processor. If you are concerned that you do not type very fast, you should practice giving yourself 30 minutes to brainstorm and type AWA essays between now and Test Day. By doing so, you will get an idea of how much you can type in the time allotted; your typing speed might also improve with practice.

Your task for the Argument essay is to assess the logic and use of evidence in an argument. It doesn't matter whether you agree or disagree with the argument's conclusion. Rather, you need to explain the ways in which the author has failed to fully support that conclusion.

Take a look at the sample prompt below:

> The following appeared in a memo from the CEO of Hula Burger, a chain of hamburger restaurants.
>
> "Officials in the video game industry report that over 60 percent of the video games released last year targeted an age 13–17 audience. Moreover, sales data indicate that, nationally, hamburgers are the favorite food among this age group. Since a branch store of Ultimate Video Games opened in town last year, hamburger sales at our restaurant next door have been higher than at any other restaurant in our chain. Because the sale and rental of video games seem to stimulate hamburger sales, the best way to increase our profits is to open new Hula Burger restaurants as near to other Ultimate Video Games stores as possible."
>
> Consider how logical you find this argument. In your essay, be sure to discuss the line of reasoning and the use of evidence in the argument. For example, you may need to consider what questionable assumptions underlie the thinking and what alternative explanations or counterpoints might weaken the conclusion. You may also discuss what types of evidence would strengthen or refute the argument, what changes in the argument would make it more logically sound, and what, if anything, would help you better evaluate its conclusion.

Where are the holes in the argument? In what ways does it fail to be completely convincing? Why might the plan fail? Not only do you have to identify its major weaknesses, you must also explain them.

The Basic Principles of Analytical Writing

You aren't being evaluated solely on the strength of your ideas. Your score will also depend on how well you express them. If your writing style isn't clear, your ideas won't come across, no matter how brilliant they are.

Good essay writing isn't just grammatically correct. It is also clear and concise. The following principles will help you express your ideas in good GMAT style.

Your Control of Language Is Important

Writing that is grammatical, concise, direct, and persuasive displays the "superior control of language" (as the test maker terms it) that earns top GMAT Analytical Writing scores. To achieve effective GMAT style in your essays, you should pay attention to the following points.

Grammar

Your writing must follow the same general rules of standard written English that are tested by Sentence Correction questions. If you're not confident of your mastery of grammar, review the Sentence Correction chapter of this book.

Diction

Diction means word choice. Do you use the words *affect* and *effect* correctly? What about *its* and *it's*, *there* and *their*, *precede* and *proceed*, *principal* and *principle*, and *whose* and *who's*? In addition to avoiding errors of usage, you will need to demonstrate your ability to use language precisely and employ a formal, professional tone.

Syntax

Syntax refers to sentence structure. Do you construct your sentences so that your ideas are clear and understandable? Do you vary the length and structure of your sentences?

Keep Things Simple

Perhaps the single most important piece of advice to bear in mind when writing a GMAT essay is to keep everything simple. This rule applies to word choice, sentence structure, and organization. If you obsess about how to use or spell an unusual word, you can lose your way. The more complicated your sentences are, the more likely they'll be plagued by errors. The more complex your organization becomes, the more likely your argument will get bogged down in convoluted sentences that obscure your point.

Keep in mind that simple does not mean *simplistic*. A clear, straightforward approach can still be sophisticated and convey perceptive insights.

Minor Grammatical Flaws Won't Harm Your Score

Many test takers mistakenly believe they'll lose points over a few mechanical errors. That's not the case. GMAT essays should be final first drafts. This means that a couple of misplaced commas, misspellings, or other minor glitches aren't going to affect your score. Occasional mistakes of this type are acceptable and inevitable, given that you have only 30 minutes to construct your essay. In fact, according to the scoring rubric, a top-scoring essay may well have a few minor grammatical flaws.

But if your essay is littered with misspellings and grammar mistakes, the graders may conclude that you have a serious communication problem. Keep in mind that sentence fragments are not acceptable, nor are informal structures such as bullet points or numerical enumeration (e.g., *(1)* instead of *first*). So be concise, forceful, and correct. An effective essay wastes no words; makes its point in a clear, direct way; and conforms to the generally accepted rules of grammar and style.

Use a Logical Structure

Good essays have a straightforward, linear structure. The problem is that we rarely think in a straightforward, linear way. That's why it's so important to plan your response before you begin typing. If you type while planning, your essay will likely loop back on itself, contain redundancies, or fail to follow through on what it sets up.

Logical structure consists of three things:

Paragraph Unity

Paragraph unity means each paragraph discusses one thing and all the discussion of that one thing happens in that paragraph. Let's say that you're responding to the essay prompt we just saw and one of your points is that there may have been reasons for the success of the Hula Burger restaurant other than its proximity to the

Ultimate Video Games store. Your next paragraph should move on to another idea—perhaps something about the expense of opening a new Hula Burger restaurant near every other Ultimate Video Games store. If, in the middle of that next paragraph, you went back to your point about other possible reasons for the success of the Hula Burger restaurant, you'd be violating paragraph unity.

Train of Thought

This is similar to paragraph unity, but it applies to the whole essay. It's confusing to the reader when an essay keeps jumping back and forth between the different weaknesses of an argument. Discuss one point fully, and then address the next. Don't write another paragraph about a topic you've already discussed.

Flow

The basic idea of flow is that you should deliver on what you promise and not radically change the subject. If your introductory paragraph says that you will mention reasons why Hula burgers might be less popular among the 8- to 12-year-old demographic than regular hamburgers are, you need to make sure that you actually do so. Similarly, avoid suddenly expanding the scope of the essay in the last sentence.

TAKEAWAYS

- Your control of language is important.
- Keep things simple.
- Minor grammatical flaws won't harm your score.
- Use a logical structure.

How the AWA Is Scored

Your essays will be graded on a scale from 0 to 6 (highest). You'll receive one score, which will be an average of the scores that you receive from each of the two graders, rounded up to the nearest half point. Your essay will be graded by a human grader as well as a computerized essay grader (the IntelliMetric™ system). The two grade completely independently of each other—IntelliMetric isn't told the human's score, nor is the human told the computer's.

If the two scores are identical, then that's your score. If the scores differ by one point, those scores are averaged. If they differ by more than one point, a second human will grade the essay to resolve any differences. IntelliMetric and the human grader agree on the same grade about 55 percent of the time and agree on identical or adjacent grades 97 percent of the time. (Only 3 percent of essays need rereading.) These figures are equivalent to how often two trained human graders agree.

IntelliMetric was designed to make the same judgments that a good human grader would. In fact, part of the Graduate Management Admission Council's (GMAC's) argument for the validity of IntelliMetric is that its performance is statistically indistinguishable from a human's. Still, you should remember that it is not a human and write accordingly.

IntelliMetric's grading algorithm was designed using 400 officially graded essays for each prompt. That's a huge sample of responses, so don't worry about whether IntelliMetric will understand your ideas—it's highly likely that someone out of those 400 responses made a similar point.

Before you begin to write, outline your essay. Good organization always counts, but with a computer grader, it's more important than ever. Use transitional phrases like *first*, *therefore*, *since*, and *for example* so that the computer can recognize structured arguments. The length of your essay is not a factor; the computer does not count the number of words in your response.

Furthermore, computers are not good judges of humor or creativity. (The human judges don't reward those either. The standard is business writing, and you shouldn't be making overly witty or irreverent remarks in, say, an email to a CEO.)

Though IntelliMetric doesn't grade spelling per se, it could give you a lower score if it can't understand you or thinks you used the wrong words.

Here's what your essay will be graded on:

Structure: Does your essay have good paragraph unity, organization, and flow?

Evidence: It's not enough simply to assert good points. Do you develop them well? How strong are the examples you provide?

Depth of Logic: Did you take apart the argument and analyze its major weaknesses effectively?

Style: The GMAC calls this "control of the elements of standard written English." How well do you express your ideas?

Now let's take a more in-depth look at the scoring scale so you get a sense of what to aim for. The following rubric shows how the GMAC will grade your essay based on the four categories of Structure, Evidence, Depth of Logic, and Style:

	1 Seriously Deficient	2 Substantially Flawed	3 Inadequate	4 Satisfactory	5 Good	6 Excellent
Structure	Lacks length and organization; *does not adhere* to topic.	Lacks length and organization; *unclear understanding* of topic.	Lacks length enough for real analysis; *strays from topic* or is partially unfocused.	Has *good basic organization* and sufficient paragraphing.	Has *well-developed paragraphs* and structure; stays on topic.	Has well-developed paragraphs and structure; *paragraphing works with examples*.
Evidence	Provides *few, if any, examples* to back up claims.	Provides *very sparse examples* to back up claims.	Provides *insufficient examples* to back up claims.	Provides *sufficient examples* to back up claims.	Provides *strong examples* to back up claims.	Provides *very strong examples* to back up claims.
Depth of Logic	Shows *very little understanding of the argument* and gives no analysis of/takes no position on it.	Presents the writer's views, but *fails to give any analytical critique*.	Analyzes somewhat, but *fails to show some key parts of the argument*.	Shows key parts of the argument adequately with *some analysis*.	Shows key parts of the argument and *analyzes them thoughtfully*.	Shows key parts of the argument and *analyzes them with great clarity*.

(Continued)

	1 Seriously Deficient	2 Substantially Flawed	3 Inadequate	4 Satisfactory	5 Good	6 Excellent
Style	Has *severe and persistent errors* in sentence structure and use of language; meaning is lost.	*Frequently uses language incorrectly* and sentence structure, grammar, and usage errors inhibit meaning.	*Uses language imprecisely* and is deficient in variety; some major errors or a number of small errors.	*Controls language adequately*, including syntax and diction; a few flaws.	*Controls language with clarity*, including variety of syntax and diction; may have a flaw here and there.	*Controls language extremely well*, including variety of syntax and diction; may have a small flaw here and there.

GMAC will grade your essay holistically based on the above rubric to arrive at your final score:

- **6: Excellent.** Essays that earn the top score must be insightful, well supported by evidence, logically organized, and skillfully written. A 6 need not be "perfect," just very good.
- **5: Good.** A 5 essay is well written and well supported but may not be as compellingly argued as a 6. There may also be more frequent or more serious writing errors than in a 6.
- **4: Satisfactory.** The important elements of the argument are addressed but not explained robustly. The organization is good, and the evidence provided is adequate. The writing may have some flaws but is generally acceptable.
- **3: Inadequate.** A 3 response misses important elements of the argument, has little or no evidence to support its ideas, and doesn't clearly express its meaning.
- **2: Substantially Flawed.** An essay scoring a 2 has some serious problems. It may not use any examples whatsoever or support its ideas in any way. Its writing will have many errors that interfere with the meaning of the sentences.
- **1: Seriously Deficient.** These essays are rare. A 1 score is reserved for essays that provide little or no evidence of the ability to analyze an argument or to develop ideas in any way. A 1 essay will have so many writing errors that the essay may be unintelligible.
- **0: No Score.** A score of 0 signifies an attempt to avoid addressing the prompt at all, either by writing only random or repeating characters or by copying the prompt. You could also score a 0 by not writing in English or by addressing a completely different topic.
- **NR: Blank.** This speaks for itself. This is what you get if you write no essay at all. Some schools will not consider your GMAT score if your essay receives an NR.

TAKEAWAYS

- Your AWA score does not count toward the 200–800 score for the rest of the test.
- Business schools receive the text of your essay along with your score report.
- The essay grading is almost pass/fail in nature: there's a clear line between 1–3 (bad) and 4–6 (good).
- A writer with a solid plan should earn a score of 4 or higher on the AWA.

The Kaplan Method for Analytical Writing

You have a limited amount of time to show the business school admissions officers that you can think logically and express yourself in clearly written English. They don't care how many syllables you can cram into a sentence or how fancy your phrases are. They care that you make sense. Whatever you do, don't hide beneath a lot of hefty words and abstract language. Make sure that everything you say is clearly written and relevant to the topic. Get in there, state your main points, back them up, and get out. The Kaplan Method for Analytical Writing—along with Kaplan's recommendations for how much time you should devote to each step of the Method—will help you produce the best essay you're capable of writing in 30 minutes.

Step 1: Take apart the argument.
Step 2: Select the points you will make.
Step 3: Organize using Kaplan's essay template.
Step 4: Write your essay.
Step 5: Proofread your work.

STEP 1: TAKE APART THE ARGUMENT

- Read through the prompt to get a sense of its scope.

- Identify the author's conclusion and the evidence used to support it.

- You can take about 2 minutes on this step.

STEP 2: SELECT THE POINTS YOU WILL MAKE

- Identify all the important gaps (assumptions) between the evidence and the conclusion.

- Think of how you'll explain or illustrate those gaps and under what circumstances the author's assumptions would not hold true.

- Think about how the author could remedy these weaknesses. This part of the Kaplan Method is very much like predicting the answer to a Critical Reasoning Strengthen or Weaken question.

- Step 2 should take about 5 minutes.

STEP 3: ORGANIZE USING KAPLAN'S ESSAY TEMPLATE

- Outline your essay.

- Lead with your best arguments.

- If you practice with the Kaplan template for the Argument essay before Test Day, organizing the essay will go smoothly and predictably. Using the Kaplan template will help you turn vague thoughts about the prompt into organized, developed paragraphs.

- The organization process should take less than 1 minute.

ORGANIZING THE ARGUMENT ESSAY: THE KAPLAN TEMPLATE

PARAGRAPH 1:

SHOW that you understand the argument by putting it in your own words.

PARAGRAPH 2:

POINT OUT one flawed assumption in the author's reasoning; explain why it is questionable.

PARAGRAPH 3:

IDENTIFY another source of the author's faulty reasoning; explain why it is questionable.

ADDITIONAL PARAGRAPHS AS APPROPRIATE:

CONTINUE to bring in points of fault in the argument, as time permits.

Time Valve #1:
Skip to the next paragraph without adding any additional flaws.

SECOND-TO-LAST PARAGRAPH:

DESCRIBE evidence that would—if it were provided—strengthen the argument.

Time Valve #2:
Combine this paragraph with the last paragraph.

LAST PARAGRAPH:

CONCLUDE that without such evidence, you're not persuaded.

STEP 4: WRITE YOUR ESSAY

- Be direct.
- Use paragraph breaks to make your essay easier to read.
- Use transitions and structural key words to link related ideas; they will help your writing flow.
- Finish strongly.
- You can afford no more than 20 minutes of typing. The other 10 minutes should be dedicated to planning and correcting.

STEP 5: PROOFREAD YOUR WORK

- Save enough time to read through the entire essay—2 minutes at minimum.
- Fix any spelling, grammar, syntax, or diction errors.
- Add any needed key words to improve the flow of your ideas.
- Don't add any new ideas or change the structure of your essay. There just isn't time.

Breakdown: Analysis of an Argument

The Instructions

Screen 1: General Instructions

The general instructions for the Argument essay will look like this:

Analytical Writing Assessment Instructions
Analysis of an Argument Essay
Time: 30 Minutes

In this part of the test, you will be asked to write a critical analysis of the argument in the prompt. You are not being asked to give your own views on the topic.

COMPOSING YOUR ESSAY: Before you begin to type, take a little time to look at the argument and plan your essay. Make sure your ideas are organized and clearly stated. Leave some time to read over your essay and make any changes you think are necessary. You will have 30 minutes to write your essay.

ESSAY ASSESSMENT: Qualified graders with varied backgrounds, including experience in business subject areas, will assess the overall quality of your analysis and composition. They will look at how well you:

- identify key elements of the argument and examine them
- arrange your analysis of the argument presented
- give appropriate examples and reasons for support
- master the components of written English

The instructions on Screen 1 tell you to read the argument, plan your essay before writing it, and leave a little time at the end for review. Sound familiar? The Kaplan Method mirrors these steps. While the prompts for the essay vary, the general directions are always the same. Become familiar with the essay directions now so you don't waste valuable time reading them on Test Day.

Screen 2: Specific Prompt

The next screen you go to will contain the specific essay prompt.

Read the argument and the directions that follow it, and write down any ideas that will be helpful in mapping out your essay. Begin writing your essay in the box at the bottom of this screen.

"The problem of poorly trained teachers that has plagued the state public school system is bound to become a good deal less serious in the future. The state has initiated comprehensive guidelines that oblige state teachers to complete a number of required credits in education and educational psychology at the graduate level before being certified."

Consider how logical you find this argument. In your essay, be sure to discuss the line of reasoning and the use of evidence in the argument. For example, you may need to consider what questionable assumptions underlie the thinking and what alternative explanations or counterpoints might weaken the conclusion. You may also discuss what types of evidence would strengthen or refute the argument, what changes in the argument would make it more logically sound, and what, if anything, would help you better evaluate its conclusion.

The only part of Screen 2 that will change is the specific prompt, which is in quotation marks. The instructions above and below it will stay the same. Again, practicing with these directions now will mean that you won't waste time reading them on Test Day.

The Stimulus

Analysis of an Argument topics will probably remind you of Critical Reasoning questions. The basic idea is similar. Just as in Critical Reasoning, the writer tries to persuade you of something—a conclusion—by citing some evidence. So, look for these two basic components of an argument: a conclusion and supporting evidence. You should read the argument in the Analysis of an Argument topic in much the same way you read Critical Reasoning stimuli; be on the lookout for assumptions—the ways the writer makes the leap from evidence to conclusion.

The Question Stem

The question stem instructs you to decide how convincing you find the argument, explain why, and discuss what might improve the argument. Note that there is a right answer here: the argument always has some problems. You want to focus your efforts on finding them, explaining them, and fixing them.

Exactly what are you being asked to do here? Paraphrase the following sentences of the question stem.

> Consider how logical you find this argument. In your essay, be sure to discuss the line of reasoning and the use of evidence in the argument.

Translation: Critique the argument. Discuss the ways in which it is not convincing. How and why might the evidence not fully support the conclusion?

> For example, you may need to consider what questionable assumptions underlie the thinking and what alternative explanations or counterpoints might weaken the conclusion. You may also discuss what types of evidence would strengthen or refute the argument, what changes in the argument would make it more logically sound, and what, if anything, would help you better evaluate its conclusion.

Translation: Spot weak links in the argument and offer constructive modifications that would strengthen them.

Now practice using the Kaplan Method for Analytical Writing on the Analysis of an Argument topic you saw before:

> "The problem of poorly trained teachers that has plagued the state public school system is bound to become a good deal less serious in the future. The state has initiated comprehensive guidelines that oblige state teachers to complete a number of required credits in education and educational psychology at the graduate level before being certified."
>
> Consider how logical you find this argument. In your essay, be sure to discuss the line of reasoning and the use of evidence in the argument. For example, you may need to consider what questionable assumptions underlie the thinking and what alternative explanations or counterpoints might weaken the conclusion. You may also discuss what types of evidence would strengthen or refute the argument, what changes in the argument would make it more logically sound, and what, if anything, would help you better evaluate its conclusion.

STEP 1: TAKE APART THE ARGUMENT

First, identify the conclusion—the point the argument is trying to make. Here, the conclusion is the first sentence:

> The problem of poorly trained teachers that has plagued the state public school system is bound to become a good deal less serious in the future.

Next, identify the evidence—the basis for the conclusion. Here, the evidence is the second sentence of the argument:

> The state has initiated comprehensive guidelines that oblige state teachers to complete a number of required credits in education and educational psychology at the graduate level before being certified.

Finally, paraphrase the argument in your own words: the problem of badly trained teachers will become less serious because new teachers will be required to take a certain number of graduate level classes.

If you aren't able to put the argument in your own words, you don't yet understand it well enough to analyze it sufficiently. Don't rush this step; you can afford a full 2 minutes if you need it.

STEP 2: SELECT THE POINTS YOU WILL MAKE

Now that you've found the conclusion and evidence, think about what assumptions the author is making. Also, think about any unaddressed questions that you feel would be relevant.

- The author assumes that the courses will improve teachers' classroom performance.
- What about bad teachers who are already certified? Would they also be required to retrain?
- Have currently poor-performing teachers already had this training?
- Will this plan have any unintended negative consequences?

You also will need to explain how these assumptions could be false or how the questions reveal weaknesses in the author's argument. Add to your notes:

- The author assumes that the courses will improve teachers' classroom performance. What if the problem is cultural? Or if it's a language barrier? Or if the teacher doesn't know the subject?
- What about bad teachers who are already certified? Would they also be required to retrain? If not, those bad teachers would still be in the system.
- Have currently poor-performing teachers already had this training? If so, this fact demonstrates that this training won't solve the problems.
- Will this plan have any unintended negative consequences? What does this training cost? If the state has to pay for it, will that mean there is less money available for other uses? If teachers have to pay for it, will good teachers leave the system?

Then think about evidence that would make the argument stronger or more logically sound:

- Evidence verifying that the training will make teachers better
- Evidence that currently bad teachers have not already received this training and that they either will soon receive it or will be removed from the classroom
- Evidence that the cost of the training is not prohibitive

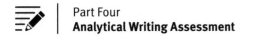

STEP 3: ORGANIZE USING KAPLAN'S ESSAY TEMPLATE

Look over the notes you've jotted down. Select the strongest point to be first, the next-strongest to be second, and so on. Two criteria determine whether a point is strong. One is how well you can explain it. If, for example, you aren't sure how to explain potential negative consequences of an expensive training program, you should use that idea last—if at all. The other is how severe a problem the weakness poses to the argument's persuasiveness. If the training doesn't work, for example, the argument is in serious trouble.

Then decide how you'll arrange your points. Follow the Kaplan template. The following is an example of an effective shorthand outline like the one you will create on Test Day:

¶ Restate argument (conc: solve problem of poorly trained teachers; evid: courses in education and ed. psychology)

¶ Assump: courses = better performance. Culture? Language? Subject matter? Need: evid. of relevance

¶ Assump: current bad teachers not already trained. If they have, training doesn't work. Need: evid. of no training

¶ Assump: bad teachers will go if not trained. If not, will be bad until they retire. Need: everyone to be trained or leave

¶ Assump: not too $. If too $, other priorities suffer. Need: evid. of low $

¶ Ways to strengthen arg. (needed evid.)

Remember, you may not have time to use all your points. Leaving your weakest for last means that if you run short on time, you'll leave out your weakest point instead of your best.

STEP 4: WRITE YOUR ESSAY

Begin typing your essay now. Keep in mind the basic principles of writing that we discussed earlier.

Keep your writing simple and clear. Choose words that you know how to use well. Avoid the temptation to make your writing "sound smarter" with overly complicated sentences or vocabulary that feels awkward.

Keep your eye on the clock and make sure that you don't run out of time to proofread. If you need to, leave out your last point or two. (Make sure that you include at least two main points.) Pretend for a moment that the writer of the following essay had only 6 minutes left on the clock after the third paragraph. Wisely, this author chooses neither to rush through the final paragraph nor to skip proofreading. Instead, this author makes the decision to leave out the point about cost and uses the time valve in the template of combining the next-to-last and last paragraphs.

> The author concludes that the present problem of poorly trained teachers will become less severe in the future because of required credits in education and psychology. However, the conclusion relies on assumptions for which the author does not supply clear evidence.

> The author assumes that the required courses will produce better teachers. In fact, the courses might be entirely irrelevant to the teachers' failings. If, for example, the prevalent problem is cultural or linguistic gaps between teacher and student, graduate-level courses that do not address these specific issues probably won't do much good. The courses also would not be heplful for a teacher who does not know their subject matter.

In addition, the author assumes that currently poor teachers have not already had this training. In fact, the author doesn't mention whether some or all of the poor teachers have had similar training. If they have, then the training seems not to have been effective and the plan should be rethought.

Finally, the author assumes that poor teachers currently working will either stop teaching in the future or will receive training. The author provides no evidence, though, to indicate that this is the case. As the argument stands, it's highly possible that only brand-new teachers will be receiving the training and the bright future to which the author refers is decades away.

To strengthen the argument, the author must provide several pieces of evidence to support his assumptions. First of all, the author's implicit claim that the courses will improve teachers could be strengthened by providing evidence that the training will be relevant to teachers' problems. The author could also make a stronger case by showing that currently poor teachers have not already had training comparable to the new requirements. Finally, the author's argument can only hold in the presence of evidence that all teachers in the system will receive the training—and will then change there teaching methods accordingly. In its current state, the argument relies too heavily on unsupported assumptions to be convincing.

STEP 5: PROOFREAD YOUR WORK

Save a few minutes to go back over your essay and catch any obvious errors. Look over the essay you just read. It has at least four grammatical errors and is missing at least one key word. By leaving herself ample proofreading time, our author will be able to find them.

- **Paragraph 1:**
  - The phrase "because of required credits" is awkward and unclear. Change to "because the state will require teachers to complete credits."

- **Paragraph 2:**
  - Add a key word to the beginning of the paragraph. Since it is the first assumption discussed, "The author assumes …" should be changed to "First, the author assumes.…"
  - The last sentence could be improved: "The courses also would not be heplful for a teacher who does not know their subject matter." For one thing, "heplful" should be "helpful."

- **Paragraph 3:** no errors

- **Paragraph 4:**
  - There's an awkward phrase about halfway through: "only brand-new teachers will be receiving the training." There's no need for anything but simple future tense: "only brand-new teachers will receive the training."

- **Paragraph 5:**
  - In the next-to-last sentence, "there teaching methods" should be "their teaching methods."

The best way to improve your writing and proofreading skills is practice. When you practice responding to AWA prompts, do so on a computer—but to mimic test conditions, don't use the automatic spell-check or grammar-check. Write practice essays using the prompts at the end of this chapter, those provided by the test maker at **mba.com**, or those in the *Official Guide for GMAT Review*. The pool of prompts provided by the test maker contains the actual prompts from which the GMAT will select your essay topic on Test Day.

GMAT Style Checklist

On the GMAT, there are three rules of thumb for successful writing: be concise, be forceful, and be correct. Following these rules is a sure way to improve your writing style—and your score. Take a look at each one in more depth.

Be Concise

- Cut out words, phrases, and sentences that don't add any information or serve a necessary purpose.
- Watch out for repetitive phrases such as "refer back" or "absolutely essential."
- Don't use conjunctions to join sentences that would be more effective as separate sentences.
- Don't use needless qualifiers such as "really" or "kind of."

Examples

> **Wordy:** The agency is not prepared to undertake expansion at this point in time.
>
> **Concise:** The agency is not ready to expand.
>
> **Redundant:** All of these problems have combined together to create a serious crisis.
>
> **Concise:** Combined, these problems create a crisis.
>
> **Too many qualifiers:** Ferrara seems to be sort of a slow worker.
>
> **Concise:** Ferrara works slowly.

Be Forceful

- Don't refer to yourself needlessly. Avoid pointless phrases like "in my personal opinion"; even phrases such as "I agree" or "I think" are considered stylistically weak.
- Avoid jargon and pompous language; it won't impress anybody. For example, "a waste of time and money" is better than "a pointless expenditure of temporal and financial resources."
- Don't use the passive voice. Use active verbs whenever possible.
- Avoid clichés and overused terms or phrases (for example, "beyond the shadow of a doubt").
- Don't be vague. Avoid generalizations and abstractions when more specific words would be clearer.
- Don't use weak sentence openings. Be wary of sentences that begin with "there is" or "there are." For example, "There are several ways in which this sentence is awkward" should be rewritten as "This sentence is awkward in several ways."
- Don't be monotonous; vary sentence length and style.
- Use transitions to connect sentences and make your essay easy to follow.

Examples

> **Needlessly references self:** Although I am no expert, I do not think privacy should be valued more than social concerns.
>
> **Speaks confidently:** Privacy should not be valued more than social concerns.
>
> **Uses passive voice:** The report was compiled by a number of field anthropologists and marriage experts.
>
> **Uses active voice:** A number of field anthropologists and marriage experts compiled the report.
>
> **Opens weakly:** It would be of no use to fight a drug war without waging a battle against demand for illicit substances.

Opens strongly: The government cannot fight a drug war effectively without waging a battle against the demand for illicit substances.

Uses cliché: A ballpark estimate of the number of fans in the stadium would be 120,000.

Employs plain English: About 120,000 fans were in the stadium.

Be Correct

- Observe the rules of standard written English. The most important rules are covered in the Sentence Correction chapter of this book.

Examples

Subject and verb disagree: Meredith, along with her associates, expect the sustainable energy proposal to pass.

Subject and verb agree: Meredith, along with her associates, expects the sustainable energy proposal to pass.

Uses faulty modification: Having worked in publishing for 10 years, Stokely's résumé shows that he is well qualified.

Uses correct modification: Stokely, who has worked in publishing for 10 years, appears from his résumé to be well qualified.

Uses pronouns incorrectly: A retirement community offers more activities than a private dwelling does, but it is cheaper.

Uses pronouns correctly: A retirement community offers more activities than a private dwelling does, but a private dwelling is cheaper.

Has unparallel structure: The dancer taught her understudy how to move, how to dress, and how to work with choreographers and deal with professional competition.

Has parallel structure: The dancer taught her understudy how to move, dress, work with choreographers, and deal with professional competition.

Fragmented sentence: You have time to invest in property. Only after you've established yourself in the business world, however.

Complete sentence: You have time to invest in property, but only after you've established yourself in the business world.

Run-on sentence: Antonio just joined the athletic club staff this year, however, because Barry has been with us since 2007, we would expect Barry to be more skilled with the weight-lifting equipment.

Correct sentence: Antonio joined the athletic club staff this year. However, because Barry has been with us since 2007, we would expect him to be more skilled with the weight-lifting equipment.

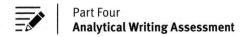

Practice Essays

Directions: Write an essay on each of the three topics that follow. The writing should be concise, forceful, and grammatically correct. After you have finished, proofread to catch any errors. Allow yourself 30 minutes to complete each essay. Practice writing under timed conditions so that you get a feel for how much you can afford to write while leaving enough time to proofread.

Essay 1

The following appeared in a memo from a staff member of a local health care clinic.

> "Many lives might be saved if inoculations against cow flu were routinely administered to all people in areas where the disease is detected. However, since there is a small possibility that a person will die as a result of the inoculations, we cannot permit inoculations against cow flu to be routinely administered."

> Consider how logical you find this argument. In your essay, be sure to discuss the line of reasoning and the use of evidence in the argument. For example, you may need to consider what questionable assumptions underlie the thinking and what alternative explanations or counterpoints might weaken the conclusion. You may also discuss what types of evidence would strengthen or refute the argument, what changes in the argument would make it more logically sound, and what, if anything, would help you better evaluate its conclusion.

After writing your essay, compare it to the sample responses on the pages that follow. Don't focus on length, as word count is not part of the grading criteria. Rather, focus on how logical the structure is and whether the essay makes its points in a clear and straightforward style.

Student Response 1 (as written, including original errors):

The writer argues that innoculations against cow flu shouldn't be administered because there is a possibility of a person dying from the innoculation. The flaw in this argument is suggested by the writer's use of the phrases "many lives" and "small possibility." These are vague words, but, they imply, that cow flu itself poses a greater risk to people in an area where the disease is present than the prevention against it. If this is the case, then the writer's argument is greatly weakened.

The writer could make the argument better by showing that the overall death rate from cow flu among those who haven't been innoculated in an area where cow flu has been detected is lower than the death rate from the vaccine among individuals who have been given the innoculation. This would show that the vaccine poses a greater risk than the disease itself. Also, it would be good to know whether some people are more likely to die from the innoculation than others and whether these people can be located. It's possible that those people who are most at risk from the innoculation are also most at risk from the disease itself, in which case the innoculation might do no greater harm than the disease would, and would also save the lives of many who were not in this high risk group. On the other hand, if those people who are most at risk from the vaccine are not at a very high risk from the disease, then maybe we can exempt them from the vaccine, but continue to administer it to those people who it will help.

Analysis 1:

Structure: The writer gives his evaluation of the argument in paragraph 1. However, the organization breaks down in paragraph 2, where the writer tries to cover too much. In this paragraph, the writer discusses ways of strengthening the argument, the need for more information, and alternative possibilities for the scenario. A better-written essay might have split paragraph 2 into several different paragraphs, each covering one topic.

Evidence: The writer does not fully support his position with specific examples. Rather, he writes vaguely of different possibilities. While this is not completely wrong, it's also not the type of concrete support that is needed here.

Depth of Logic: This is probably the weakest area in the essay. The writer fails to fully develop his ideas. He looks at the problem only through a cost-benefit lens—which way saves more lives?—as opposed to questioning whether any risk of death means that we shouldn't routinely inoculate.

Style: The writing style is flat and the first sentence in paragraph 2 is long and convoluted. The ideas in paragraph 2 seem strung together.

This essay would earn a score of 3. While the writer has some decent ideas and shows adequate writing ability, the structure of the essay is poor, the logic fails to show some parts of the author's argument, and the writer inadequately develops support for his own points. Had this student used the same ideas, but developed and organized them according to the Kaplan template, he would almost assuredly have earned a score of 4 or better.

Student Response 2 (as written, including original errors):

The argument above states that inoculations against cow flu could be useful in combating the disease, but, due to the risk of death from the inoculations themselves, the vaccines should not be widely administered. This argument relies on several unsupported assumptions and therefore fails to be persuasive.

The argument against widespread inoculations is rooted in the assumption that the risk of death from the inoculations is greater than the risk of death from cow flu. However, the author provides no evidence to support this key assumption. Without specific statistics regarding the death rates from inoculations and cow flu, we cannot assume that one outweighs the other: cow flu and the inoculations may be equally risky, or cow flu may in fact be riskier than the inoculations. In addition, the language of the argument appears to contradict its primary assumption. The author states that "many lives" could be saved by inoculations, but there is a "small possibility" of death from the inoculations. These terms suggest that the risk from cow flu is greater than that of the inoculations, further weakening the author's position that inoculations should not be routinely administered.

Additionally, the author takes an "all or nothing" position, suggesting that inoculations must be widely administered or not administered at all. This position ignores the possibility of variation in rates of infection and effects of the inoculation in different environments. The vaccine may pose a serious risk to those relatively unaffected by cow flu, while posing little risk to those most impacted by cow flu. In this case, vaccines administered to select portions of the population might save the most lives while putting the fewest lives in danger.

To make this argument persuasive, the author needs to present specific evidence to support the argument's assumptions. For instance, details regarding the number of deaths caused by cow flu and the vaccine would clarify the relative risks of the flu and the inoculations, allowing an accurate evaluation of the merits and risks of the vaccine. Also, a less extreme stance on inoculations—one that allowed for selective administration of the inoculations based upon an area's risk for the disease—would provide a more realistic solution to the challenge of balancing the dangers of cow flu and inoculations. Without such changes, the conclusion of this argument remains unconvincing.

Analysis 2:

Structure: The writer of this essay has clearly used the Kaplan template to her benefit. She frames the argument succinctly in the first paragraph. In each of the middle paragraphs, she lays out one major problem in the argument's reasoning and explains with clear support why it is a problem. In the final paragraph, the writer introduces evidence that would strengthen the argument and then draws her conclusion.

Evidence: The evidence is solid. The writer could have brought in counterexamples to support criticisms of the argument, but this is not a fatal flaw.

Depth of Logic: The logic in this essay is much stronger than in the last. The organization of the essay leaves few gaps in the reasoning.

Style: The writing style is superior, with fewer (although not zero) grammatical mistakes and much stronger flow.

This essay would receive a score of 6 from the GMAT graders. It is not perfect, but the graders do not expect perfection. The conclusion is somewhat clunky, and the writer missed one or two opportunities to strengthen her point. However, it is still a very strong essay in all four categories of evaluation, and it is a vast improvement over the earlier effort.

Essay 2

The following appeared in a memo from the regional manager of Luxe Spa, a chain of high-end salons.

"Over 75 percent of households in Parksboro have Jacuzzi bathtubs. In addition, the average family income in Parksboro is 50 percent higher than the national average, and a local store reports record-high sales of the most costly brands of hair and body care products. With so much being spent on personal care, Parksboro will be a profitable location for a new Luxe Spa—a salon that offers premium services at prices that are above average."

Consider how logical you find this argument. In your essay, be sure to discuss the line of reasoning and the use of evidence in the argument. For example, you may need to consider what questionable assumptions underlie the thinking and what alternative explanations or counterpoints might weaken the conclusion. You may also discuss what types of evidence would strengthen or refute the argument, what changes in the argument would make it more logically sound, and what, if anything, would help you better evaluate its conclusion.

After writing your essay, compare it to the sample response on the following page. Don't focus on length, as word count is not part of the grading criteria. Rather, focus on how logical the structure is and whether the essay makes its points in a clear and straightforward style.

Student Response (as written, including original errors):

Though it might seem at first glance that the regional manager of Luxe Spa has good reasons for suggesting that Parksboro would be a profitable location for a new spa, a closer examination of the arguments presented reveals numerous examples of leaps of faith, poor reasoning, and ill-defined terminology. In order to better support her claim, the manager would need to show a correlation between the figures she cites in reference to Parksboro's residents and a willingness to spend money at a spa with high prices.

The manager quotes specific statistics about the percentage of residents with Jacuzzis and the average income in Parksboro. She then uses these figures as evidence to support her argument. However, neither of these statistics as presented does much to bolster her claim. Just because 75 percent of homes have Jacuzzis doesn't mean those homeowners are more likely to go to a pricey spa. For instance, the presence of Jacuzzis in their houses may indicate a preference for pampering themselves at home. Parksboro could also be a planned development in the suburbs where all the houses are designed with Jacuzzis. If this is the case, than the mere ownership of a certain kind of bathtub should hardly be taken as a clear indication of a person's inclination to go to a spa. In addition, the fact that Parksboro's average family income is 50 percent higher than the national average is not enough on its own to predict the success or failure of a spa in the region. Parksboro may have a very small population, for instance, or a small number of wealthy people counterbalanced by a number of medium- to low-income families. We simply cannot tell from the information provided. In addition, the failure of the manager to provide the national average family income for comparison makes it unclear if earning 50 percent more would allow for a luxurious lifestyle or not.

The mention of a local store's record-high sales of expensive personal care items similarly provides scant evidence to support the manager's assertions. We are given no indication of what constitutes "record-high" sales for this particular store or what "most costly" means in this context. Perhaps this store usually sells very few personal care products and had one unusual month. Even if this one store sold a high volume of hair- and body-care products, it may not be representative of the Parksboro market as a whole. And perhaps "most costly" refers only to the most costly brands available in Parksboro, not to the most costly brands nationwide. The manager needs to provide much more specific information about residents' spending habits in order to provide compelling evidence that personal care ranks high among their priorities.

To make the case that Parksboro would be a profitable location for Luxe Spa, the regional manager should try to show that people there have a surplus of income and a tendency to spend it on indulging in spa treatments. Although an attempt is made to make this very argument, the lack of supporting information provided weakens rather than strengthens the memo. Information such as whether there are other high-end spas in the area and the presence of tourism in the town could also have been introduced as reinforcement. As it stands, Luxe Spa would be ill-advised to open a location in Parksboro based solely on the evidence provided here.

Analysis:

Structure: The use of the Kaplan template is evident here. In the first paragraph, the writer demonstrates his understanding of the argument and gives a summary of its flaws. Each paragraph that follows elaborates on one flaw in the author's reasoning. The final paragraph introduces evidence that, if provided, would strengthen the argument.

Evidence: The evidence is strong. The writer develops his points by providing examples to explain why the author's reasoning is questionable. Some minor flaws are evident, as in the second paragraph, when the writer misses an opportunity to point out that a small population might not be enough to support a spa.

Depth of Logic: Once again, the organization of the essay enhances its depth of logic. The writer takes apart the argument methodically and provides clear analysis of each part.

Style: The writing style is smooth and controlled, and grammar and syntax errors are minimal to nonexistent.

This essay would score a 6. The writer makes a very strong showing in all four categories of the grading rubric.

Essay 3

The following appeared in a document released by a community's arts bureau:

> "In a recent county survey, 20 percent more county residents indicated that they watch TV programs dedicated to the arts than was reported eight years ago. The number of visitors to our county's museums and galleries over the past eight years has gone up by a comparable proportion. Now that the commercial funding public TV relies on is facing severe cuts, which will consequently limit arts programming, it is likely that attendance at our county's art museums will also go down. Therefore, public funds that are currently dedicated to the arts should be partially shifted to public television."

> Consider how logical you find this argument. In your essay, be sure to discuss the line of reasoning and the use of evidence in the argument. For example, you may need to consider what questionable assumptions underlie the thinking and what alternative explanations or counterpoints might weaken the conclusion. You may also discuss what types of evidence would strengthen or refute the argument, what changes in the argument would make it more logically sound, and what, if anything, would help you better evaluate its conclusion.

After writing your essay, compare it to the sample response on the following page. Don't focus on length, as word count is not part of the grading criteria. Rather, focus on how logical the structure is and whether the essay makes its points in a clear and straightforward style.

Student Response (as written, including original errors):

In a time of threatened scarcity of funding, a community arts organization is asking to shift public arts funds partly to public television. The organization cites a recent survey of county residents that shows a 20 percent self-reported increase in arts TV-watching over the last eight years concomitant with a similar, documented increase in local museum and art gallery attendance. This earnest plea is understandable, but the underlying rationale for shifting funding is flawed and lacks sufficient substantiation.

First, the author may be confusing correlation with causation. Does the survey—even if we accept its findings as valid—really indicate that people went to museums as a result of seeing arts programming on television? Its quite possible that there are alternate reasons for the increase in attendance at museums, such as partnerships with schools, discount programs for senior citizens, introduction of IMAX theaters, or popular traveling exhibits. Alternatively, people may be watching more arts programming on television as a direct result of being lured into museum attendance for reasons that have nothing to do with television.

A second reason to be hesitant to adopt the recommended funding shift is that it assumes that there are only two viable sources of funding for public television: commercial and public. Before it resorts to diverting public funds from other arts organizations, public television has the option to pursue direct fundraising from viewers; these newly enthusiastic television arts program viewers may be delighted to support such programming directly. Public television has a unique opportunity to reach its audience in a way that is more elusive to smaller art museums. It is potentially in a superior position to recover from reduced corporate funding without needing to rely more heavily on public funds.

Conversely, it is possible that the author knows more than he has shared about a connection between public television watching and local museum attendance. For instance, there may have been some specific partnerships in the last eight years between local museums and local public television stations, including specific programming designed to tie in with current museum exhibitions. The recent survey to which the author alluded may have referenced direct ties between the television programming and museum attendance. Such data would make it more likely that increasing the public funding for public television would also directly benefit local museums.

Until more information is provided to us, however, we cannot accept the authors' argument for a shift in public funds to local public television as a way to support local art museums.

Analysis:

Structure: This essay is very well organized. The essayist's use of transitions is particularly strong here, as the author leads the reader through the points of fault in the argument and describes evidence that could potentially strengthen the argument.

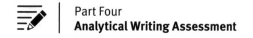

Evidence: The essayist provides multiple strong examples that strengthen the essay's major points.

Depth of Logic: The essayist accurately identifies the assumptions inherent in the argument and develops the essay by proposing plausible alternative explanations for the evidence the argument's author cites.

Style: The essayist has a few problems with misplaced apostrophes; otherwise, the grammar and syntax are strong.

This essay would score a 6. It is an excellent example of how following the Kaplan template will help you organize your ideas into a convincing essay. After the introduction, two paragraphs develop and support the author's two main points, followed by a paragraph describing how the argument could be strengthened and a clear conclusion.

CHAPTER 10

Analytical Writing Assessment Practice Set

Below are 10 Argument essay prompts for you to use to practice the Analytical Writing Assessment. Allow yourself 30 minutes to complete each essay. The writing should be concise, forceful, and grammatically correct. Use the Kaplan Method for Analytical Writing to guide your process and the Kaplan template for the Argument essay to structure your ideas into a well-organized essay. After you have finished, proofread to catch any errors. Practice writing under timed conditions so that you get a feel for how much you can afford to write while leaving enough time to proofread. High-scoring sample essays for each prompt are found at the end of the chapter.

The following general instructions apply to all of the practice essays:

Analytical Writing Assessment Instructions

Analysis of an Argument Essay

Time: 30 Minutes

In this part of the test, you will be asked to write a critical analysis of the argument in the prompt. You are not being asked to give your own views on the topic.

COMPOSING YOUR ESSAY: Before you begin to type, take a little time to look at the argument and plan your essay. Make sure your ideas are organized and clearly stated. Leave some time to read over your essay and make any changes you think are necessary. You will have 30 minutes to write your essay.

ESSAY ASSESSMENT: Qualified graders with varied backgrounds, including experience in business subject areas, will assess the overall quality of your analysis and composition. They will look at how well you:

- identify key elements of the argument and examine them
- arrange your analysis of the argument presented
- give appropriate examples and reasons for support
- master the components of written English

Practice Essay Prompts

Essay 1

The following appeared in the events column of a municipal magazine:

"In a recent survey, adults under the age of 50 reported spending 55 percent of their free time at the local community center, while those aged 50 or older reported spending only 35 percent of their free time there. As major employers continue to bring jobs for younger people into our area, we can expect a significant increase in usage of the facility in the near future. We should therefore begin allocating a much larger portion of the city budget toward the upkeep of the community center."

Consider how logical you find this argument. In your essay, be sure to discuss the line of reasoning and the use of evidence in the argument. For example, you may need to consider what questionable assumptions underlie the thinking and what alternative explanations or counterpoints might weaken the conclusion. You may also discuss what types of evidence would strengthen or refute the argument, what changes in the argument would make it more logically sound, and what, if anything, would help you better evaluate its conclusion.

Essay 2

The following appeared in a report delivered at a recent corporate board meeting:

"Three weeks ago, 27 engineers from our Research and Development department stormed the corporate headquarters to protest against poor working conditions, low wages, and a lack of benefits, while over 500 engineers from the same department went to work as usual. As the group of engineers who are satisfied with their working conditions, wages, and benefits far outnumbers the group of protesters, we can conclude that we are currently providing adequate wages and benefits, as well as good working conditions. The board of directors should therefore ignore this incident."

Consider how logical you find this argument. In your essay, be sure to discuss the line of reasoning and the use of evidence in the argument. For example, you may need to consider what questionable assumptions underlie the thinking and what alternative explanations or counterpoints might weaken the conclusion. You may also discuss what types of evidence would strengthen or refute the argument, what changes in the argument would make it more logically sound, and what, if anything, would help you better evaluate its conclusion.

Essay 3

The following appeared in a statement by the director of a local superstore:

"Ever since Big Box Mart opened across the street two years ago, our store's foot traffic has been steadily declining. The best way to counter this trend is to undercut Big Box Mart's prices on several key items that are popular this holiday season. Doing so will bring back our former customers, and any revenue lost due to the lower prices will be made up for by sales of non-discounted items."

Consider how logical you find this argument. In your essay, be sure to discuss the line of reasoning and the use of evidence in the argument. For example, you may need to consider what questionable assumptions underlie the thinking and what alternative explanations or counterpoints might weaken the conclusion. You may also discuss what types of evidence would strengthen or refute the argument, what changes in the argument would make it more logically sound, and what, if anything, would help you better evaluate its conclusion.

Essay 4

The following appeared as part of a presentation by Reese Key Capital, an investment group:

"Our company invests under the guiding principle that the stock market behaves according to a balancing effect—the more violently a stock's price moves in one direction, the more powerful the eventual correction in the other. In 2012, shares of Whiplash Incorporated (WLI) plummeted 27 percent over the course of three weeks. The fourth week, however, saw a massive 20 percent appreciation in share price, and Whiplash is now one of the most valuable companies on the exchange. As some of you may know, Bargain Liquidation Enterprises (BLE) shares have just fallen 45 percent over the last few weeks, so we can expect our recent investment in BLE to yield significant profits in the near and distant future."

Consider how logical you find this argument. In your essay, be sure to discuss the line of reasoning and the use of evidence in the argument. For example, you may need to consider what questionable assumptions underlie the thinking and what alternative explanations or counterpoints might weaken the conclusion. You may also discuss what types of evidence would strengthen or refute the argument, what changes in the argument would make it more logically sound, and what, if anything, would help you better evaluate its conclusion.

Essay 5

The following appeared in an announcement by a local community group organizer:

"In a recent interview, the owner of our local Fit and Fashionable sporting goods store stated that sales of the Red Runner Sneakers line are grossing roughly 20 percent higher than they were three years ago when the sneakers were first introduced here. During this time, we've seen a comparable percentage increase in runners from our community placing well at regional track competitions. However, the owner goes on to mention her desire to sharpen the business's focus by eliminating several product lines. As the Red Runners will be one of the discontinued lines, we can expect to see a decline in our community's newfound enthusiasm for running. We should therefore petition the owner of Fit and Fashionable to reconsider this decision."

Consider how logical you find this argument. In your essay, be sure to discuss the line of reasoning and the use of evidence in the argument. For example, you may need to consider what questionable assumptions underlie the thinking and what alternative explanations or counterpoints might weaken the conclusion. You may also discuss what types of evidence would strengthen or refute the argument, what changes in the argument would make it more logically sound, and what, if anything, would help you better evaluate its conclusion.

Essay 6

The following is an excerpt from a memo written by the vice president of Innovatronic Corp.:

"In the six months that Samuels has served as executive director of marketing, market share and net profits have plummeted. Product sales have hit a five-year low. During the previous six months, when Nichols served as executive director, our market share was number four in an industry with dozens of competitors, and sales and profits were on the rise. It is clear that we need to replace Samuels with someone of Nichols's caliber immediately."

Consider how logical you find this argument. In your essay, be sure to discuss the line of reasoning and the use of evidence in the argument. For example, you may need to consider what questionable assumptions underlie the thinking and what alternative explanations or counterpoints

might weaken the conclusion. You may also discuss what types of evidence would strengthen or refute the argument, what changes in the argument would make it more logically sound, and what, if anything, would help you better evaluate its conclusion.

Essay 7

The following is part of an article in the local news section of a newspaper:

"Fifteen middle school children were sent home sick last Friday. An investigation has revealed that all 15 students had been served school lunches containing pepper jack cheese. What's particularly worrisome is the presence of abnormally colored specks embedded in the cheese's surface. Health officials have thus far refused to release a public statement acknowledging the danger posed by pepper jack but, given the facts, it would not be wise to allow your children to consume pepper jack cheese."

Consider how logical you find this argument. In your essay, be sure to discuss the line of reasoning and the use of evidence in the argument. For example, you may need to consider what questionable assumptions underlie the thinking and what alternative explanations or counterpoints might weaken the conclusion. You may also discuss what types of evidence would strengthen or refute the argument, what changes in the argument would make it more logically sound, and what, if anything, would help you better evaluate its conclusion.

Essay 8

The following is an excerpt from a factory manager's report:

"Ten years ago, my staff of 20 employees was sufficient to keep our facilities operating at 50 percent capacity. During this time, I've gradually instituted certain changes in policy that have clearly worked for the better: The same 20 employees are now able to keep our facilities operating at 85 percent capacity. All of this was done while keeping their salaries at roughly the same level, adjusted for inflation. Therefore, we do not need to award any substantial raises at this time."

Consider how logical you find this argument. In your essay, be sure to discuss the line of reasoning and the use of evidence in the argument. For example, you may need to consider what questionable assumptions underlie the thinking and what alternative explanations or counterpoints might weaken the conclusion. You may also discuss what types of evidence would strengthen or refute the argument, what changes in the argument would make it more logically sound, and what, if anything, would help you better evaluate its conclusion.

Essay 9

The following is part of an internal sales memo for The Groomed Man, a reseller of men's hygiene products:

"Sales of the XP2500 electric razor have been well above expectations, but sales of its replacement cartridges have been rather disappointing. If our company is serious about success, we must either make changes to reduce the durability of the cartridges so that consumers would need to replace them more often or increase their price."

Consider how logical you find this argument. In your essay, be sure to discuss the line of reasoning and the use of evidence in the argument. For example, you may need to consider what questionable assumptions underlie the thinking and what alternative explanations or counterpoints might weaken the conclusion. You may also discuss what types of evidence would strengthen or refute the argument, what changes in the argument would make it more logically sound, and what, if anything, would help you better evaluate its conclusion.

Essay 10

The following is an excerpt from the regional director's report:

"Regarding the district manager position, both Ibrahim and Einhorn have shown interest, but Ibrahim is clearly the more qualified of the two. Over the past few years, Ibrahim has improved employee retention by 40 percent and greatly boosted the morale of his team, and performance metrics are at a multi-year high. When polled, the majority of Ibrahim's employees had nothing but praise for Ibrahim's management style. Promoting Einhorn to the position would be a mistake, as her management style differs markedly from Ibrahim's."

Consider how logical you find this argument. In your essay, be sure to discuss the line of reasoning and the use of evidence in the argument. For example, you may need to consider what questionable assumptions underlie the thinking and what alternative explanations or counterpoints might weaken the conclusion. You may also discuss what types of evidence would strengthen or refute the argument, what changes in the argument would make it more logically sound, and what, if anything, would help you better evaluate its conclusion.

Sample Essays and Analyses

Compare your essays to the corresponding sample responses on the pages that follow. Don't focus on length, as word count is not part of the grading criteria. Rather, focus on how logical the structure is and whether the essay makes its points in a clear and straightforward style. Following each sample essay is an analysis that discusses what makes the essay successful and what could still be improved upon.

Essay 1

The following appeared in the events column of a municipal magazine:

"In a recent survey, adults under the age of 50 reported spending 55 percent of their free time at the local community center, while those aged 50 or older reported spending only 35 percent of their free time there. As major employers continue to bring jobs for younger people into our area, we can expect a significant increase in usage of the facility in the near future. We should therefore begin allocating a much larger portion of the city budget toward the upkeep of the community center."

Student Response (as written, including original errors):

The author of the argument above believes that the city should allocate a larger portion of the city budget toward the upkeep of the local community center. The author believes that this should be done because he expects major employers to continue bringing jobs for younger people into the area and, that as a result, usage of the community center will increase significantly. The author also notes that in a recent survey, adults under the age of 50 reported spending a larger percentage of their free time at the community center than those aged 50 or older. However, because the author's argument contains a number of assumptions, the argument is not persuasive.

First, the author seems to assume that simply because people under the age of 50 spend 55 percent of their free time at the local community center, that they actually spend a significant amount of time at the center. If, however, the total amount of free time available to a young person is severely limited, then the actual amount of time that a young person spends at the community center may be quite low, regardless of what percent of his or her free time such a person spends at the center.

The author also assumes that simply because major employers may continue to bring jobs for younger people into the area that more young people will begin to use the local community center. However, this may not be the case. For example, if such employers hire mostly young people who already live in the community and who are currently unemployed, then the total amount of free time available to young people in the community may decrease, and thus, their usage of the community center may decrease as well.

The author also assumes that the survey respondents under the age of 50 are representative of the people under 50 who actually use the community center. For example, if the percent of survey respondents who were between the ages of 30 and 50 is much higher than the percent of community center visitors who are also in that age group, the results of the survey may not provide an appropriate yardstick for gauging whether to accept the author's proposal.

Moreover, while the author seeks to increase the percent of the city's budget that is allocated to the community center, the author does not address where the funds for this allocation will come from. For example, will the funds allocated to other city services be reduced, or does the author believe that the city's total revenues will increase enough that his proposal would not result in city having to reduce its other expenditures? It would likely make sense to evaluate whether allocating these funds to the community center is an optimal use of the city's funds.

This argument could be greatly strengthened if the author were to address some of the deficiencies outlined above. For example, if the author were to demonstrate that the employers he or she expects to continue hiring younger people are likely to hire many young people from outside the area, then this would increase the likelihood that more young people will begin moving to the area, or at least communting to it, and thus would increase the likelihood that more young will begin to use the community center. However, because the author failed to do so, this argument is not persuasive.

Analysis:

Structure: This is a great example of following the Kaplan template. The opening paragraph lays out the author's argument, several body paragraphs explore major flaws, then the writer wraps up with a paragraph outlining possible strengtheners. The writer fleshes out the essay using no less than six paragraphs, a rather ambitious number. While the GMAT does not require this much content to score well, the ability to write at length without sacrificing quality is certainly a bonus.

Evidence: Thanks in part to the large number of paragraphs used, evidence is specific and compelling.

Depth of Logic: Depth of logic is strong. Each body paragraph maintains a clear focus on a separate flaw, and clear examples flesh out the writer's thoughts. Time does seem to be an issue by the end. The final paragraph feels a bit rushed as it only provides a strengthener for one of the mentioned flaws.

Style: Style is clean but grammatical and syntax errors are present, particularly near the end. However, they are rare and their effect on clarity is minimal, so there will be no reduction in score.

This is a 6 essay. While it isn't perfect, GMAT graders are not expecting a first draft to be perfect. Better time management would allow the writer to round out the final paragraph more fully and proofread more thoroughly.

Essay 2

The following appeared in a report delivered at a recent corporate board meeting:

"Three weeks ago, 27 engineers from our Research and Development department stormed the corporate headquarters to protest against poor working conditions, low wages, and a lack of benefits, while over 500 engineers from the same department went to work as usual. As the group of engineers who are satisfied with their working conditions, wages, and benefits far outnumbers the group of protesters, we can conclude that we are currently providing adequate wages and benefits, as well as good working conditions. The board of directors should therefore ignore this incident."

Student Response (as written, including original errors)

The report argues that the 27 engineers who protested should be ignored. The recommendation is based on the large number of engineers who did not protest, positing that these workers' behavior demonstrated satisfaction with conditions. As written, the argument suffers from several key assumptions and fails to be convincing.

The most questionable logic lies in equating a lack of protest with job satisfaction. While it is true that only about 5 percent of workers protested, it is entirely possible that a much larger proportion is dissatisfied. For instance, the 27 protesting workers may have been chosen to represent a greater number, and many of those who went to work as normal could have been protesting by proxy. Another possibility is that workers who did not protest were unaware that a protest was taking place, and that there would have been a greater turnout with increased dissemination. The only way to make the connection effectively true would be to establish that those who protest were the only members of the company with those feelings, and the argument as written does not make this necessary link.

Conversely, the argument also does not address any potential differences in those 27 protesters' compensation and that of those who did not protest. Were it demonstrated that the protesters were compensated differently than other employees at the company, the assertion of adequate wages and recommendation to ignore the complaints would not be justified. Likewise, were the 27 employees all members of one team or sub-committee within the Research and Development department, it could point to a local deficiency in treatment. However, the argument would be strengthened if it were demonstrated that the protesters were treated similarly in all facets to other employees.

The next problematic assumption is that implicit satisfaction with conditions, pay, and benefits is sufficient to say that those are adequate. A copasetic employee does not establish that an employer is offering a positive or competitive package, as that would be a more objective measurement. This aspect of the argument could be strengthened or weakened by comparing the conditions, wages, and benefits with those of similar engineering firms and establishing whether or not the compensation and benefits are in line with the market.

It remains possible that the report is correct in both its recommendations and assertions. However, as written, there are many assumptions that question the validity of both the conclusion and the logic leading up to it. Without providing a greater depth of information on the protesters and the potential disparities, the argument fails to be convincing.

Analysis:

Structure: The essay begins with a very concise introduction paragraph. The writer then lays out each identified flaw in separate paragraphs, from strongest to weakest, before concluding that more information is needed before the argument can be convincing.

Evidence: Evidence is clear and specific. The writer explores an abundance of possible alternative explanations in great clarity, each of which would cast doubt upon the original argument.

Depth of Logic: Thanks to the detailed support provided, it is very easy to follow the writer's train of thought.

Style: The style is concise yet detailed and descriptive at the same time. The essay is devoid of grammatical and syntactical errors, evidence that the writer was thorough in his proofreading.

This is a 6 essay. Although the writer elected to mention strengtheners at the end of each body paragraph rather than have a separate strengthener paragraph at the end, this does not negatively impact the clarity of the essay.

Essay 3

The following appeared in a statement by the director of a local superstore:

"Ever since Big Box Mart opened across the street two years ago, our store's foot traffic has been steadily declining. The best way to counter this trend is to undercut Big Box Mart's prices on several key items that are popular this holiday season. Doing so will bring back our former customers, and any revenue lost due to the lower prices will be made up for by sales of non-discounted items."

Student Response (as written, including original errors):

The director of the local superstore notes that his store has attracted fewer customers over the last two years, a trend that he attributes to the opening of a competing store, Big Box Mart, nearby. In order to address this issue, the director has concluded that, during the holiday season, his store should charge less for key products than does Big Box Mart. According to the director, this strategy will enable the store to draw former customers and to make up lost revenue. Although the temporary price cuts may in fact appeal to former patrons, the director needs more information to determine if this plan will ensure lasting success for his store.

First and foremost, the director needs to determine why his store has suffered a steady loss of customers over the last two years. The director speculates that these consumers have been drawn to Big Box Mart because it offers lower prices on certain popular items; however, the loss of clientele for the superstore may have been due to a different reason entirely. Possibly, Big Box Mart offers better customer service, has more product variety, or guarantees a more pleasant shopping environment. The director must also consider the possibility that the loss of superstore customers and the opening of Big Box Mart are completely coincidental, and that another factor, such as a change in local demographics, economics, or traffic patterns, may be the cause of the superstore's situation. Without more information to support his assessment, the director should not assume that changing the superstore's prices on popular products would necessarily bring former consumers back to shop.

Secondly, before implementing his plan, the director must consider the impact of temporarily dropping the prices of just a few products. He assumes that briefly offering savings on these key items will be enough of an incentive for former customers to visit the store, purchase both the sale items and full-priced products, and then return as regular customers. The director fails to consider the possibility that patrons, especially during the holiday season when many shoppers are bargain-hunting, will make a special trip to the superstore to purchase the sale items and then leave without making any other purchases. If this occurs, the superstore will actually lose revenue from this scheme, and when the holiday season concludes, consumers will resume their normal shopping habits at other establishments.

In order to determine whether or not the director's strategy will encourage former customers to return to the superstore on a regular basis, the director needs to gather information as to why these consumers first stopped patronizing the store. A survey of previous customers will offer valuable information about whether or not prices were the primary incentive for these individuals to shop elsewhere. If prices were the chief reason why customers switched stores, then the director's plan would provide only a short-term solution. Rather than offering limited price cuts, however, the superstore would likely experience a better outcome with a long-term plan to price the majority of their products more competitively. If other factors, such as customer service or product selection, were the primary reasons why the superstore has lost customers, addressing these issues must take precedence over a short-term price-cutting scheme. Overall, until the director of the superstore determines the ultimate cause of his store's loss of clients, he will be unable to deal with the problem effectively.

Analysis:

Structure: Structure in this essay is sound. The writer lays out the argument before laying out its faults in the body paragraphs, then concludes the essay with specific suggestions on what the director needs to consider before making his argument.

Evidence: Evidence is presented well. The writer uses very specific real-world examples to show why the director's logic is flawed.

Depth of Logic: Organization is excellent. The flaws are not only presented in separate paragraphs, they're also organized chronologically—a paragraph on flaws before implementing and one on flaws if implemented—and that makes this essay even easier to follow.

Style: Writing style is very clean and down to earth. Some minor flaws are evident, as in the last sentence of the first paragraph, when the writer makes it seem like it is the director and not the writer who feels that he needs more information before making his argument. This is a very minor issue in an otherwise solid essay and would not result in a score reduction.

This is a 6 essay. The writer's argument is clear and compelling, with a strong showing in all four categories of the rubric.

Essay 4

The following appeared as part of a presentation by Reese Key Capital, an investment group:

"Our company invests under the guiding principle that the stock market behaves according to a balancing effect—the more violently a stock's price moves in one direction, the more powerful the eventual correction in the other. In 2012, shares of Whiplash Incorporated (WLI) plummeted 27 percent over the course of three weeks. The fourth week, however, saw a massive 20 percent appreciation in share price, and Whiplash is now one of the most valuable companies on the exchange. As some of you may know, Bargain Liquidation Enterprises (BLE) shares have just fallen 45 percent over the last few weeks, so we can expect our recent investment in BLE to yield significant profits in the near and distant future."

Student Response (as written, including original errors):

The argument by Reese Key Capital presents its principle that stock prices are subject to balanced corrections, offers a single example of one company's stock price history supporting that principle, and based on that principle and single example predicts that a different company's stock price will rebound dramatically and "yield significant profits in the near and distant future." This prediction is tenuous since it is based on a "guiding principle," which itself is supported only by a single example. The argument makes a number of unsupported assumptions in applying the principle and in extrapolating from the example company to the subject company.

Initially, reliance on this "guiding principle" is highly suspect without access to the data and experiences that underlay its development. The argument does not indicate if this guiding principle is based on ideology, general impression, anecdotal evidence, or scientific research and analysis. A single example is presented in which a company's stock prices rebounded as the principle predicts. However, a single example out of the hundreds of thousands, even millions, of stock price movements and patterns over the course of recent history is hardly a basis for guiding investment decisions. Any "principle" that one could dream up would almost certainly yield at least one example from that sea of data.

The argument's prediction assumes that Bargain Liquidation Enterprises (BLE) will follow the rule, as Whiplash Incorporated (WLI) did, rather than be an exception to the rule. Notably, WLI rebounded from a 27 percent drop in stock prices, while the argument predicts that BLE will rebound from an approximately double 45 percent drop in price. The data supporting the balancing principle should be analyzed to ascertain whether there is a point at which price drops become too large so that the balancing principle ceases to bear out.

Finally, the argument predicts great profits in both the near and distant future. However, based on the principle itself the recent downturn should be balanced by an upcoming upswing, which in turn should be balanced by a future downturn. The principle actually predicts an absence of profits and of losses, since all reactions in price are balanced by counter-reactions. Thus, presuming the principle is correct, what is really needed is guidance as to when to get on and off the anticipated roller coaster ride of up and down stock prices, i.e. what is the normal high point of this stock's price at which to sell off and the normal low point of this stock's price at which to buy.

The argument would be greatly strengthened if data and analysis supporting the formation of the guiding principle were presented. Clearly, not every company's stock price that declines dramatically rebounds, as some companies do fail and go out of business. Therefore, the principle that a stock price's movement in one direction will be balanced at some point by an equal and opposite movement in the future must be a generalization, with exceptions to the rule. However, it then becomes imperative to know the frequency with which exceptions occur and, moreover, if there are any factors that could be used to identify exceptions to the rule. Without such supporting information, the argument as presented is not convincing.

Analysis:

Structure: The writer does a great job in presenting all of the pieces necessary for a strong essay. Background on the argument is provided, flaws are revealed in individual paragraphs, and a full paragraph is dedicated to strengtheners.

Evidence: Evidence provided is specific and strong. The writer presents compelling points regarding the lack of a comparable stock example and the failure of the author to consider the short-term fluctuation as part of a longer trend that continues in the wrong way.

Depth of Logic: Depth of logic is solid. The use of key words does an excellent job of guiding the reader along.

Style: The essay is fairly clean. Errors in grammar and syntax are few and not enough to significantly impair understanding. With a bit of proofreading to clean up missing punctuation and the like, this essay has the potential to read flawlessly.

This is a 6 essay. The writer makes a very compelling case for why the author's argument is not only weak but also possibly wrong. The essay is not without mistakes, but it is well written for a first draft.

Essay 5

The following appeared in an announcement by a local community group organizer:

"In a recent interview, the owner of our local Fit and Fashionable sporting goods store stated that sales of the Red Runner Sneakers line are grossing roughly 20 percent higher than they were three years ago when the sneakers were first introduced here. During this time, we've seen a comparable percentage increase in runners from our community placing well at regional track competitions. However, the owner goes on to mention her desire to sharpen the business's focus by eliminating several product lines. As the Red Runners will be one of the discontinued lines, we can expect to see a decline in our community's newfound enthusiasm for running. We should therefore petition the owner of Fit and Fashionable to reconsider this decision."

Student Response (as written, including original errors):

The community organizer argues that the decision made by the owner of Fit and Fashionable to discontinue the Red Runners line will cause a decline in the community's "newfound enthusiasm for running," as evidenced in the percent increase in local runners placing well at regional track competitions. As written, the community organizer's argument is less than compelling due to a number of faulty assumptions and missing data.

The organizer's most profound error is to mistake a correlation for proof of a causal relationship. Red Runners sales are up, and so is the percentage of local runners placing well at track meets: this is the organizer's only evidence for the conclusion that the Red Runners are causing the improved local performance at competitions. In fact, there could be any number of other explanations for the observed correlation between Red Runners sales and improved local running performance. Perhaps there is an alternate reason for local runners' achievement, such as promotion of running by a local health organization, or the recent formation of a running club, or the availability of new trails or an indoor track. It is also entirely possible that there has been a recent influx of runners from other communities, and that those athletes happen to prefer Red Runners sneakers, or that once local runners are drawn to the sport, they develop a preference for the Red Runners line.

Secondly, having erroneously declared Red Runners to be the cause for improved local runners' performance, the organizer assumes that once the Red Runners are discontinued at Fit and Fashionable, those local runners who have been placing well at track competitions will lose their enthusiasm for the sport. Even if Red Runners are the cause of the improved "enthusiasm" and hence the improved performance, it is preposterous to presume that in this day and age, one cannot obtain a particular brand of sneakers anywhere except at a single local sporting goods store. Almost certainly, there are other regional sporting goods stores that compete with Fit and Fashionable and that carry Red Runners. Even if there is no other local or regional sporting goods store that does, just about anything can be purchased via the Internet or through mail-order catalogues, often at discounted prices. If runners genuinely are "enthusiastic" about their sport, and if they really like Red Runners, they will find a way to procure these favored sneakers.

Finally, the community organizer's evidence of the percent increase in local runners placing well at regional track competitions may well be misleading. Is the number of local runners who have improved their performance increasing, or is the number of non-local runners who are performing poorly increasing? It might also simply be the case that the number of non-local runners overall is decreasing. Any of these scenarios would create a percent increase in local runners placing well at regional track meets, but only the first of them would actually support the community organizer's argument.

In order for the community organizer's argument to be convincing, he would need to provide numerical data to show that the number of local runners placing well at regional track meets has in fact increased. Unfortunately, he would also have to rule out other causes for local running prowess other than the Red Runners sneakers line and demonstrate that Red Runners are only available through the local Fit and Fashionable sporting goods store. In all probability, ruling out other causes and demonstrating that there is no other way to obtain Red Runners sneakers would be difficult or impossible. Hence, it is probable that the community organizer's argument cannot be salvaged. Due to the argument's faulty assumptions, it remains unconvincing.

Analysis:

Structure: The writer clearly follows the Kaplan template for this by succinctly paraphrasing the argument in the first paragraph before dedicating a paragraph to each of the argument's major flaws. In the final paragraph, the writer provides examples of what it would take to strengthen the argument before concluding that it is likely beyond salvage.

Evidence: Evidence is solid and plentiful. In each case, the writer presents a plethora of possible alternative explanations.

Depth of Logic: The essay is organized incredibly well. An abundance of key words make transitions extremely easy to follow. While the essay does not get to every single flaw in the original argument (i.e., do the regional track stars mentioned in the prompt even wear Red Runner sneakers?), this will not affect the essay's score. The GMAT graders are looking for a well-developed essay, not one that leaves nothing unexplored.

Style: The writer's style is strong and the lack of grammatical and spelling errors is indicative of time spent proofreading.

This essay would score a 6. The one minor issue with the essay is that the writer's original position of "less than compelling" turns into "impossible to salvage" by the time the essay wraps up. But this is certainly not enough to detract from the score. It is a very strong essay in all four categories of evaluation.

Essay 6

The following is an excerpt from a memo written by the vice president of Innovatronic Corp.:

"In the six months that Samuels has served as executive director of marketing, market share and net profits have plummeted. Product sales have hit a five-year low. During the previous six months, when Nichols served as executive director, our market share was number four in an industry with dozens of competitors, and sales and profits were on the rise. It is clear that we need to replace Samuels with someone of Nichols's caliber immediately."

Student Response (as written, including original errors):

The argument above asserts that Innovatronic's current executive director of marketing, Samuels, should be replaced because the company's profits and market share have dropped significantly during his tenure. However, this argument relies on several unsupported assumptions and is therefore not persuasive.

First, the recommended course of action—replacing Samuels with "someone of Nichols's caliber"—suggests that Samuels, and no one else, is responsible for the decline in market share and net profits. However, this assumption ignores the possibility that other employees could be equally responsible for the problem, if not more so. For instance, while the executive director of marketing likely has some impact on market share and net profits, the directors of other divisions of the company, such as finance or operations, may have greater or equal impacts. Additionally, lower-level employees may be to blame for the company's decline: salespeople may be falling short of their sales goals, manufacturing workers may be producing defective goods, and delivery people may be missing deadlines. Without specific details explaining how or why Samuels himself is responsible for the company's decline, we cannot rule out the possibility of other directors, managers, or lower-level employees being the cause of the problem.

Additionally, this argument rests upon the assumption that no outside factor was responsible for the company's troubles. For example, a depressed local or national economy could result in a decline in sales or profits; an increase in the price of a manufacturing component could cause a reduction in profits; and the introduction of new competitors into the market could lead to a lower market share and profits. Similarly, the goods and services that Innovatronic produces may not be in demand due to a shift in technology, rather than any mismanagement on Samuels's part. For instance, audio electronics technology (such as mp3 technology) evolves rapidly, and products relying on older or outdated technology can quickly fall out of favor with the public. If Innovatronic is producing outdated goods, then Samuels may have little, if any, ability within his position of director of marketing to generate sales of a product that is no longer in demand. Without evidence demonstrating that these alternative scenarios are not responsible for the company's problems, we cannot assume that Samuels is to blame simply because his tenure coincided with the decline in company profits.

Finally, this argument assumes the company's performance reflects the influence of its current leadership. The argument suggests that because performance dropped during the six months that Samuels has been director of marketing, it must be actions taken during those six months that are responsible for the drop in profits and market share. However, it is equally likely that policies implemented before Samuels became director of marketing are in fact to blame for the company's current performance. If this is the case, Nichols's performance might be the cause of the company's decline, and the conclusion that Samuels be replaced with someone of Nichols's caliber becomes completely invalid.

To make this argument persuasive, the author needs to include additional evidence to address these assumptions. In particular, this argument needs specific details regarding Samuels's actions and decisions as director of marketing and an explanation of how they are the direct cause of the company's drop in market share and profits. The argument would also benefit from details demonstrating that there are no other causes of Innovatronic's current performance, such as outside factors or the performance of other employees, as these details would strengthen the claim that Samuels is the primary cause. Without this additional evidence, this argument cannot be persuasive, and the recommendation to replace Samuels cannot be acted upon.

Analysis:

Structure: The structure in this essay is strong. The writer begins with a paragraph that clearly lays out the argument before introducing flaws in several subsequent body paragraphs and rounding out the essay with a paragraph that lays out possible strengtheners.

Evidence: Evidence, for the most part, is solid. It is not as compelling in the second paragraph, which explores blaming lower-level employees rather than the executive director for a loss of profits and market share in a company. However, the wealth of compelling evidence renders this one weak spot a minor issue.

Depth of Logic: The writer's logic is clear and easy to follow. Points are clear and illustrated with specific examples. Key words are used to great effect for transitioning from one paragraph to the next.

Style: The style is explanatory and forceful. Minor issues of syntax are present, such as referring to the executive director simply as a director, but this does not merit a reduction in score.

This essay would earn a 6. The writer presents a strong and compelling argument in a well-written essay. The writer did not pick up on certain opportunities, such as the possibility that Samuels is taking a calculated short-term risk for a long-term play, but what was discussed and covered is already enough to merit a top score.

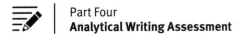

Essay 7

The following is part of an article in the local news section of a newspaper:

"Fifteen middle school children were sent home sick last Friday. An investigation has revealed that all 15 students had been served school lunches containing pepper jack cheese. What's particularly worrisome is the presence of abnormally colored specks embedded in the cheese's surface. Health officials have thus far refused to release a public statement acknowledging the danger posed by pepper jack but, given the facts, it would not be wise to allow your children to consume pepper jack cheese."

Student Response (as written, including original errors):

The author of this article advises his readers against giving their children pepper jack cheese. He bases this advice on the fact that over a dozen students fell ill the previous week, and that all had received school lunches containing pepper jack cheese that had irregularly-colored specks. While the author's argument may have some merit, as written it relies on unsubstantiated assumptions and is unconvincing.

Firstly, the author presupposes that the pepper jack cheese is in fact the source of the students' illness. However, all that he tells the reader is that these students were served lunches containing pepper jack, and in so doing, he ignores the multitude of other possible causes of sickness. Perhaps it was another ingredient that was served as part of the same school meal, or perhaps a group of students who coincidentally had eaten the same lunch decided to fake being sick in order to go home early. Without additional evidence to prove that the cheese in fact caused the students to become ill, there is little reason to believe that parents should avoid giving similar food to their children.

Secondly, the author cites the fact that the cheese in the children's meals had specks of an abnormal color to further his theory, without demonstrating to the reader that these specks increase the likelihood that the cheese was poisonous. It is entirely possible that the cheese had colors that are not considered "normal" for pepper jack, but that this did not make it any less healthy to eat than cheese without specks. Until he can provide information to prove that the specks made the cheese unhealthy for consumption, the reader must remain open to the possibility that the pepper jack played no role in the outbreak of sickness.

If the author were to offer additional facts surrounding this situation, he would be more likely to sway his readers to not feed children pepper jack. Specifically, much more information is needed either from the health officials mentioned, or from a doctor that treated the sick students, demonstrating that the cheese (and not some other food or ailment) did in fact cause the students to be sent home. Alternatively, he could bolster his theory by further explaining the link between the irregularly-colored specks and the health of the cheese—if these specks were in fact a sign that the pepper jack had turned rotten, this would make his conclusion much more believable. Without the inclusion of such data, however, the argument remains flimsy and is unlikely to have a significant effect on parents.

Analysis:

Structure: The writer closely followed the Kaplan template. The first paragraph clearly lays out the argument. Each of the next two paragraphs fleshes out a major flaw in the author's argument. The final paragraph provides specific suggestions for what is needed to bolster the argument.

Evidence: The provided evidence is strong. While some minor flaws are present, such as missing the opportunity to mention that the health officials' refusal to release a public statement is actually a pretty strong argument against the original author's position, overall the writer of this essay presents specific, plausible alternatives.

Depth of Logic: Organization is strong. Transitional key words are put to good use, making the essay very easy to follow.

Style: The writing style is smooth and fluid. Grammatical errors are minimal and certainly not present to the extent that they affect understanding.

This essay would receive a score of 6. The essay is compelling and well written, and flaws are minor and few.

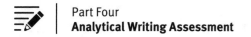

Essay 8

The following is an excerpt from a factory manager's report:

"Ten years ago, my staff of 20 employees was sufficient to keep our facilities operating at 50 percent capacity. During this time, I've gradually instituted certain changes in policy that have clearly worked for the better: The same 20 employees are now able to keep our facilities operating at 85 percent capacity. All of this was done while keeping their salaries at roughly the same level, adjusted for inflation. Therefore, we do not need to award any substantial raises at this time."

Student Response (as written, including original errors):

The factory manager who wrote the above report has concluded that his factory does not need to award substantial raises to its employees. He bases this claim on a steadily increased rate of factory operation over the past decade, despite wages of factory workers remaining flat (in terms of real dollars). However, this argument fails to address too many factors for it to make a compelling case.

For one, the information about capacity is given in a vacuum. The manager takes credit for his factory running at 85 percent capacity, 35 percent higher than it ran 10 years ago. But without knowing what 100 percent capacity is, we can't place any value on that improvement. Technological advances could have increased the factory's maximum output. If workers are not just keeping pace with but gaining on modern technology, and they've done so on a budget, then the manager's accomplishments are impressive. But conversely, if the product itself is increasing in technological complexity, production might have slowed down considerably. 85 percent of maximum today might represent the same or lower volume than did 50 percent of the old cap—and if things are slowing down, judicious raises to motivate employees might be necessary to boost productivity.

Additionally, the manager fails to consider factors outside his own factory. While salary in absolute terms is a useful metric, it's far more useful to know how those wages changed relative to the industry, and to the population as a whole. If the 10-year span described in the text covered an economic recession, it's possible that almost no one was getting raises. And, if the factory produced for a flagging industry, lost profits and competition with outsourcing might have resulted in industry-wide salary cuts. In other words, the "flat" salaries might have actually represented de facto raises relative to everyone else in the factory workers' community. And of course, economic and industry slumps tend to be temporary. If the economy has since picked up and the industry recovered, then continuing to subject workers to austerity measures would be inappropriate and could even prove self-destructive.

To be convincing, the proposal must consider all these possibilities. Its author must establish that the improvements in output are not just in percentage terms but also in real terms. The factory needs to be meeting it parent company's needs. The manager must also establish the business and economic environment has not changed significantly over the past 10 years. Even if we assume that his policy changes and flat wages worked in the past, we need to know that it will still work today. However, none of this data is included. For these reasons, although the author's conclusions may prove correct with further analysis, the proposal in its current form should be rejected.

Analysis:

Structure: This is a great example of the Kaplan template in action. The essay opens with a succinct paraphrase of the argument, fleshes out two major flaws in separate body paragraphs, then closes with recommendations for a stronger argument.

Evidence: Evidence provided is strong and relevant. The writer presents several types of real-world information data whose presence could have an effect on the author's argument.

Depth of Logic: The writer's logic is solid. Relevant possible economic conditions are presented to clearly show the impact that missing data is having on the author's argument.

Style: The writing style is professional, though perhaps a bit highbrow. While such a style could result in reduced clarity, this is generally not the case in this essay.

This essay would earn a 6. The writer uses a concise and professional tone, resulting in an essay that is clear and compelling.

Essay 9

The following is part of an internal sales memo for The Groomed Man, a reseller of men's hygiene products:

"Sales of the XP2500 electric razor have been well above expectations, but sales of its replacement cartridges have been rather disappointing. If our company is serious about success, we must either make changes to reduce the durability of the cartridges so that consumers would need to replace them more often or increase their price."

Student Response (as written, including original errors):

The author of the memo asserts that The Groomed Man must either reduce the durability or increase the retail price of replacement cartridges for its popular electric razor, the XP2500. The only evidence presented is that sales of the razor have exceeded expectations while sales of the cartridges have not met their target. This reasoning is not persuasive, as it neglects to consider several important possibilities.

The first of these unconsidered possibilities is the potential for the proposed plan to further reduce sales. If the replacement cartridges are made less durable, consumers may be disappointed in the product. Word of the cartridges' low quality may spread quickly via online user reviews, thus creating a bad reputation for the company, hurting overall sales.

The author of the memo has also failed to consider what other factors may have contributed to the low sales of replacement cartridges. If durability is not the issue, then the proposed plan will have little impact. Perhaps the XP2500 can use another brand's cartridges. If this is the case, then making The Groomed Man's cartridges a less appealing product will not improve sales.

The author of the memo also fails to consider whether the sales expectations themselves were reasonable. Perhaps the XP2500 is a new product—if the razor has not been on the market long, consumers would not yet have needed to purchase many replacement cartridges.

Lastly, the author of the memo is not clear about what are the appropriate criteria for "success." If the company's success relies upon a high volume of cartridge sales, then perhaps change is needed. But if cartridges provide very low profit margins, and razors provide very high profit margins, then perhaps the best path to profitability is to focus on selling razors and to not be concerned with cartridge sales.

For the argument to be more convincing, the author must show that the sales targets for the replacement razors was reasonable, and that the success of The Groomed Man relies upon a high volume of cartridge sales. Further, the author must show that high durability was the only factor responsible for the low sales of cartridges. Lastly, the author must demonstrate that lowering the quality will not ultimately lead to further reduction of sales. Until these considerations are addressed, the memo's argument will not be convincing.

Analysis:

Structure: This essay makes excellent use of the Kaplan template. An opening paragraph succinctly lays out the argument, each of several body paragraphs focuses on a specific flaw in the author's reasoning, and a closing paragraph provides suggestions to strengthen the logic.

Evidence: Evidence provided is specific and solid. The writer explores a number of alternative explanations to the scenario, from using other brands of replacements to the product possibly being brand new. Minor issues are present, such as missing the possibility that crippling the replacement cartridges could damage the strong razor sales, which would in turn further cripple cartridge sales. What is presented, however, is sufficient to provide a compelling argument in its own right, so this does not negatively impact the score.

Depth of Logic: The use of key words and the clarity of supporting details make this essay easy to follow.

Style: Style is clear and compact. The lack of jargon and grammatical errors makes this a very fluid essay.

This is a 6 essay. It evaluates well in all four criteria and its quality stays consistent and error-free throughout despite the impressive number of paragraphs.

Essay 10

The following is an excerpt from the regional director's report:

"Regarding the district manager position, both Ibrahim and Einhorn have shown interest, but Ibrahim is clearly the more qualified of the two. Over the past few years, Ibrahim has improved employee retention by 40 percent and greatly boosted the morale of his team, and performance metrics are at a multi-year high. When polled, the majority of Ibrahim's employees had nothing but praise for Ibrahim's management style. Promoting Einhorn to the position would be a mistake, as her management style differs markedly from Ibrahim's."

Student Response (as written, including original errors):

A person in charge of hiring a new district manager is currently evaluating two possible candidates for the position. While both Ibrahim and Einhorn have shown interest, the author of the argument clearly advocates for the hiring of Ibrahim over Einhorn, based off of a number of seemingly logical positions. However, upon closer inspection, the author's argument as currently written does not hold up to scrutiny. In addition to a glaring lack of details regarding the qualifications of Einhorn, the author also makes a number of assumptions in describing Ibrahim's performance metrics. In order to endorse the author's suggestion, some additional information is needed.

First of all, although the author is comparing Ibrahim to Einhorn, there is a complete failure on the part of the author to discuss the merits—or lack thereof—of one of the candidates entirely. Indeed, the principal reason the author declares Ibrahim the more qualified candidate is a series of performance metrics showing solid improvement across a number of measures. Admittedly, the stats are impressive. Ibrahim has improved employee retention, boosted the morale of his team, and improved in other key areas. Unfortunately, no such record of Einhorn's performance is given. It's entirely possible that during the same time period, Einhorn met or exceeded Ibrahim's performance in each category. Without that information, it is difficult to determine who is the more qualified candidate.

Additionally, the assumptions underlying Ibrahim's impressive performance metrics are numerous. Though employee retention within his division has improved by 40 percent under his management, it is not clear if this is the result of Ibrahim's decisions and managerial style, or if this is a company-wide phenomenon. It's possible that the economy has suffered in the last few years, and more employees are staying at the same company out of fear of not finding another job. Another unwarranted assumption made by the author is that the effusive praise for Ibrahim is a sincere expression of praise for his managerial style, but if the employees were concerned that Ibrahim would see their comments, for example, then they would be less likely to honestly appraise his ability as a manager.

Finally, the author mentions that promoting Einhorn over Ibrahim would be a mistake, considering the fact that the managerial styles of the two candidates differ markedly. However, without an understanding of the different managerial styles, it is difficult to determine who would make a better district manager. It's entirely possible that Ibrahim's abilities lend themselves to his current position, while Einhorn's managerial style is more suited for the role of the district manager. Ultimately, without an understanding of the skills and talents that Einhorn brings to the table, and without a more complete picture of the demands required of the district manager, it is difficult to evaluate the merits of this particular argument.

In order to persuasively argue that Ibrahim is a better candidate, the author needs to first present the performance metrics of Einhorn. If it is clear from the statistics that Einhorn is a poor manager, for example, then the argument becomes more credible. Moreover, the author needs to tie together the abilities and talents of Ibrahim with the demands of the district manager position. Boosting employee morale and getting along with employees may be great in his current position, but the demands of the district manager don't require such people skills. It's possible that the job requires more analytics and coordination, which might better suit Einhorn's managerial style. Until these issues are clarified, the argument that Ibrahim should be hired over Einhorn seems flimsy at best.

Analysis:

Structure: The essay makes heavy use of the Kaplan template. The argument is clearly detailed in the first paragraph. The writer then spends three more paragraphs fleshing out three of the argument's main flaws before concluding with a paragraph that specifies what would be needed to make this a compelling argument.

Evidence: The evidence provided is strong. The writer acknowledges the few merits of the original author's argument before providing solid evidence as to why these alone do not make the argument compelling.

Depth of Logic: Organization enhances the depth of logic in this essay. The writer lays out all of the original argument's merits before attacking it, resulting in a very persuasive essay. Transitional key words are used effectively.

Style: The style is very calm and purposeful, with a clear focus on the goal from the start. The prose is clean and mostly devoid of even minor errors, a sign that the writer budgeted time efficiently enough to proofread.

This is a 6 essay with no major flaws. Argumentation is clear and purposeful from the start, and the writer clearly took the time to present a clean first draft.

Appendixes

Grammar Reference Guide

Sentence Structure

Understanding the basic rules of sentence structure enables you to spot the classic GMAT errors quickly. The fundamental principles described here will play a role in nearly every Sentence Correction item you see, whether in the original version or among some of the answer choices. It's important to learn this basic material, especially if English is not your native language.

Run-On Sentences

When a sentence consists of more than one clause (a group of words that contains a subject and a verb), those clauses must be joined properly. It is never acceptable to hook two clauses together with just a comma, as the "sentence" below does. That's called a **run-on sentence**.

Wrong: Nietzsche moved to Basel in 1869, he planned to teach classical philology.

There are a number of acceptable ways to fix a run-on.

Correct: Nietzsche moved to Basel in 1869; he planned to teach classical philology.

Also Correct: Nietzsche planned to teach classical philology; therefore, he moved to Basel in 1869.

Also Correct: Nietzsche moved to Basel in 1869, and he planned to teach classical philology. (The words *for, and, nor, but, or, yet,* and *so* are known as coordinating conjunctions. You can remember them by the acronym FANBOYS.)

Also Correct: Because Nietzsche planned to teach classical philology, he moved to Basel in 1869. (Words such as *because, although, if,* and *though* are known as subordinating conjunctions.)

Also Correct: Nietzsche, who planned to teach classical philology, moved to Basel in 1869. (Words such as *who, whom, which, where, that,* and *whose* are known as relative pronouns.)

Sentence Fragments

Every sentence must contain at least one complete independent clause. If there is no independent clause at all, or if what's supposed to be the independent clause is incomplete, you've got a **sentence fragment**.

Wrong: While most people, who have worked hard for many years, have not managed to save any money.

This sentence fragment consists of nothing but subordinate clauses. There has to be an independent clause.

Correct: Most people, who have worked hard for many years, have not managed to save any money, although they are trying to be more frugal now.

Also Correct: While most people, who have worked hard for many years, have not managed to save any money, they are trying to be more frugal now.

Subject-Verb Agreement

Remember, in English, a subject and its verb must **agree** in number and person. **Number** refers to whether a subject (or a verb) is singular or plural. **Person** refers to first person (*I, we*), second person (*you*), and third person (*he, she, it, one, they*).

Intervening Phrases

When the subject of a sentence is followed by a phrase (a group of words that does not have a subject and verb) or relative clause, the words are not part of the subject. They simply add information about that subject.

Learn to recognize groups of words that can come between the subject and verb!

1. **Relative clauses**, which contain important information about the subject of another clause, are very often placed in between a subject and verb. (The previous sentence contains a relative clause.)

Wrong: John Clare, *who during the mid-nineteenth century wrote many fine poems on rural themes,* were confined for decades to an insane asylum.

The subject is *John Clare*, which is singular, but the verb is *were*, which is plural. The fact that the relative clause ends with a plural noun (*themes*) is supposed to distract you from the fact that the subject and verb don't agree.

Correct: John Clare, who during the mid-nineteenth century wrote many fine poems on rural themes, *was* confined for decades to an insane asylum.

2. **Appositives** often come between a subject and a verb. Appositives are nouns, pronouns, or noun phrases that are placed next to nouns to describe them further.

Wrong: John Smith, *the man who led British expeditions to several American sites,* have left several written accounts of dramatic events there.

Correct: John Smith, the man who led British expeditions to several American sites, *has* left several written accounts of dramatic events there.

Relative clauses and appositives are sometimes set off from the rest of the sentence by commas. When this is the case, it's a dead giveaway that those words are not part of the subject. That makes checking for subject-verb agreement much easier; just ignore the words set off by commas and concentrate on the subject and the verb.

3.   The **prepositional phrase** is an all-time favorite.

Wrong: Wild animals *in jungles all over the world* is endangered.

Correct: Wild animals in jungles all over the world *are* endangered.

Prepositional phrases, and some relative clauses and appositives, are not set off by commas. It's harder to recognize intervening phrases and clauses when they're not set off by commas, but if you remember to check each sentence carefully for such things, you'll be able to pick them out anyway.

Compound Subjects

When two nouns or groups of nouns are joined by *and*, they're called a **compound subject** and are therefore plural.

Correct: *Ontario and Quebec* contain about two-thirds of the population of Canada.

Some connecting phrases may look as though they should make a group of words into a compound subject— but they don't result in a compound subject.

Wrong: George Bernard Shaw, as well as Mahatma Gandhi and River Phoenix, were vegetarians.

And is the only connecting word that results in a compound and plural subject. The following words and phrases do not create compound subjects:

along with	*as well as*
together with	*besides*
in addition to	

Correct: *George Bernard Shaw*, as well as Mahatma Gandhi and River Phoenix, *was* a vegetarian.

Wrong: Neither Thomas Jefferson nor Alexander Hamilton were supportive of Aaron Burr's political ambitions.

When words in the subject position are connected by *either . . . or* or *neither . . . nor*, the verb agrees with the last word in the pair. If the last word is singular, the verb must be singular. If the last word is plural, the verb must be plural.

Correct: Neither Thomas Jefferson nor *Alexander Hamilton was* supportive of Aaron Burr's political ambitions.

Correct: Neither Thomas Jefferson nor *the Federalists were* supportive of Aaron Burr's political ambitions.

Both . . . and is the only pair that always results in a plural subject.

Correct: *Both* Thomas Jefferson *and* Alexander Hamilton *were* unsupportive of Aaron Burr's political ambitions.

Unusual Sentence Patterns

When you're checking for subject-verb disagreement, remember that the subject doesn't always appear before the verb.

Wrong: Dominating the New York skyline is the Empire State Building and the Chrysler Building.

The subject of this sentence is a compound subject, *the Empire State Building and the Chrysler Building*. The verb should be plural.

Correct: Dominating the New York skyline *are* the Empire State Building and the Chrysler Building.

Subjects That Are Not Nouns or Pronouns

An entire clause can serve as the subject of a sentence. When used as subject, a clause always takes a singular verb:

Whether the economy will improve in the near future *is* a matter of great concern.

Infinitives and gerunds can be used as subjects. Remember that they're singular subjects:

To err is human.
Rollerblading is dangerous.

See the section on verbs for more on infinitives and gerunds.

Modification

Adjectives and adverbs aren't the only sentence elements whose job it is to modify. Phrases and even relative clauses can act as modifiers in a sentence. The following sentence contains several types of modifiers:

Waiting to regain enough strength to eat, a cheetah, which expends most of its energy in the chase, must rest beside its prey.

Waiting to regain enough strength to eat is a phrase that describes the cheetah, as does the relative clause *which expends most of its energy in the chase*. The phrase *beside its prey* modifies the verb *rest*.

English depends heavily on word order to establish modifying relationships. When a sentence's modifiers violate the conventions of word order, confusion often results.

Introductory Modifiers

Wrong: Sifting the sand of a riverbed, gold was discovered by prospectors in California in 1848.

A modifying phrase that begins a sentence refers to the noun or pronoun immediately following the phrase. But if we apply that rule here, the sentence says that the *gold was sifting sand*. See the problem? The author presumably meant to say that the prospectors were sifting sand. There are several ways to correct the sentence so that it expresses the intended meaning.

Correct: Sifting the sand in a riverbed, prospectors discovered gold in California in 1848.
Also Correct: Prospectors, sifting the sand in a riverbed, discovered gold in California in 1848.

Also Correct: Gold was discovered by prospectors, who were sifting the sand in a riverbed, in California in 1848.

In all three cases, the phrase or clause directly precedes or follows the noun it describes.

Dangling Modifiers

A modifying phrase or clause should clearly refer to a particular word in the sentence. A modifying phrase or clause that does not sensibly refer to any word in the sentence is called a **dangling modifier.** The most common sort of dangler is an introductory modifying phrase that's followed by a word it can't logically refer to.

Wrong: Desiring to free his readers from superstition, the theories of Epicurus are expounded in Lucretius's poem *De rerum natura.*

The problem with this sentence is that the phrase that begins the sentence seems to modify the noun following it: *theories.* In fact, there is really nowhere the modifier can be put to make it work properly and no noun to which it can reasonably refer (*Lucretius's,* the possessive, is functioning as an adjective modifying *poem*). Get rid of dangling constructions by clarifying the modification relationship or by making the dangler into a subordinate clause.

Correct: Desiring to free his readers from superstition, Lucretius expounded the theories of Epicurus in his poem *De rerum natura.*

Now the phrase *desiring to free his readers from superstition* clearly refers to the proper noun *Lucretius.*

Other Modifiers

In correcting some misplaced introductory modifiers, we move the modifier to a position inside the sentence rather than at the beginning. This is perfectly acceptable, but just remember that modifying phrases inside a sentence can also be misplaced.

Wrong: That night they sat discussing when the cow might calve in the kitchen.

The problem here is the phrase *in the kitchen,* which seems to refer to where the cow might have her calf. What the author probably meant to say is the following correct sentence:

Correct: That night they sat in the kitchen discussing when the cow might calve.

This sentence is correct because the phrase comes directly after the word it modifies: the verb *sat.*

Wrong: As a young man, the French novelist Gustave Flaubert traveled in Egypt, which was a fascinating experience.

It's not that *Egypt* itself was a fascinating experience, but that traveling there was fascinating.

Correct: Traveling in Egypt as a young man was a fascinating experience for the French novelist Gustave Flaubert.

Pronouns

When doing Sentence Correction questions, always try to locate the antecedent of a pronoun (that is, the word to which the pronoun refers). Most of the pronoun problems you'll encounter on the test result from a problem in the relationship of the pronoun and its antecedent.

Pronoun Reference

In GMAT English, a pronoun must refer clearly to one and only one antecedent.

1. Watch out for sentences in which pronouns refer to indefinite antecedents, paying particular attention to the pronoun *they*. (Avoid references to some vague *they*.)

Wrong: They serve meals on many of the buses that run from Santiago to Antofagasta. (Who are *they*?)

Better: Meals are served on many of the buses that run from Santiago to Antofagasta.

In the preceding sentence, it's acceptable to use the passive voice because you don't know who is doing the action. Also note that it's quite all right to use *it* like this:

> *It* seldom rains in Death Valley.

2. Sometimes a sentence is structured so that a pronoun can refer to more than one thing, and as a result the reader doesn't know what the author intended.

Wrong: Pennsylvania Governor William Keith encouraged the young Benjamin Franklin to open his own printing shop because he perceived that the quality of printing in Philadelphia was poor. (*Which* man perceived that the quality of printing in Philadelphia was poor?)

Pronouns are assumed to refer to the nearest reasonable antecedent. Nonetheless, it is best to avoid structural ambiguity of the sort that occurs in this sentence.

Better: Because *he* perceived that the quality of printing in Philadelphia was poor, Pennsylvania Governor *William Keith* encouraged the young Benjamin Franklin to open his own printing shop. (*Keith* perceived that the quality of printing was poor.)

Better: Because the young *Benjamin Franklin* perceived that the quality of printing in Philadelphia was poor, Pennsylvania Governor William Keith encouraged *him* to open *his* own printing shop. (In this version, *Franklin* is the one who perceived that the printing was poor.)

3. Sometimes it's easy to see what the author meant to use for the antecedent, but when you examine the sentence more closely, that antecedent is nowhere to be found. Correct the problem either by replacing the pronoun with a noun or by providing a clear antecedent.

Poor: The proslavery writer A. C. C. Thompson questioned Frederick Douglass's authorship of *The Narrative*, claiming that he was too uneducated to have written such an eloquent book.

What's the antecedent of *he*? It should be the noun *Frederick Douglass*, but the sentence contains only the possessive form *Douglass's*. As a rule, avoid using a possessive form as the antecedent of a personal pronoun.

Better:	The proslavery writer A. C. C. Thompson questioned whether Frederick Douglass actually wrote *The Narrative*, claiming that *he* was too uneducated to have written such an eloquent book.

Oddball Problems

Here are two oddball pronoun reference problems to watch out for:

DO SO

Wrong:	It is common for a native New Yorker who has never driven a car to move to another part of the country and have to learn to do it.
Better:	It is common for a native New Yorker who has never driven a car to move to another part of the country and have to learn to *do so*.

ONE AND *YOU*

When we give advice to others or make general statements, we often use the pronouns *one* and *you*. "You should brush your teeth every day." "One never knows what to do in a situation like that."

It is never acceptable to mix *one* and *you*, or *one* and *yours*, or *you* and *one's* in a sentence together.

Wrong:	One shouldn't eat a high-fat diet and avoid exercise, and then be surprised when you gain weight.
Correct:	*One* shouldn't eat a high-fat diet and avoid exercise, and then be surprised when *one* gains weight.
Also Correct:	*You* shouldn't eat a high-fat diet and avoid exercise, and then be surprised when *you* gain weight.

Also, never use *one* or *one's* to refer to any antecedent except *one*.

Wrong:	A person should leave a light on in an empty house if one wants to give the impression that someone is at home.
Correct:	A *person* should leave a light on in an empty house if *he or she* wants to give the impression that someone is at home.
Also Correct:	*One* should leave a light on in an empty house if *one* wants to give the impression that someone is at home.
Also Correct:	*One* should leave a light on in an empty house if *he or she* wants to give the impression that someone is at home.

Pronoun Agreement

Always use singular pronouns to refer to singular entities and plural pronouns to refer to plural entities. First, identify the antecedent of a given pronoun, and don't allow yourself to be distracted by a phrase that comes between the two. The GMAT will frequently try to confuse you by inserting a phrase containing plural nouns between a pronoun and its singular antecedent, or vice versa.

Wrong:	A cactus will flower in spite of the fact that they receive little water.
Correct:	A *cactus* will flower in spite of the fact that *it* receives little water.
Wrong:	The number of people with college degrees is many times what they were last summer.
Correct:	The *number* of people with college degrees is many times what *it* was last summer.

Note: The number is always singular. (The number of cookies he ate *was* impressive.) *A number* is always plural. (A number of turkeys *were* gathered outside the shed.)

Pronoun Case

One type of pronoun problem you can't catch by looking at the relationship between a pronoun and its antecedent is wrong case.

	Subjective Case	Objective Case
First Person:	*I, we*	*me, us*
Second Person:	*you*	*you*
Third Person:	*he, she, it, they, one*	*him, her, it, them, one*
Relative Pronouns:	*who, that, which*	*whom, that, which*

When to Use Subjective Case Pronouns

1. Use the subjective case for the subject of a sentence:
    She is falling asleep.
2. Use the subjective case after forms of *to be*:
    It is *I*.
3. Use the subjective case in comparisons between the subjects of understood verbs:
    Gary is taller than *I* (am tall).

When to Use Objective Case Pronouns

1. Use the objective case for the object of a verb:
    I called *him*.
2. Use the objective case for the object of a preposition:
    I laughed at *her*.
3. Use the objective case after infinitives and gerunds:
    Asking *him* to go was a big mistake.
4. Use the objective case in comparisons between objects of understood verbs:
    She calls you more than (she calls) *me*.

There probably won't be many times when you are in doubt as to which case of a pronoun is correct. However, the following hints may prove helpful:

When two or more nouns or pronouns are functioning the same way in a sentence, determine the correct case of any pronoun by considering it separately:

Beatrice and (*I* or *me*) are going home early.

Without *Beatrice*, should the sentence read: *Me am going home early* or *I am going home early*? *I am going*, of course, so *Beatrice and I are going home early*.

A common mistake in the use of relative pronouns is using *who* (subject case) when *whom* (object case) is needed, or vice versa. If you tend to confuse the two, try the following system.

Scholars have disagreed over (*who* or *whom*) is most likely to have written *A Yorkshire Tragedy*, but some early sources attribute it to Shakespeare.

1. Isolate the relative pronoun in its own clause: *Whom is most likely to have written* A Yorkshire Tragedy.

2. Ask yourself the question: Who or whom wrote *A Yorkshire Tragedy*?

3. Answer with an ordinary personal pronoun: *He* did. (If you are a native speaker of English, your ear undoubtedly tells you that *him did* is wrong.)

4. Since *he* is in the subjective case, we need the subjective case relative pronoun: *who*. Therefore, this sentence should read:
    Scholars have disagreed over *who* is most likely to have written *A Yorkshire Tragedy*, but some early sources attribute it to Shakespeare.

Verbs

Here are some important terms and concepts to review before you read this section:

Verb: A word that expresses an action or a state of being.

Verbal: A word that is formed from a verb but is not functioning as a verb. There are three kinds of verbals: *participles*, *gerunds*, and *infinitives*.

It is important to realize that a verbal is not a verb, because a sentence must contain a verb, and a verbal won't do. A group of words containing a verbal but lacking a verb is not a sentence.

Participle: Usually ends in *–ing* or *–ed*. It is used as an adjective in a sentence:

Let *sleeping* dogs lie.
It is difficult to calm a *frightened* child.
Peering into his microscope, Robert Koch saw the tuberculosis bacilli.

Gerund: Always ends in *–ing*. It is used in a sentence as a noun:

Skiing can be dangerous.
Raising a family is a serious task.
I was surprised at his *acting* like such a coward.

Note from the third sentence that a noun or pronoun that comes before a gerund is in the possessive form: *his*, not *him*.

Infinitive: The basic form of a verb, generally preceded by *to*. It is usually used as a noun but may be used as an adjective or an adverb:

> Winston Churchill liked *to paint*. (Infinitive used as a noun.)
> The will *to conquer* is crucial. (Infinitive used as an adjective—modifies the *will*.)
> Students in imperial China studied the Confucian classics *to excel* on civil service exams. (Infinitive used as an adverb—modifies *studied*.)

Verb Tense

On the GMAT, you'll find items that are wrong because a verb is in the wrong tense. To spot this kind of problem, you need to be familiar with both the way each tense is used individually and the ways the tenses are used together.

Present Tense

Use the present tense to describe a state or action occurring in the present time:

> Congress *is* debating health policy this session.

Use the present tense to describe habitual action:

> Many Americans *jog* every day.

Use the present tense to describe "general truths"—things that are always true:

> The earth *is* round and *rotates* on its axis.

Past Tense

Use the simple past tense to describe an event or state that took place at a specific time in the past, and is now over and done with:

> Hundreds of people *died* when the *Titanic* sank.
> Few people *bought* new cars last year.

There are two other ways to express past action:

> Bread *used to* cost a few cents per loaf.
> The presidential candidate *did promise* not to raise taxes.

Future Tense

Use the future tense for intended actions or actions expected in the future:

> The 22nd century *will begin* in the year 2101.

We often express future actions with the expression *to be going to*:

> I *am going to move* to another apartment as soon as possible.

The simple present tense is also used to speak of future events. This is called the **anticipatory future.** We often use the anticipatory future with verbs of motion, such as *come, go, arrive, depart,* and *leave*:

> The senator *is leaving* for Europe tomorrow.

We also use the anticipatory future in two-clause sentences when one verb is in the regular future tense:

> The disputants will announce the new truce as soon as they *agree* on its terms.

Present Perfect Tense

Use the present perfect tense for actions and states that started in the past and continue up to and into the present time:

> Hawaii *has been* a state since 1959.

Use the present perfect for actions and states that happen a number of times in the past and may happen again in the future:

> Italy *has had* many changes in government since World War II.

Use the present perfect for something that happened at an unspecified time in the past. Notice the difference in meaning between the two sample sentences below:

Present Perfect: Susan Sontag *has written* a critical essay about Leni Riefenstahl. (We have no idea when—we just know she wrote it.)

Simple Past: Susan Sontag *wrote* a critical essay about Leni Riefenstahl in 1974. (We use the simple past because we're specifying when Sontag wrote the essay.)

Past Perfect Tense

The past perfect tense is used to represent past actions or states that were completed before other past actions or states. The more recent past event is expressed in the simple past, and the earlier past event is expressed in the past perfect:

> After he came to America, Vladimir Nabokov translated novels that *he had* written in Russian while he was living in Europe.

Note the difference in meaning between these two sentences:

> The Civil War *had ended* when Lincoln was shot. = *The war was over by the time of Lincoln's death.*
> The Civil War *ended* when Lincoln was shot. = *The war ended when Lincoln died.*

Future Perfect Tense

Use the future perfect tense for a future state or event that will take place before another future event:

> By the time the next election is held, the candidates *will have debated* at least once. (Note that the present tense form [anticipatory future] is used in the first clause.)

Sequence of Tenses

When a sentence has two or more verbs in it, you should always check to see whether the tenses of those verbs correctly indicate the order in which things happened. As a general rule, if two things happened at the same time, the verbs should be in the same tense.

Wrong: Just as the sun rose, the rooster crows.

Rose is past tense, and *crows* is present tense, but the words *just as* indicate that both things happened at the same time. The verbs should be in the same tense.

Correct: Just as the sun *rose*, the rooster *crowed*.

Also Correct: Just as the sun *rises*, the rooster *crows*.

When we're talking about the past or the future, we often want to indicate that one thing happened or will happen before another. That's where the past perfect and the future perfect come in.

Use the past perfect for the earlier of two past events and the simple past for the later event.

Wrong: Mozart finished about two thirds of the Requiem when he died.

Putting both verbs of the sentence in the simple past tense makes it sound as if Mozart wrote two thirds of the Requiem after dying. If we put the first verb into the past perfect, though, the sentence makes much more sense.

Correct: Mozart *had finished* about two thirds of the Requiem when he *died*.

Note: Occasionally, the GMAT won't use the past perfect for the earlier event. They'll use a word like *before* or *after* to make the sequence of events clear. You should always look for the past perfect, but if it's not there, you can settle for the simple past with a time word such as *before* or *after*.

Use the future perfect for the earlier of two future events.

Wrong: By the time I write to Leo, he will probably move.

The point the author is trying to get across is not that Leo will move when he gets the letter, but that by the time the letter arrives he'll be living somewhere else.

Correct: By the time I write to Leo, he *will* probably *have moved*.

When you use a participial phrase in a sentence, the action or the situation that phrase describes is assumed to take place at the same time as the action or state described by the verb of the sentence.

Wrong: *Being* a French colony, Senegal is a Francophone nation.

This implies that Senegal is still a French colony. We can make the information in the participial phrase refer to an earlier time than does the verb by changing the regular participle to what's called a **perfect participle.** The way to do it is to use *having + the past participle.*

Correct: *Having been a French colony*, Senegal is a Francophone nation.

You can do the same thing with infinitives by replacing the regular infinitive with *to have + the past participle:*

I'm glad *to meet* you. (I'm glad to be in the process of meeting you right now.)
I'm glad *to have met* you. (I'm glad now that I met you earlier today, last week, or whenever.)

Subjunctive Mood

On the GMAT, you may come across an item that tests your knowledge of the subjunctive. Subjunctive verb forms are used in two ways.

The subjunctive form *were* is used in statements that express a wish or situations that are contrary to fact:

I wish I *were* a rich man. (But I'm not.)
If I *were* you, I wouldn't do that. (But I'm not you.)

The **subjunctive of requirement** is used after verbs such as *ask, demand, insist,* and *suggest*—or after expressions of requirement, suggestion, or demand. A subjunctive verb of requirement is in the base form of the verb: the infinitive without *to:*

> Airlines insist that each passenger *pass* through a metal detector.
>
> It's extremely important that silicon chips *be made* in a dust-free environment.

Conditional Sentences

Conditional sentences are if-then statements:

> *If* you go, *then* I'll go, too.

Note that many conditional sentences imply rather than state the word *then,* and this is also correct usage:

> *If* you go, I'll go too.

We use conditional sentences when we want to speculate about the results of a particular situation. There are three types of conditional sentences.

Statements of Fact: There is a real possibility that the situation described in the *if* clause really happened, or is happening, or will happen:

> If top military officials resign, there will be protests in the capital city.
>
> If John Milton met Galileo, they probably discussed astronomy.

Contrary to Fact: The situation in the *if* clause never happened, so what is said in the *then* clause is pure speculation:

> Blaise Pascal wrote that if Cleopatra's nose had been shorter, the face of the world would have changed.
>
> Alexander the Great said, "If I were not Alexander, I would want to be Diogenes."

Future Speculation: Some conditional sentences speculate about the future, but with the idea that the situation in the *if* clause is extremely unlikely to happen:

> If Shakespeare's manuscripts were to be discovered, the texts of some of his plays would be less uncertain.

Parallelism

Remember, when you express a number of ideas of equal importance and function in the same sentence, you should always be careful to make them all the same grammatical form (that is, all nouns, all adjectives, all gerunds, all clauses, or whatever). That's called **parallel structure** or **parallelism.**

Coordinate Ideas

Coordinate ideas occur in pairs or in a series, and they are linked by conjunctions such as *and, but, or,* and *nor,* or, in certain instances, by linking verbs such as *is.*

Wrong:	To earn credits, an American college student can take up folk dancing, ballet, or study belly dancing.
Correct:	To earn credits, an American college student can take up *folk dancing, ballet,* or *belly dancing.*

Note that once you begin repeating a word in a series like the following, you must follow through:

Wrong:	A wage earner might invest her money in stocks, in bonds, or real estate.
Correct:	A wage earner might invest her money *in* stocks, *in* bonds, or *in* real estate.
Also Correct:	A wage earner might invest her money *in* stocks, bonds, or real estate.

This principle applies equally to prepositions (*in, on, by, with*, etc.), articles (*the, a, an*), helping verbs (*had, has, would*, etc.), and possessive pronouns (*his, her*, etc.). You must either repeat the appropriate item in front of each element in the series or include it only in front of the first item in the series.

Correlative Constructions

There is a group of words in English that are called **correlative conjunctions.** They are used to relate two ideas in some way. Here's a list of them:

> *both . . . and*
>
> *either . . . or*
>
> *neither . . . nor*
>
> *not only . . . but (also)*

You should always be careful to place correlative conjunctions immediately before the terms they're coordinating.

Wrong:	Isaac Newton not only studied physics but also theology.

The problem here is that the author intends to coordinate the two nouns *physics* and *theology*, but makes the mistake of putting the verb of the sentence (*studied*) after the first element of the construction (*not only*), and in so doing destroys the parallelism. Note that the solution to an error like this is usually to move one of the conjunctions.

Correct:	Isaac Newton studied not only *physics* but also *theology*.

Compared or Contrasted Ideas

Frequently, two or more ideas are compared or contrasted within the same sentence. Compared or contrasted ideas should be presented in the same grammatical form.

Certain phrases should clue you in that the sentence contains ideas that should be presented in parallel form. These phrases include *as . . . as* and *more (or less)* x *than* y.

Wrong:	Skiing is as strenuous as to run.
Correct:	*Skiing* is as strenuous as *running*.
Wrong:	Skiing is less dangerous than to rappel down a cliff.
Correct:	*To ski* is less dangerous than *to rappel* down a cliff.

In certain cases, sentences with forms of *to be* must be expressed in parallel form.

Wrong:	To drive while intoxicated is risking grave injury and criminal charges.

When an infinitive is the subject of *to be*, don't use a gerund after the verb, and vice versa. Pair infinitives with infinitives and gerunds with gerunds.

Correct: *To drive* while intoxicated is *to risk* grave injury and criminal charges.

Note that we wouldn't change both words to gerunds in this sentence because it wouldn't sound idiomatic.

Comparisons

On the GMAT, you will see a number of sentences that make comparisons. A sentence that makes a comparison must do two things: it must be clear about what is being compared, and it must compare things that logically can be compared. A sentence that makes an unclear or illogical comparison is grammatically unacceptable. When you see a comparative expression such as *like, as, more than, unlike, less than, similar to*, or *different from*, it should remind you to ask yourself two questions about the comparison in the sentence: Is it clear? Is it logical?

Unclear Comparisons

Sometimes it isn't clear what the author is trying to compare.

Wrong: Byron admired Dryden more than Wordsworth.

There are two ways to interpret this sentence: that Dryden meant more to Byron than Wordsworth did, or that Byron thought more highly of Dryden than Wordsworth did. Whichever meaning you choose, the problem can be cleared up by adding more words to the sentence.

Correct: Byron admired Dryden more than *he did* Wordsworth.

Also Correct: Byron admired Dryden more than *Wordsworth did*.

Illogical Comparisons

Sometimes what the author meant to say is clear enough, but what the author meant to say is not what he ended up saying.

Wrong: The peaches here are riper than any other fruit stand.

This sentence is comparing *peaches* to *fruit stands*, even though that's clearly not the intention of the author. We can correct it so that we're comparing peaches to peaches by inserting the phrase *those at*.

Correct: The peaches here are riper than *those at* any other fruit stand.

Now the pronoun *those* is standing in for *peaches*, so the sentence is accurately comparing things that can be reasonably compared: the peaches here and some other peaches.

Incomplete comparisons like this one are normally corrected by inserting a phrase like *those of, those in, those at, that of, that in*, and *that at*.

Incomplete comparisons can also be corrected by use of the possessive.

Wrong:	Many critics considered Enrico Caruso's voice better than any other tenor. (This is comparing a voice to a person.)
Correct:	Many critics considered Enrico Caruso's voice better than *any other tenor's*. (Note that this is a shortened version of: *Many critics considered Enrico Caruso's voice better than any other tenor's voice*.)

The second sort of incomplete comparison occurs when one thing is being compared to a group it is a part of. This error is corrected by inserting either the word *other* or the word *else*.

Wrong:	Astaire danced better than any man in the world.

This is wrong because he couldn't have danced better than himself.

Correct:	Astaire danced better than any *other* man in the world.

Comparative Forms

The comparative form is used when comparing only two members of a class, and the superlative for three or more.

Loretta's grass grows *more vigorously* than Jim's.
Loretta's grass grows the *most vigorously* of any in the neighborhood.

Of Buchanan and Lincoln, the *latter* was *taller*.
Of McKinley, Roosevelt, and Taft, the *last* was *heaviest*.

Idiom

Sometimes the right way to say something isn't a matter of grammar but is a matter of **idiom**: an accepted, set phrase or usage that's right for no other reason than that's just the way we say it.

Most of what we call "idioms" are pairs of words that are used together to convey a particular meaning, and many "idiom errors" result from substituting an unacceptable word—usually a preposition—for a word that is always part of the idiom.

Wrong:	Brigitte Bardot has joined an organization that is concerned in preventing cruelty to animals.

The adjective *concerned* is followed by either *about* or *with*, either of which would be idiomatic here. But the expression *concerned in* simply isn't idiomatic—we just don't say it that way.

Correct:	Brigitte Bardot has joined an organization that is *concerned with* preventing cruelty to animals.
Also Correct:	Brigitte Bardot has joined an organization that is *concerned about* preventing cruelty to animals.

There are so many possible idiom errors of this kind that we can't list them all. The most frequently tested errors, however, are contained in Appendix 3 of this book, Common GMAT Idioms.

Ellipsis

An **ellipsis** is the omission from a sentence of words that are clearly understood. Ellipsis is perfectly acceptable as long as it's done properly—in fact, we do it all the time. Not many people would make a statement like:

> I've seen more movies this year than you have seen movies this year.

Instead, we would automatically shorten the statement to the much more concise and natural sounding:

> I've seen more movies this year than you have.

In the following sentence, ellipsis is properly used:

> *The Spectator* was written by Addison and Steele.

This is a shorter way of saying:

> *The Spectator* was written by Addison and by Steele.

It's all right to leave the second *by* out of the sentence because the same preposition appears before *Addison* and before *Steele*, so you need to use it only once.

Now watch what happens when ellipsis is improperly used.

Wrong: Ezra Pound was interested but not very knowledgeable about economics.

This is wrong because the preposition that's needed after the word *interested* (*in*) is not the same as the preposition that follows the word *knowledgeable* (*about*).

Correct: Ezra Pound was *interested in* but not very *knowledgeable about* economics.

Wrong: London always has and always will be the capital of the United Kingdom.

This is wrong because the verb form that's needed after *has* is not the same as the one that's needed after *will*, so both must be included.

Correct: London always *has been* and always *will be* the capital of the United Kingdom.

Negatives

You will probably run across at least one item that tests your ability to recognize the difference between idiomatic and unidiomatic ways to express negative ideas. You already know that a double negative is a no-no in standard written English. You wouldn't have any trouble realizing that a sentence such as "I don't want no help" is unacceptable. But the incorrect negatives you will probably see on the exam won't be quite that obvious.

The obviously negative words are *neither, nobody, nor, nowhere, never, none, not, no one*, and *nothing*. But don't forget that *barely, rarely, without, hardly, seldom*, and *scarcely* are also grammatically negative.

In Sentence Correction, you'll find problems with these words where sentences connect two or three negative ideas. Read through the following example sentences carefully:

> There were *neither* threats *nor* bombing campaigns.
> There were *no* threats *or* bombing campaigns.
> There were *no* threats *and no* bombing campaigns.
> There were *no* threats, *nor* were there bombing campaigns.

These are the most common idiomatic ways to join two negative ideas. If you can remember these patterns, you can probably eliminate many wrong answers, because they in some way violate these idiomatic patterns.

Wrong: When Walt Whitman's family moved to Brooklyn, there were no bridges nor tunnels across the East River.

The phrase *no bridges nor tunnels* is just not idiomatic—it contains a double negative. The sentence can be rewritten to correct the problem in several ways.

Correct: There were *no bridges or tunnels* across the East River.

Also Correct: There were *neither bridges nor tunnels* across the East River.

Also Correct: There were *no bridges and no tunnels* across the East River.

Another situation in which negatives can cause problems is in a series. Words like *no*, *not*, and *without* must follow the same rules as prepositions, articles, helping verbs, and the like.

Wrong: After the floods in the Midwest, many farmers were left without homes, businesses, and huge bills to replace all they had lost.

When a preposition, such as *without* in this sentence, is used in front of only the first member of a series, it's taken to refer to all three members of the series. Here, that causes the sentence to say that the farmers were left without homes, without businesses, and without huge bills to replace what they had lost, which makes no sense. There are several ways to rewrite the sentence so that it makes sense.

Correct: After the floods in the Midwest, many farmers were left *without* homes, *without* businesses, and *with* huge bills to replace all they had lost.

Also Correct: After the floods in the Midwest, many farmers were left *with no* homes, *with no* businesses, and *with* huge bills to replace all they had lost.

Also Correct: After the floods in the Midwest, many farmers were left *with no* homes, *no* businesses, and huge bills to replace all they had lost.

Guide to Usage and Style

In Part Four, we discussed how to analyze a GMAT essay topic, organize your thoughts, and outline an essay. Once you have an overall idea of what you want to say in your essay, you can start thinking about how to say it. This appendix emphasizes the skills you need for the second stage of the writing process: producing clearly developed and well-organized essays. The best strategy is to study this section and tackle the exercises in short, manageable blocks, interspersed with the study of other subjects in preparation for the GMAT.

Perhaps the single most important thing to bear in mind when writing essays is this: *keep it simple*. This applies to word choice, sentence structure, and argument. Obsession about how to spell a word correctly can throw off your flow of thought. The more complicated (and wordy) your sentences, the more likely they will contain errors. The more convoluted your argument, the more likely you will get bogged down in convoluted sentence structure. Yet recall that simple does *not* mean simplistic. A clear, straightforward approach can be sophisticated.

Many students mistakenly believe that their essays will be "downgraded" by such mechanical errors as misplaced commas, poor choice of words, misspellings, faulty grammar, and so on. Occasional problems of this type will not significantly affect your GMAT essay score. The test readers understand that you are writing first-draft essays. They will *not* be looking to take points off for such errors, unless you make them repeatedly. If an essay is littered with misspellings, incorrect usage, and the like, then a more serious communication problem is indicated.

Bottom line: don't worry excessively about writing mechanics, but do try to train yourself out of poor habits and do proofread your essays for obvious errors. Your objective in taking the GMAT is admission to business school. To achieve that objective, give the business schools what they want. They do not expect eloquence in a 30-minute assignment, but they do want to see effective writing.

To write an effective essay, there are three things you need to do:

1. **Be concise.**

2. **Be forceful.**

3. **Be correct.**

An effective essay is concise; it wastes no words. An effective essay is forceful; it makes its point. And an effective essay is correct; it conforms to the generally accepted rules of grammar and form.

The following pages break down the three broad objectives of concision, forcefulness, and correctness into 16 specific principles. Don't panic! Many of them will already be familiar to you. Besides, you will have many chances to practice in the exercises we provide.

Principles 1 through 4 aim primarily at the first objective: concise writing; principles 5 through 10 aim primarily at the second objective: forceful writing; and principles 11 through 16 aim primarily at the third objective: grammatically correct writing. (For a thorough understanding of the third of these objectives, though, you should consult Appendix 1, Grammar Reference Guide.) In this appendix, we concentrate on principles that are rarely tested in Sentence Correction but become important when you do your writing. Each principle is illustrated by exercises. (Answers to these exercises are at the end of this section.)

The principles of concise and forceful writing are generally not as rigid as the principles of grammatically correct writing. Concision and forcefulness are matters of art and personal style as well as common sense and tradition. But if you are going to disregard a principle, we hope you will do so out of educated choice. On the GMAT Analytical Writing Assessment, sticking closely to the principles of standard English writing should produce a concise, forceful, and correct essay.

Be Concise

The first four principles of good writing relate to the goal of expressing your points clearly in as few words as possible. Each principle represents a specific way to tighten up your writing.

Principle 1: Avoid Wordiness

Do not use several words when one will do. Wordy phrases are like junk food: they add only fat, not muscle. Many people make the mistake of writing phrases such as *at the present time* or *at this point in time* instead of the simpler *now*, or *take into consideration* instead of simply *consider*, in an attempt to make their prose seem more scholarly or formal. It does not work. Instead, their prose ends up seeming inflated and pretentious. Don't waste your words or your time.

Wordy:	I am of the opinion that the aforementioned managers should be advised that they will be evaluated with regard to the utilization of responsive organizational software for the purpose of devising a responsive network of customers.
Concise:	We should tell the managers that we will evaluate their use of flexible computerized databases to develop a customer network.

Exercise 1: Wordy Phrases

Improve the following sentences by omitting or replacing wordy phrases.

1. In view of the fact that John has prepared with much care for this presentation, it would be a good idea to award him with the project.

    _____

2. The airline has a problem with always having arrivals that come at least an hour late, despite the fact that the leaders of the airline promise that promptness is a goal that has a high priority for all the employees involved.

    _____

3. In spite of the fact that she only has a little bit of experience in photography right now, she will probably do well in the future because she has a great deal of motivation to succeed in her chosen profession.

    _____

4. Accuracy is a subject that has great importance to English teachers and company presidents alike.

    _____

5. The reason why humans kill each other is that they experience fear of those whom they do not understand.

    _____

Principle 2: Don't Be Redundant

Redundancy means that the writer needlessly repeats an idea. It's redundant to speak of "a beginner lacking experience." The word *beginner* implies lack of experience by itself. You can eliminate redundant words or phrases without changing the meaning of the sentence. Watch out for words that add nothing to the sense of the sentence.

Here are some common redundancies:

Redundant	Concise
refer back	*refer*
few in number	*few*
small-sized	*small*
grouped together	*grouped*

Redundancy often results from carelessness, but you can easily eliminate redundant elements when proofreading.

Exercise 2: Redundancy

Repair the following sentences by crossing out or rephrasing redundant elements.

1. All these problems have combined together to create a serious crisis.

   _____

2. A staff that large in size needs an effective supervisor who can get the job done.

   _____

3. He knows how to follow directions, and he knows how to do what he is told.

   _____

4. The recently observed trend of spending on credit has created a middle class that is poorer and more impoverished than ever before.

   _____

5. Those who can follow directions are few in number.

   _____

Principle 3: Avoid Needless Qualification

Since the object of your essay is to convince your reader, you will want to adopt a reasonable tone. There will likely be no single, clear-cut "answer" to the essay topic, so don't overstate your case. Occasional use of qualifiers such as *fairly, rather, somewhat,* and *relatively,* and expressions such as *seems to be, a little,* and *a certain amount of* will let the reader know you are reasonable, but overusing such modifiers weakens your argument. Excessive qualification makes you sound hesitant. Like wordy phrases, qualifiers can add bulk without adding substance.

Wordy:	This rather serious breach of etiquette may possibly shake the very foundations of the corporate world.
Concise:	This serious breach of etiquette may shake the foundations of the corporate world.

Just as bad is the overuse of the word *very*. Some writers use this intensifying adverb before almost every adjective in an attempt to be more forceful. If you need to add emphasis, look for a stronger adjective (or verb).

Weak:	Novak is a very good pianist.
Strong:	Novak is a virtuoso pianist.
	or
	Novak plays beautifully.

And don't try to qualify words that are already absolute.

Wrong	Correct
more unique	*unique*
the very worst	*the worst*
completely full	*full*

Exercise 3: Excessive Qualification

Practice achieving concision by eliminating needless qualification in the sentences below.

1. She is a fairly excellent teacher.

   _____

2. Ferrara seems to be sort of a slow worker.

   _____

3. You yourself are the very best person to decide what you should do for a living.

   _____

4. Needless to say, children should be taught to cooperate at home and in school.

   _____

5. The travel agent does not recommend the trip to Tripoli, since it is possible that one may be hurt.

   _____

Principle 4: Do Not Write Sentences Just to Fill Up Space

This principle suggests several things:

- Don't write a sentence that gets you nowhere.
- Don't ask a question only to answer it.
- Don't merely copy the essay's directions.
- Don't write a whole sentence only to announce that you're changing the subject.

If you have something to say, say it without preamble. If you need to smooth over a change of subject, do so with a transitional word or phrase, rather than with a meaningless sentence. If your proofreading reveals unintentional wasted sentences, delete them.

Wordy: Which idea of the author's is more in line with what I believe? This is a very interesting . . .

Concise: The author's beliefs are similar to mine.

The author of the wordy example above is just wasting words and time. Get to the point quickly and stay there. Simplicity and clarity win points.

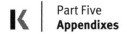
Exercise 4: Unnecessary Sentences

Rewrite each of these multiple-sentence statements as one concise sentence.

1. What's the purpose of getting rid of the chemical pollutants in water? People cannot safely consume water that contains chemical pollutants.

    _____

2. I do not believe those who argue that some of Shakespeare's plays were written by others. There is no evidence that other people had a hand in writing Shakespeare's plays.

    _____

3. Which point of view is closest to my own? This is a good question. I agree with those who say that the United States should send soldiers to areas of conflict.

    _____

4. Frank Lloyd Wright was a famous architect. He was renowned for his ability to design buildings that blend into their surroundings.

    _____

5. A lot of people find math a difficult subject to master. They have trouble with math because it requires very precise thinking skills.

    _____

Be Forceful

The next group of principles aims at the goal of producing forceful writing. If you follow these principles, your writing will be much more convincing to the reader.

Principle 5: Avoid Needless Self-Reference

Avoid such unnecessary phrases as *I believe*, *I feel*, and *in my opinion*. There is no need to remind your reader that what you are writing is your opinion.

Weak:	I am of the opinion that air pollution is a more serious problem than the government has led us to believe.
Forceful:	Air pollution is a more serious problem than the government has led us to believe.

Self-reference is another form of qualifying what you say—a very obvious form. One or two self-references in an essay might be appropriate, just as the use of qualifiers like *probably* and *perhaps* can be effective if you practice using them *sparingly*. Practice is the only sure way to improve your writing.

Exercise 5: Needless Self-Reference

Eliminate needless self-references in these sentences.

1. I do not think this argument can be generalized to most business owners.

   _____

2. My own experience shows me that food is the best social lubricant.

   _____

3. Although I am no expert, I do not think privacy should be valued more than social concerns.

   _____

4. My guess is that most people want to do good work, but many are bored or frustrated with their jobs.

   _____

5. I must emphasize my belief that the author does in fact have a valid point.

   _____

Principle 6: Use the Active Voice

Using the passive voice is a way to avoid accountability. Put verbs in the active voice whenever possible. In the active voice, the subject performs the action (e.g., we write essays). In the passive voice, the subject is the receiver of the action and the performer of the action is often only implied (e.g., essays are written).

You should avoid the passive voice EXCEPT in the following cases:

- When you do not know who performed the action: _The letter was opened before I received it._ (Here, the subject _the letter_ is the receiver of the action; the performer of the action is unknown.)
- When you prefer not to refer directly to the person who performs the action: _An error has been made in computing this data._

Passive:	The estimate of this year's tax revenues was prepared by the General Accounting Office.
Active:	The General Accounting Office prepared the estimate of this year's tax revenues.

Exercise 6: Undesirable Passives

Replace passive voice with active wherever possible.

1. The politician's standing in the polls has been hurt by recent allegations of corruption.

   _____

2. The bill was passed in time, but it was not signed by the president until the time for action had passed.

   _____

3. Advice is usually requested by those who need it least; it is not sought out by the truly lost and ignorant.

   _____

4. The minutes of the City Council meeting should be taken by the city clerk.

_____

5. The report was compiled by a number of field anthropologists and marriage experts.

_____

Principle 7: Avoid Weak Openings

Try not to begin a sentence with *there is*, *there are*, or *it is*. These roundabout expressions usually indicate that you are trying to distance yourself from the position you are taking.

Exercise 7: Weak Openings

Rewrite these sentences to eliminate weak openings.

1. It would be unwise for businesses to ignore the illiteracy problem.

_____

2. It would be of no use to fight a drug war without waging a battle against demand for illicit substances.

_____

3. There are many strong points in the candidate's favor; intelligence, unfortunately, is not among them.

_____

4. It has been decided that we, as a society, can tolerate homelessness.

_____

5. There seems to be little doubt that Americans like watching television better than conversing.

_____

Principle 8: Avoid Needlessly Vague Language

Don't just ramble on when you're writing your GMAT essays. Choose specific, descriptive words. Vague language weakens your writing because it forces the reader to guess what you mean instead of concentrating fully on your ideas and style. The essay topics you're given aren't going to be obscure. You will be able to come up with specific examples and concrete information about the topics. Your argument will be more forceful if you stick to this information.

Weak:	Brown is highly educated.
Forceful:	Brown has a master's degree in business administration.
Weak:	She is a great communicator.
Forceful:	She speaks persuasively.

Notice that sometimes, to be more specific and concrete, you will have to use more words than you might with vague language. This principle is not in conflict with the general objective of concision. Being concise may mean eliminating unnecessary words. Avoiding vagueness may mean adding necessary words.

Exercise 8: Needlessly Vague Language

Rewrite these sentences to replace vague language with specific, concrete language.

1. Water is transformed into steam when the former is heated to a high temperature.

   _____

2. The diplomat was required to execute an agreement that stipulated that he would live in whatever country the federal government thought necessary.

   _____

3. The principal told John that he should not even think about coming back to school until he changed his ways.

   _____

4. The police detective had to seek the permission of the lawyer to question the suspect.

   _____

5. Lots of species of animals were destroyed when the last ice age occurred.

   _____

Principle 9: Avoid Clichés

Clichés are overused expressions, expressions that may once have seemed colorful and powerful but are now dull and worn out. Time pressure and anxiety may make you lose focus; that's when clichés may slip into your writing. A reliance on clichés will suggest you are a lazy thinker. Keep them out of your essay.

Weak: Performance in a crisis is the acid test for a leader.

Forceful: Performance in a crisis is the best indicator of a leader's abilities.

Putting a cliché in quotation marks in order to indicate your distance from the cliché does not strengthen the sentence. If anything, it just makes weak writing more noticeable. Notice whether you use clichés. If you do, ask yourself if you could substitute more specific language for the cliché.

Exercise 9: Clichés

Make the following sentences more forceful by replacing clichés.

1. Beyond the shadow of a doubt, Jefferson was a great leader.

   _____

2. Trying to find the employee responsible for this embarrassing information leak is like trying to find a needle in a haystack.

   _____

3. The military is putting all its eggs in one basket by relying so heavily on nuclear missiles for the nation's defense.

   _____

4. Older doctors should be required to update their techniques, but you can't teach an old dog new tricks.

_____

5. A ballpark estimate of the number of fans in the stadium would be 120,000.

_____

Principle 10: Avoid Jargon

Jargon includes two categories of words that you should avoid. First is the specialized vocabulary of a group, such as that used by doctors, lawyers, or baseball coaches. Second is the overly inflated and complex language that burdens many students' essays. You will not impress anyone with big words that do not fit the tone or context of your essay, especially if you misuse them.

If you are not certain of a word's meaning or appropriateness, leave it out. An appropriate word, even a simple one, will add impact to your argument. As you come across words you are unsure of, ask yourself, "Would a reader in a different field be able to understand exactly what I mean from the words I've chosen?" "Is there any way I can say the same thing more simply?"

Weak:	The marketing team should think outside the box to help raise interest in the company's new product.
Forceful:	The marketing team should experiment with new ideas to help raise interest in the company's new product.

The following are commonly used jargon words:

prioritize	_parameter_
optimize	_time frame_
utilize	_input/output_
finalize	_maximize_
designate	_facilitate_
bottom line	

Exercise 10: Jargon

Replace the jargon in the following sentences with more appropriate language.

1. We anticipate utilizing hundreds of paper clips in the foreseeable future.

_____

2. Education-wise, our schoolchildren have been neglected.

_____

3. Foreign diplomats should always interface with local leaders.

_____

4. There is considerable evidentiary support for the assertion that Vienna sausages are good for you.

_____

5. In the case of the recent railway disaster, it is clear that governmental regulatory agencies obfuscated in the preparation of materials for release to the public through both the electronic and print media.

_____

Be Correct

Correctness is perhaps the most difficult objective for writers to achieve. The complex rules of standard English usage can leave you feeling unsure of your writing and more than a bit confused. But remember, the most important lesson you can take from this section is how to organize your thoughts into a strong, well-supported argument. Style and grammar are important but secondary concerns. Your readers will *not* mark you down for occasional errors common to first-draft writing. So just think of this section, together with the Grammar Reference Guide, as helping you to improve the details of good writing. If it begins to overwhelm you, stop and take a break. You need time to absorb this information.

Do the exercises and then compare your answers to ours. Make sure you understand what the error was in each sentence. Use what you learn in this section to help you proofread your practice essays; later, return to your practice essays and edit them. Better yet, ask a friend to edit them, paying special attention to correctness.

Principle 11: Avoid Slang and Colloquialisms

Conversational speech is filled with slang and colloquial expressions. However, you should avoid slang on the GMAT Analytical Writing Assessment. Slang terms and colloquialisms can be confusing to the reader since these expressions are not universally understood.

Inappropriate:	He is really into gardening.
Correct:	He enjoys gardening.
Inappropriate:	She plays a wicked game of tennis.
Correct:	She excels in tennis.
Inappropriate:	Myra has got to go to Memphis for a week.
Correct:	Myra must go to Memphis for a week.
Inappropriate:	Joan has been doing science for eight years now.
Correct:	Joan has been a scientist for eight years now.

With a little thought, you will find the right word. Using informal language is risky. Play it safe by sticking to standard usage.

Part Five
Appendixes

Exercise 11: Slang and Colloquialisms

Replace the informal elements of the following sentences with more appropriate terms.

1. Cynthia Larson sure knows her stuff.

   _____

2. Normal human beings literally can't even with repeated humiliation.

   _____

3. If you want a good cheesecake, you must make a top-notch crust.

   _____

4. International organizations should try and cooperate on global issues like hunger.

   _____

5. The environmentalists aren't in it for the prestige; they really care about protecting the yellow-throated hornswoggler.

   _____

Principle 12: Use Commas Correctly

When using the comma, follow these rules:

A. Use commas to separate items in a series. If more than two items are listed in a series, they should be separated by commas.

Correct:	My recipe for buttermilk biscuits contains flour, baking soda, salt, shortening, and buttermilk.

B. If there is no clause preceding or following a series, then do not place commas before the first element of a series or after the last element.

Wrong:	My investment adviser recommended that I construct a portfolio of, stocks, bonds, commodities futures, and precious metals.
Wrong:	The elephants, tigers, and dancing bears, were the highlights of the circus.

C. Use commas to separate two or more adjectives that modify the same noun; do not use a comma after the last adjective in the series.

Wrong:	I can't believe you sat through that long, dull, uninspired, movie three times.
Correct:	I can't believe you sat through that long, dull, uninspired movie three times.

D. Use commas to set off parenthetical clauses and phrases. (A parenthetical expression is one that is not necessary to the main idea of the sentence.)

Correct:	Gordon, who is a writer by profession, bakes an excellent cheesecake.

The main idea is that Gordon bakes an excellent cheesecake. The intervening clause merely serves to identify Gordon; thus, it should be set off with commas.

Correct: The newspaper that has the most insipid editorials is the *Daily Times*.

Correct: The newspaper, which has the most insipid editorials of any I have read, won numerous awards last week.

In the first of these examples, the clause beginning with *that* defines which paper the author is discussing. In the second example, the main point is that the newspaper won numerous awards, and the intervening clause beginning with *which* identifies the paper.

E. Use commas after introductory participial or prepositional phrases.

Correct: Having watered his petunias every day during the drought, Harold was very disappointed when his garden was destroyed by insects.

Correct: After the banquet, Harold and Martha went dancing.

F. Use commas to separate independent clauses (clauses that could stand alone as complete sentences) connected by coordinate conjunctions such as *and*, *but*, *nor*, and *yet*.

Correct: Susan's old car has been belching blue smoke from the tailpipe for two weeks, but it has not broken down yet.

Note: Make sure the comma separates two *independent* clauses joined by a conjunction. It is incorrect to use a comma to separate the two parts of a compound verb.

Wrong: Barbara went to the grocery store, and bought two quarts of milk.

Exercise 12: Commas

Correct the punctuation errors in the following sentences.

1. It takes a friendly energetic person to be a successful salesman.

   _____

2. I was shocked to discover that a large, modern, glass-sheathed, office building had replaced my old school.

   _____

3. The country club, a cluster of ivy-covered whitewashed buildings was the site of the president's first speech.

   _____

4. Pushing through the panicked crowd the security guards frantically searched for the suspect.

   _____

5. Despite careful analysis of the advantages and disadvantages of each proposal Harry found it hard to reach a decision.

   _____

Principle 13: Use Semicolons Correctly

When using a semicolon, follow these rules:

A. Use a semicolon *instead of* a coordinate conjunction such as *and*, *or*, or *but* to link two closely related independent clauses.

Wrong:	Whooping cranes are an endangered species; and they are unlikely to survive if we continue to pollute.
Correct:	Whooping cranes are an endangered species; there are only 50 whooping cranes in New Jersey today.
Correct:	Whooping cranes are an endangered species, and they are unlikely to survive if we continue to pollute.

B. A semicolon can be used between independent clauses that are connected by words like *therefore*, *nevertheless*, and *moreover*.

Correct:	Farm prices have been falling rapidly for two years; nevertheless, the traditional American farm is not in danger of disappearing.

C. Use semicolons to separate items in a list in which the items themselves contain commas.

Correct:	Three important dates in the history of the company are December 16, 1999; April 4, 2003; and June 30, 2011.

Exercise 13: Semicolons

Correct the punctuation errors in the following sentences.

1. Morgan has five years' experience in karate; but Thompson has even more.

   _____

2. Very few students wanted to take the class in physics, only the professor's kindness kept it from being canceled.

   _____

3. You should always be prepared when you go on a camping trip, however you must avoid carrying unnecessary weight.

   _____

4. Before this evening's party, I need to purchase crackers, cheese, and salami from the Italian butcher shop on the corner, spinach and zucchini from the farmer's market, and wine glasses, plates, and serving spoons from the department store.

   _____

Principle 14: Use Colons Correctly

When using a colon, follow these rules:

A. In formal writing, the colon is used only as a means of signaling that what follows is a list, definition, explanation, or concise summary of what has gone before. The colon usually follows an independent clause, and it will frequently be accompanied by a reinforcing expression like *the following*, *as follows*, or *namely*, or by an explicit demonstrative like *this*.

Correct:	Your instructions are as follows: read the passage carefully, answer the questions on the last page, and turn over your answer sheet.
Correct:	This is what I found in the refrigerator: a moldy lime, half a bottle of stale soda, and a jar of peanut butter.
Correct:	The biggest problem with America today is apathy: the corrosive element that will destroy our democracy.

B. Be careful not to put a colon between a verb and its direct object.

Wrong:	I want: a slice of pizza and a small green salad.
Correct:	This is what I want: a slice of pizza and a small green salad. (The colon serves to announce that a list is forthcoming.)
Correct:	I don't want much for lunch: just a slice of pizza and a small green salad. (Here, what follows the colon defines what "don't want much" means.)

C. Context will occasionally make clear that a second independent clause is closely linked to its predecessor, even without an explicit expression like those used above. Here, too, a colon is appropriate, although a period will always be correct also.

Correct:	We were aghast: the "charming country inn" that had been advertised in such glowing terms proved to be a leaking cabin full of mosquitoes.
Correct:	We were aghast. The "charming country inn" that had been advertised in such glowing terms proved to be a leaking cabin full of mosquitoes.

Exercise 14: Colons

Edit these sentences so they use colons correctly.

1. I am sick and tired of: your whining, your complaining, your nagging, your teasing, and, most of all, your barbed comments.

_____

2. The chef has created a masterpiece, the pasta is delicate yet firm, the mustard greens are fresh, and the medallions of veal are melting in my mouth.

_____

3. In order to write a good essay, you must: practice, get plenty of sleep, and eat a good breakfast.

_____

Principle 15: Use Hyphens and Dashes Correctly

When using a hyphen or a dash, follow these rules:

A. Use the hyphen with the compound numbers twenty-one through ninety-nine and with fractions used as adjectives.

Correct:	Sixty-five students constituted a majority.
Correct:	A two-thirds vote was necessary to carry the measure.
Wrong:	Only two-thirds of the students passed the final exam.

B. Use the hyphen with the prefixes *ex*, *all*, and *self*, and with the suffix *elect*.

Correct:	The constitution protects against self-incrimination.
Correct:	The president-elect was invited to chair the meeting.

C. Use the hyphen with a compound adjective when it comes before the word it modifies, but not when it comes after the word it modifies.

Correct:	The no-holds-barred argument continued into the night.
Correct:	The argument continued with no holds barred.

D. Use the hyphen with any prefix used before a proper noun or adjective.

Correct:	They believed that his activities were un-American.

E. Use a hyphen to separate component parts of a word in order to avoid confusion with other words.

Correct:	The sculptor was able to re-form the clay after the dog knocked over the bust.

F. Use the dash to indicate an abrupt change of thought. In general, however, formal writing is best when you think out what you want to say in advance and avoid abrupt changes of thought.

Correct:	To get a high score—and who doesn't want to get a high score?—you need to devote yourself to prolonged and concentrated study.

Exercise 15: Hyphens and Dashes

Edit these sentences so they use hyphens and dashes correctly.

1. The child was able to count from one to ninety nine.

   _____

2. After another tough loss, the captain of the basketball team called for a players only meeting.

   _____

3. Before each game, the locker rooms are to be used by players-only.

   _____

4. A two thirds majority would be needed to pass the budget reforms.

   _____

5. The house, and it was the most dilapidated house that I had ever seen was a bargain because the land was so valuable.

   _____

Principle 16: Use the Apostrophe Correctly

When using an apostrophe, follow these rules:

A. Use the apostrophe with contracted forms of verbs to indicate that one or more letters have been eliminated in writing. But try to avoid contractions altogether on the GMAT. (See also Principle 11: Avoid Slang and Colloquialisms.)

Full Forms:

you are	*it is*	*you have*	*the boy is*
Harry has	*we would*	*was not*	

Contracted:

you're	*it's*	*you've*	*the boy's*
Harry's	*we'd*	*wasn't*	

One of the most common errors involving use of the apostrophe is using it in the contraction *you're* or *it's* to indicate the possessive form of *you* or *it*. When you write *you're*, ask yourself whether you mean *you are*. If not, the correct word is *your*. Similarly, are you sure you mean *it is* or *it has*? If not, use the possessive form *its*. You spell *his* or *hers* without an apostrophe, so you should spell *its* without an apostrophe.

Incorrect:	You're chest of drawers is ugly.
Incorrect:	The dog hurt it's paw.
Correct:	Your chest of drawers is ugly.
Correct:	The dog hurt its paw.

B. Use the apostrophe to indicate the possessive form of a noun.

Not Possessive:

the boy	*Harry*	*the children*	*the boys*

Possessive Form:

the boy's	*Harry's*	*the children's*	*the boys'*

Correct:	Ms. Fox's office is on the first floor. (One person possesses the office.)
Correct:	The Foxes' apartment has a wonderful view. (There are several people named Fox living in the same apartment. First, you must form the plural; then, add the apostrophe to indicate possession.)

C. The apostrophe is used to indicate possession only with nouns; in the case of pronouns, there are separate possessives for each person and number.

my, mine	*our, ours*
your, yours	*your, yours*
his, his	*their, theirs*
her, hers	
its its	

The exception is the neutral *one*, which forms its possessive by adding an apostrophe and an *s*.

Exercise 16: Apostrophes

Edit these sentences so they use apostrophes correctly.

1. The presidents limousine had a flat tire.

   _____

2. You're tickets for the show will be at the box office.

   _____

3. The opportunity to change ones lifestyle does not come often.

   _____

4. The desks' surface was immaculate, but it's drawers were messy.

   _____

5. The cat on the bed is hers'.

   _____

Answers to Exercises (Note: The answers you see below are not the *only* correct improvements, but they are examples that demonstrate proper grammar and strong writing.)

Answers to Exercise 1: Wordy Phrases

1. Since John has prepared for this presentation so carefully, we should award him the project.
2. Flights are always at least an hour late on this airline, though its leaders promise that promptness is a high priority for all its employees.
3. Although she is inexperienced in photography, she will probably succeed because she is motivated.
4. Accuracy is important to English teachers and company presidents alike.
5. Humans kill each other because they fear those whom they do not understand.

Answers to Exercise 2: Redundancy

1. All these problems have combined to create a crisis.
2. A staff that large needs an effective supervisor.
3. He knows how to follow directions.
4. The recent trend of spending on credit has created a poorer middle class.
5. Few people can follow directions.

Answers to Exercise 3: Excessive Qualification

1. She is a good teacher.

2. Ferrara is a slow worker.

3. You are the best person to decide what you should do for a living.

4. Children should be taught to cooperate at home and in school. (If there's no need to say it, don't!)

5. The travel agent said not to go to Tripoli, since one may be hurt. (Saying *it is possible that one may be hurt* is an example of redundant qualification, since both *possible* and *may* indicate uncertainty.)

Answers to Exercise 4: Unnecessary Sentences

1. People cannot safely consume water that contains chemical pollutants.

2. No present evidence suggests that Shakespeare's plays were written by others.

3. The United States should send soldiers to areas of conflict.

4. The architect Frank Lloyd Wright was famous for his ability to design buildings that blend into their surroundings.

5. A lot of people find math a difficult subject because it requires very precise thinking skills.

Answers to Exercise 5: Needless Self-Reference

1. This argument cannot be generalized to most business owners.

2. Food is the best social lubricant.

3. Privacy should not be valued more than social concerns.

4. Most people want to do good work, but many are bored or frustrated with their jobs.

5. The author has a valid point.

Answers to Exercise 6: Undesirable Passives

1. Recent allegations of corruption have hurt the politician's standing in the polls.

2. Congress passed the bill in time, but the president did not sign it until the time for action had passed.

3. Those who need advice least usually request it; the truly lost and ignorant do not seek it.

4. The city clerk should take the minutes of the City Council meeting.

5. A number of field anthropologists and marriage experts compiled the report.

Answers to Exercise 7: Weak Openings

1. Businesses ignore the illiteracy problem at their own peril.

2. The government cannot fight a drug war effectively without waging a battle against demand for illicit substances.

3. The candidate has many strong points; intelligence, unfortunately, is not among them.

4. We, as a society, have decided to tolerate homelessness.

5. Americans must like watching television better than conversing.

Answers to Exercise 8: Needlessly Vague Language

1. When water is heated to 100 °C, it turns into steam.

2. The diplomat had to agree to live wherever the government sent him.

3. The principal told John not to return to school until he was ready to behave.

4. The police detective had to ask the lawyer for permission to question the suspect.

5. The last ice age destroyed thousands of animal species.

Answers to Exercise 9: Clichés

1. Jefferson was a great leader.

2. Trying to find the employee responsible for this embarrassing information leak may be impossible.

3. The military should diversify its defense rather than rely so heavily on nuclear missiles.

4. Older doctors should be required to update their techniques, but many seem resistant to changes in technology.

5. I estimate that 120,000 fans were in the stadium. (Even when a cliché is used in its original context, it sounds old.)

Answers to Exercise 10: Jargon

1. We expect to use hundreds of paper clips in the next two months.

2. Our schoolchildren's education has been neglected.

3. Foreign diplomats should always talk to local leaders.

4. Recent studies suggest that Vienna sausages are good for you.

5. Government regulatory agencies lied in their press releases about the recent railway disaster.

Answers to Exercise 11: Slang and Colloquialisms

1. Cynthia Larson is an expert.

2. Normal human beings cannot tolerate repeated humiliation.

3. If you want a good cheesecake, you must make a superb crust.

4. International organizations should try to cooperate on global issues like hunger. (Note: While *try and* might be a common verbal expression, the correct written expression is always *try to*.)

5. The environmentalists are not involved in the project for prestige; they truly care about protecting the yellow-throated hornswoggler.

Answers for Exercise 12: Commas

1. It takes a friendly, energetic person to be a successful salesman.

2. I was shocked to discover that a large, modern, glass-sheathed office building had replaced my old school.

3. The country club, a cluster of ivy-covered whitewashed buildings, was the site of the president's first speech.

4. Pushing through the panicked crowd, the security guards frantically searched for the suspect.

5. Despite careful analysis of the advantages and disadvantages of each proposal, Harry found it hard to reach a decision.

Answers for Exercise 13: Semicolons

1. Morgan has five years' experience in karate; Thompson has even more.

2. Very few students wanted to take the class in physics; only the professor's kindness kept it from being canceled.

3. You should always be prepared when you go on a camping trip; however, you must avoid carrying unnecessary weight.

4. Before this evening's party, I need to purchase crackers, cheese, and salami from the Italian butcher shop on the corner; spinach and zucchini from the farmer's market; and wine glasses, plates, and serving spoons from the department store.

Answers to Exercise 14: Colons

1. I am sick and tired of the following: your whining, your complaining, your nagging, your teasing, and, most of all, your barbed comments.

2. The chef has created a masterpiece: the pasta is delicate yet firm, the mustard greens are fresh, and the medallions of veal are melting in my mouth.

3. In order to write a good essay, you must do the following: practice, get plenty of sleep, and eat a good breakfast.

Answers to Exercise 15: Hyphens and Dashes

1. The child was able to count from one to ninety-nine.

2. After another tough loss, the captain of the basketball team called for a players-only meeting.

3. Before each game, the locker rooms are to be used by players only.

4. A two-thirds majority would be needed to pass the budget reforms.

5. The house—and it was the most dilapidated house that I had ever seen—was a bargain because the land was so valuable.

Answers to Exercise 16: Apostrophes

1. The president's limousine had a flat tire.

2. Your tickets for the show will be at the box office.

3. The opportunity to change one's lifestyle does not come often.

4. The desk's surface was immaculate, but its drawers were messy.

5. The cat on the bed is hers.

APPENDIX 3

Common GMAT Idioms

Note: All of the following have been known to appear on more than one GMAT. Entries with double ellipses (such as *between . . . and . . .*) indicate that the idiom also sets up a parallelism (between A and B).

able to (ability to)

> No one has been *able to* prove that the person who wrote Shakespeare's plays was named Shakespeare.

among versus **between**

Use *between* when referring to two items or groups, *among* when referring to three or more.

> Don't make me choose *between* Tweedledum and Tweedledee.
> *Among* the five candidates, he's by far the best qualified.

amount versus **number**

Use *amount* when referring to an uncountable quantity, like soup or love, and *number* when referring to countable things, like jelly beans or people.

> The *amount* of work you put into your studies will affect the *number* of points you will add to your GMAT score.

as versus **like**

Use *like* to compare nouns; use *as* to compare actions—in other words, use *as* when what follows is a clause.

> *Like* fine wine, fruitcake tastes better after it has aged.
> Dogs don't scratch up furniture, *as* cats often do.

as . . . as . . .

> She actually is *as* naïve *as* she appears.

associate with

> Many people *associate* the smell of vinegar *with* coloring Easter Eggs.

at least as . . . as . . .

> The Eiffel Tower is *at least as* tall *as* the Statue of Liberty.

attribute to

> I *attribute* his success *to* having good friends in high places.

believe to be

> The expert *believes* the painting *to be* a fraud.

between . . . and . . .

> You must decide *between* wealth *and* fame.

both versus **each**

Use *both* when pointing out similarities; use *each* when pointing out differences. Note that *each* is always singular.

Although *both* cooks enjoy making goulash, *each* has a different take on this classic dish.

both . . . and . . .

He is *both* an artist *and* a rogue.

compare to versus **compare with**

On the GMAT, *compare with* is the generally preferred form. Use *compare to* to point out an abstract or figurative likeness and *compare with* to consider likenesses and differences in general.

Shall I *compare* thee *to* a summer's day?
Compared with a summer's day, it's cold outside.

connection between

I saw little *connection between* her words and her deeds.

consequence of

One *consequence of* the Supreme Court decision was increased public distrust in the judicial system.

consider

I *consider* you a very good friend.

Note: Although *consider to be* is also correct, the GMAT prefers the more concise and simple *consider*.

continue to

Do not *continue to* deny the obvious.

contrast with

I like to *contrast* my plaid pants *with* a lovely paisley jacket.

credit with

James Joyce is often *credited with* the invention of the literary form called stream of consciousness.

debate over

This idiom only applies when *debate* is used as a noun.

They held a lively *debate over* whom to throw off the island.

decide to

She *decided to* go to the party after all.

define as

My dictionary *defines* a clause *as* a group of words containing a subject and a verb.

different from

John Major's policies were not very *different from* those of Margaret Thatcher.

difficult to

It's *difficult to* disagree with such a persuasive argument.

dispute over

This idiom applies only when *dispute* is used as a noun.

> The *dispute over* how to read the punch cards was never properly resolved.

distinguish between . . . and . . .

> Some colorblind people cannot *distinguish between* red *and* green.

distinguish . . . from . . .

> Other colorblind people find it difficult to *distinguish* blue *from* purple.

double versus **twice** (**triple** versus **three times**, etc.)

On the GMAT, *double* (*triple*, *quadruple*, etc.) is only used as a verb; when making a comparison, the preferred form is *twice* (*three times*, etc.).

> He promised to *double* the company's profits in less than a year.
> I ate *twice* as much as you did.

each (See **both** versus **each** above.)

each other versus **one another**

In GMAT English, *each other* is used to refer to two things, and *one another* is used for three or more.

> Those two theories contradict *each other*.
> Those three theories contradict *one another*.

either . . . or . . .

> Today I will *either* look for a job *or* watch the Boston marathon on TV.

–er than

> Winston Churchill was a bett*er* dancer *than* Neville Chamberlain ever was.

extent to which

> You should appreciate the *extent to which* the same idioms repeatedly appear on the GMAT.

estimate to be

> The oldest cave paintings known to exist are *estimated to be* over 50,000 years old.

fewer versus **less**

Use *fewer* to describe countable things, like jelly beans or people, and *less* to describe an uncountable quantity, like soup or love. (See **amount** versus **number** above.)

> I ate *fewer* hotdogs and *less* potato salad than I did at last year's picnic.

forbid to

> I was *forbidden to* discuss politics at the dinner table.

from . . . to . . .

> *From* the Redwood forest *to* the Gulf Stream waters, this land was made for you and me.

just as . . . so too . . .

> *Just as* sand flows through an hourglass, *so too* flow the days of our lives.

if versus **whether**

If you're ever given a choice on the GMAT, choose *whether*. The actual rule states that whenever you're discussing a choice between alternatives, you should use *whether* (as in *whether or not* to do something) rather than *if*. On the GMAT, *if* is reserved for conditional "if-then" statements.

> Let me know *if* I behave inappropriately in front of the royal family. (Translation: I may or may not behave inappropriately, but if I do, I should be informed).
> Tell me *whether* I behaved inappropriately in front of the royal family. (Translation: Either I behaved inappropriately or I didn't; tell me the truth.)

in danger of

> Conservationists fear that the West Indian manatee is *in danger of* becoming extinct.

less (See **fewer** versus **less** above.)

like versus **such as**

> If you're ever given a choice on the GMAT, choose *such as*. The GMAT writers prefer *such as* to *like* when what follows are examples; to these writers, *like* means "similar to."
> I prefer salty snacks *such as* potato chips to sweet snacks *such as* candy bars.
> I've never met anyone *like* him before.

likely to

> You're *likely to* do well on the GMAT Verbal Section.

link to

> Exposure to classical music has been *linked to* improved performance on mathematical aptitude tests.

model after

> Louisiana's legal system is *modeled after* the Napoleonic Code.

more than

> I was *more* prepared this time *than* I was the last time I took the test.

native

Use *native to*, meaning "indigenous to," when discussing plants, animals, and the like. Use *a native of* when discussing people and where they were born.

> The sugar maple is *native to* Canada.
> Brendan is *a native of* Canada.

neither . . . nor . . .

Note that when a sentence has a *neither . . . nor . . .* subject, whatever follows *nor* determines whether the verb is singular or plural. (The same thing is true of *either . . . or . . .* subjects.)

> *Neither* the players *nor* the coach was surprised by the team's victory.

not . . . but [rather, merely] . . .

> It's *not* a bother *but rather* an honor to serve you.

not only . . . but also . . .

> I am *not only* charming *but also* modest to a fault.

not so . . . as . . .

It's *not so* bad *as* it seems.

not so much . . . as . . .

The company's recent success is due *not so much* to better management *as* to an improved economy.

number (See **amount** versus **number** above.)

Also note that on the GMAT, *the number of* will always be singular, while *a number of* will always be plural.

The number of stars in our galaxy *is* huge.
A number of guests *are* waiting in the foyer.

one another (See **each other** versus **one another** above.)

opposition to

There has been far less *opposition* in the United States than in Europe *to* the use of genetically modified foods.

perceive as

I didn't mean for my comments to be *perceived as* criticism.

prohibit from

People are *prohibited from* entering the park after 10 p.m.

range from . . . to . . .

Scores on the GMAT *range from* 200 *to* 800.

regard as

I *regard* him *as* little more than a common criminal.

require to

The laws in many states *require* couples *to* have their blood tested before getting married.

resistance to

Stress can lower one's *resistance to* cold and flu viruses.

same as

I got the *same* score *as* he did.

seem to

He *seemed to* be at a loss for words.

so . . . as to be . . .

My new game is *so* entertaining *as to be* genuinely addictive.

so . . . that . . .

In fact, it's *so* addictive *that* I spend several hours every day playing it.

such as (See **like** versus **such as** above.)

superior to

Superman's powers are clearly *superior to* those of Batman.

target at

> I sometimes suspect that junk food ads are *targeted at* children.

the –er . . . the –er . . .

> *The* bigg*er* they come, *the* hard*er* they fall, or so I have heard.

try to

> *Try to* write a short story based on your travel experiences.

twice (See **double** versus **twice** above.)

use as

> Lacking cooking implements, we *used* one of the car's hubcaps *as* a makeshift pan.

view as

> Many *view* the former publishing magnate *as* a con artist extraordinaire.

whether (See **if** versus **whether** above.)

worry about

> There's no need to *worry about* idioms on the GMAT; just study the ones you don't recognize.

Idioms Quiz

1. The actor skillfully portrays not only a politician (and also, and as well, but also) a father in this film.

2. She is widely respected, both as an athlete (and also, and as, but also as) a role model.

3. I must have either cupcakes (or else, or, and) cookies for lunch.

4. You must decide (between, among) the hot and sour soup (or, and) the egg drop soup.

5. (Between, Among) the three professors, Steiner is generally (considered, considered to be, considered as) the (more, most) entertaining lecturer.

6. There were (less, fewer) immigrants entering the country last year than the previous year.

7. The (number, amount) of students in my class (has, have) gone up.

8. I regard the movies of Orson Welles (as, to be, as being) superior (when compared to, over, to) those of Alfred Hitchcock.

9. Zeppo is often perceived (as, to be, as being) the least talented of the Marx Brothers.

10. According to exit polls, a majority of those who voted for the winning candidate viewed him (as, to be, as being) the lesser of two evils.

11. The mountains of Switzerland are very different (than, from) those of Peru.

12. It was so quiet (you, that you, as a result you) could hear a pin drop.

13. Eva and Bharat (each, both) went to the same high school.

14. Giovanni and Daniel (both had their, each had his) own take on why the negotiations were unsuccessful.

15. Some pundits like to associate the 1960s (with, and) the decline of Western civilization.

16. We held a spirited debate (over, about, concerning) the criteria a movie must meet in order to join the pantheon of classic horror films.

17. I can assure you that it was not a dispute (over, about, concerning) trivial issues.

18. Visitors are forbidden (to enter, from entering) the park after dusk.

19. They are also prohibited (to visit, from visiting) the ancient religious site.

20. I hereby define a "baker's dozen" (to be, as, as being) thirteen.

21. Polar bears are clearly more intelligent (compared to, as, than) most primates.

22. Studying grammar is about as pleasant (when compared to, as, than) going to the dentist.

23. I attribute my stunning success (as due to, because of, to) good looks and native intelligence.

24. I attribute my good looks not so much to exquisite grooming (as, but, but rather) to an inner radiance.

25. Most historians credit Philo Taylor Farnsworth (as, for, with) having invented the television back in the1920s while he was still a teenager.

26. Swing dances (like, such as) the Jitterbug and the Hucklebuck were especially popular in the 1940s.

27. (Similar to, Like, As with) many American pop singers, he (is also, is) adored by fans around the globe.

28. I did not try the clam dip, (as, like) my roommate who got sick did.

29. I've finally decided (on going, to go) camping over the holidays, but I still haven't figured out (whether, if) I need to buy a tent.

30. Disease-causing microbes that have developed a resistance (against, to) antibiotics are difficult to combat.

Answers

1. The actor skillfully portrays *not only* a politician *but also* a father in this film.

2. She is widely respected both as an athlete *and as* a role model.

3. I must have either cupcakes *or* cookies for lunch.

4. You must decide *between* the hot and sour soup *and* the egg drop soup.

5. *Among* the three professors, Steiner is generally *considered* the *most* entertaining lecturer.

6. There were *fewer* immigrants entering the country last year than the previous year.

7. The *number* of students in my class *has* gone up.

8. I regard the movies of Orson Welles *as* superior *to* those of Alfred Hitchcock.

9. Zeppo is often *perceived as* the least talented of the Marx Brothers.

10. According to exit polls, a majority of those who voted for the winning candidate viewed him *as* the lesser of two evils.

11. The mountains of Switzerland are very different *from* those of Peru.

12. It was so quiet *that you* could hear a pin drop.

13. Eva and Bharat *both* went to the same high school.

14. Giovanni and Daniel *each had his* own take on why the negotiations were unsuccessful.

15. Some pundits like to associate the 1960s *with* the decline of Western civilization.

16. We held a spirited debate *over* the criteria a movie must meet in order to join the pantheon of classic horror films.

17. I can assure you that it was not a dispute *over* trivial issues.

18. Visitors are forbidden *to enter* the park after dusk.

19. They are also prohibited *from visiting* the ancient religious site.

20. I hereby define a "baker's dozen" *as* thirteen.

21. Polar bears are clearly more intelligent *than* most primates.

22. Studying grammar is about *as* pleasant as going to the dentist.

23. I attribute my stunning success *to* good looks and native intelligence.

24. I attribute my good looks not so much to exquisite grooming *as* to an inner radiance.

25. Most historians credit Philo Taylor Farnsworth *with* having invented the television back in the 1920s while he was still a teenager.

26. Swing dances *such as* the Jitterbug and the Hucklebuck were especially popular in the 1940s.

27. *Like* many American pop singers, he *is* adored by fans around the globe.

28. I did not try the clam dip, *as* my roommate who got sick did.

29. I've finally decided *to go* camping over the holidays, but I still haven't figured out *whether* I need to buy a tent.

30. Disease-causing microbes that have developed a resistance *to* antibiotics are difficult to combat.

GMAT STRATEGY SHEET

Use this sheet to review the Kaplan Methods for the different question types you'll see on Test Day.

TEST PREP

The Analytical Writing Assessment

The Kaplan Method

1) Take apart the argument.
2) Select the points you will make.
3) Organize using Kaplan's essay template.
4) Write your essay.
5) Proofread your work.

Kaplan Argument Essay Template

Paragraph 1: Show that you understand the argument by putting it in your own words.

Paragraph 2: Point out one flawed assumption in the author's reasoning; explain why it is questionable.

Paragraph 3: Identify another source of the author's faulty reasoning; explain why it is questionable.

In additional paragraphs, describe other points of fault in the argument, as time permits.

Second-to-last paragraph: Describe evidence that would—if it were provided—strengthen the argument.

Final paragraph: Conclude that without such evidence, you're not persuaded.

The Verbal Methods

The Kaplan Method for Reading Comprehension

1) Read the passage strategically.
2) Analyze the question stem.
3) Research the relevant text.
4) Make a prediction.
5) Evaluate the answer choices.

Kaplan Reading Comprehension Strategies

Global questions: Use Topic, Scope, and Purpose, and your Passage Map to predict the correct answer.

Detail questions: Use your Passage Map to target your research.

Inference questions: Use clues in the question stem or answer choices to research; the correct answer will follow from the passage.

Logic questions: Use your Passage Map and keywords to determine why or how the author uses the reference.

The Kaplan Method for Critical Reasoning

1) Identify the question type.
2) Untangle the stimulus.
3) Predict the answer.
4) Evaluate the choices.

Kaplan Critical Reasoning Strategies

Assumption: Identify the conclusion and evidence; determine the central assumption; predict the answer.

Strengthen or Weaken: Identify the conclusion and evidence; determine the central assumption; predict the answer that confirms (strengthens) or denies (weakens) the central assumption.

Evaluation: Identify the conclusion and evidence; determine the central assumption; predict an answer that identifies missing information that would help in assessing the assumption's validity.

Flaw: Identify the conclusion and evidence; determine the central assumption; predict a choice that describes the logical fallacy of
the assumption.

Explain: Search the answer choices for a statement that, if true, could explain how the statements in the stimulus could all be true.

Inference: Accept the statements in the stimulus as true; locate the answer choice that must follow from the stimulus.

Bolded Statement: Identify the purpose of every sentence in the stimulus and select the answer that matches your desription of the bolded statements.

The Kaplan Method for Sentence Correction

1) Read the original sentence carefully, looking for errors.
2) Scan and group the answer choices.
3) Eliminate choices until only one remains.

Six Classic Sentence Correction Errors

Verbs: Check for number agreement and tense.

Pronouns: Check for antecedent and number agreement.

Modification: Check for proper placement and intended reference.

Parallel Structure: Be consistent; use parallel constructions.

Comparisons: Use parallel construction; make sure items are logically comparable.

Usage/style: Avoid redundancy and passive voice; use idioms correctly.